THE WORKS OF
HENRIK IBSEN

THE VIKING EDITION
VOLUME
VIII

Fru Hennings as Hedvig in "The Wild Duck"

HENRIK IBSEN

AN ENEMY OF THE PEOPLE
THE WILD DUCK

WITH INTRODUCTIONS BY

WILLIAM ARCHER

NEW YORK
CHARLES SCRIBNER'S SONS
1911

CONTENTS

ILLUSTRATIONS

AN ENEMY OF THE PEOPLE

AN ENEMY OF THE PEOPLE

INTRODUCTION*

FROM *Pillars of Society* to *John Gabriel Borkman*, all Ibsen's plays, with one exception, succeeded each other at intervals of two years. The single exception was *An Enemy of the People*. The storm of obloquy which greeted *Ghosts* stirred him to unwonted rapidity of production. *Ghosts* had appeared in December, 1881; already, in the spring of 1882, Ibsen, then living in Rome, was at work upon its successor; and he finished it at Gossensass, in the Tyrol, in the early autumn. It appeared in Copenhagen at the end of November. Perhaps the rapidity of its composition may account for the fact that we find no sketch or draft of it in the poet's *Literary Remains*.

John Paulsen[1] relates an anecdote of Ibsen's extreme secretiveness during the process of composition, which may find a place here: "One summer he was travelling by rail with his wife and son. He was engaged upon a new play at the time; but neither Fru Ibsen nor Sigurd had any idea as to what it was about. Of course they were both very curious. It happened that, at a station, Ibsen left the carriage for a few moments. As he did so he dropped a scrap of paper. His wife picked it up, and read on it only the words, 'The doctor says. . . .' Noth-

* Copyright, 1907, by Charles Scribner's Sons.

[1] *Samliv med Ibsen*, p. 173.

3

ing more.   Fru Ibsen showed it laughingly to Sigurd, and
said, 'Now we will tease your father a little when he comes
back.   He will be horrified to find that we know anything of his play.'   When Ibsen entered the carriage his
wife looked at him roguishly, and said, 'What doctor is
it that figures in your new piece?   I am sure he must have
many interesting things to say.'   But if she could have
foreseen the effect of her innocent jest, Fru Ibsen would
certainly have held her tongue.   For Ibsen was speechless
with surprise and rage.   When at last he recovered his
speech, it was to utter a torrent of reproaches.   What did
this mean?   Was he not safe in his own house?   Was he
surrounded with spies?   Had his locks been tampered
with, his desk rifled?   And so forth, and so forth.   His
wife, who had listened with a quiet smile to the rising
tempest of his wrath, at last handed him the scrap of
paper.   'We know nothing more than what is written
upon this slip which you let fall.   Allow me to return it
to you.'   There stood Ibsen crestfallen.   All his suspicions had vanished into thin air.   The play on which he
was occupied proved to be *An Enemy of the People*, and
the doctor was none other than our old friend Stockmann,
the good-hearted and muddleheaded reformer, for whom
Jonas Lie partly served as a model."

The indignation which glows in *An Enemy of the People* was kindled, in the main, by the attitude adopted
towards *Ghosts* by the Norwegian Liberal press and the
"compact majority" it represented.   But the image on
which the play rings the changes was present to the poet's
mind before *Ghosts* was written.   On December 19, 1879
—a fortnight after the publication of *A Doll's House*—

Ibsen wrote to Professor Dietrichson: "It appears to me doubtful whether better artistic conditions can be attained in Norway before the intellectual soil has been thoroughly turned up and cleansed, and all the swamps drained off." Here we have clearly the germ of *An Enemy of the People*. The image so took hold of Ibsen that after applying it to social life in this play, he recurred to it in *The Wild Duck*, in relation to the individual life.

The mood to which we definitely owe *An Enemy of the People* appears very clearly in a letter to George Brandes, dated January 3, 1882, in which Ibsen thanks him for his criticism of *Ghosts*. "What are we to say," he proceeds, "of the attitude taken up by the so-called Liberal press—by those leaders who speak and write about freedom of action and thought, and at the same time make themselves the slaves of the supposed opinions of their subscribers? I am more and more confirmed in my belief that there is something demoralising in engaging in politics and joining parties. I, at any rate, shall never be able to join a party which has the majority on its side. Björnson says, 'The majority is always right'; and as a practical politician he is bound, I suppose, to say so. I, on the contrary, of necessity say, 'The minority is always right.' Naturally I am not thinking of that minority of stagnationists who are left behind by the great middle party, which with us is called Liberal; I mean that minority which leads the van, and pushes on to points which the majority has not yet reached. I hold that that man is in the right who is most closely in league with the future."

The same letter closes with a passage which foreshadows not only *An Enemy of the People*, but *Rosmersholm*: "When I think how slow and heavy and dull the general intelligence is at home, when I notice the low standard by which everything is judged, a deep despondency comes over me, and it often seems to me that I might just as well end my literary activity at once. They really do not need poetry at home; they get along so well with the *Parliamentary News* and the *Lutheran Weekly*. And then they have their party papers. I have not the gifts that go to make a good citizen, nor yet the gift of orthodoxy; and what I possess no gift for I keep out of. Liberty is the first and highest condition for me. At home they do not trouble much about liberty, but only about liberties, a few more or a few less, according to the standpoint of their party. I feel, too, most painfully affected by the crudity, the plebeian element, in all our public discussion. The very praiseworthy attempt to make of our people a democratic community has inadvertently gone a good way towards making us a plebeian community. Distinction of soul seems to be on the decline at home."

So early as March 16, 1882, Ibsen announces to his publisher that he is "fully occupied with preparations for a new play." "This time," he says, "it will be a peaceable production which can be read by Ministers of State and wholesale merchants and their ladies, and from which the theatres will not be obliged to recoil. Its execution will come very easy to me, and I shall do my best to have it ready pretty early in the autumn." In this he was successful. From Gossensass on September 9, he wrote to Hegel: "I have the pleasure of sending you herewith the remainder of the manuscript of my new play. I have enjoyed writing this piece, and I feel quite lost and lonely now that it is out of hand. Dr. Stockmann and I got on excellently together; we agree on so many subjects. But the Doctor is a more muddleheaded person than I am, and he has, moreover, several other characteristics because of which people will stand hearing a good many things from him which they might perhaps not have taken in such very good part had they been said by me."

A letter to Brandes, written six months after the appearance of the play (June 12, 1883), answers some objection which the critic seems to have made—of what nature we can only guess: "As to *An Enemy of the People*, if we had a chance to discuss it I think we should come to a tolerable agreement. You are, of course, right in urging that we *must* all work for the spread of our opinions. But I maintain that a fighter at the intellectual outposts can never gather a majority around him. In ten years, perhaps, the majority may occupy the standpoint which Dr. Stockmann held at the public meeting. But during these ten years the Doctor will not have been standing still; he will still be at least ten years ahead of the majority. The majority, the mass, the multitude, can never overtake him; he can never have the majority with him. As for myself, at all events, I am conscious of this incessant progression. At the point where I stood when I wrote each of my books, there now stands a fairly compact multitude; but I myself am there no longer; I am elsewhere, and, I hope, further ahead." This is a fine saying, and as just as it is fine, with respect to the series of social plays, down to, and including, *Rosmersholm*.

To the psychological series, which begins with *The Lady from the Sea*, this law of progression scarcely applies. The standpoint in each is different; but the movement is not so much one of intellectual advance as of deepening spiritual insight.

As Ibsen predicted, the Scandinavian theatres seized with avidity upon *An Enemy of the People*. Between January and March, 1883, it was produced in Christiania, Bergen, Stockholm, and Copenhagen. It has always been very popular on the stage, and was the play chosen to represent Ibsen in the series of festival performances which inaugurated the National Theatre at Christiania. The first evening, September 1, 1899, was devoted to Holberg, the great founder of Norwegian-Danish drama; *An Enemy of the People* followed on September 2; and on September 3 Björnson held the stage, with *Sigurd Jorsalfar*. Oddly enough, *Ein Volksfeind* was four years old before it found its way to the German stage. It was first produced in Berlin, March 5, 1887, and has since then been very popular throughout Germany. It has even been presented at the Court Theatres of Berlin and Vienna—a fact which seems remarkable when we note that in France and Spain it has been pressed into the service of anarchism as a revolutionary manifesto. When first produced in Paris in 1895, and again in 1899, it was made the occasion of anarchist demonstrations. It was the play chosen for representation in Paris on Ibsen's seventieth birthday, March 29, 1898. In England it was first produced by Mr. Beerbohm Tree at the Haymarket Theatre on the afternoon of June 14, 1893. Mr. (now Sir Herbert) Tree has repeated his performance of Stock-

mann a g l many times in London, the provinces, and
America. He revived the play at His Majesty's Theatre in 1 /5. Mr. Louis Calvert played Stockmann at
the Ge eman's Concert Hall in Manchester, January
27, 18S I can find no record of the play in America,
save C man performances and those given by Mr. Tree;
but it eems incredible that no American actor should
have een attracted by the part of Stockmann. *Een
Vij d des Volks* was produced in Holland in 1884, be-
for it had even been seen in Germany; and in Italy *Un
N nico del Popolo* holds a place in the repertory of the
d inguished actor Ermete Novelli.

Of all Ibsen's plays, *An Enemy of the People* is the least
oetical, the least imaginative, the one which makes least
ppeal to our sensibilities. Even in *The League of Youth*
there is a touch of poetic fancy in the character of Selma;
while *Pillars of Society* is sentimentally conceived throughout, and possesses in Martha a figure of great, though
somewhat conventional, pathos. In this play, on the
other hand, there is no appeal either to the imagination
or to the tender emotions. It is a straightforward satiric
comedy, dealing exclusively with the everyday prose of
life. We have only to compare it with its immediate
predecessor, *Ghosts*, and its immediate successor, *The
Wild Duck*, to feel how absolutely different is the imaginative effort involved in it. Realising this, we no longer
wonder that the poet should have thrown it off in half the
time he usually required to mature and execute one of
his creations.

Yet *An Enemy of the People* takes a high place in the
second rank of the Ibsen works, in virtue of its buoyant

vitality, its great technical excellence, and the geniality
of its humour. It seems odd, at first sight, that a dis-
tinctly polemical play, which took its rise in a mood of ex-
asperation, should be perhaps the most amiable of all the
poet's productions. But the reason is fairly obvious.
Ibsen's nature was far too complex, and far too specifi-
cally dramatic, to permit of his giving anything like direct
expression to a personal mood. The very fact that Dr.
Stockmann was to utter much of his own indignation and
many of his own ideas forced him to make the worthy
Doctor in temperament and manner as unlike himself as
possible. Now boisterous geniality, loquacity, irrepres-
sible rashness of utterance, and a total absence of self-
criticism and self-irony were the very contradiction of
the poet's own characteristics—at any rate, after he had
entered upon middle life. He doubtless looked round
for models who should be his own antipodes in these respects. John Paulsen, as we have seen, thinks that he
took many traits from Jonas Lie; others say[1] that one of
his chief models was an old friend named Harald Thau-
low, the father of the great painter. Be this as it may,
the very effort to disguise himself naturally led him to at-
tribute to his protagonist and mouthpiece a great superficial amiability. I am far from implying that Ibsen's
own character was essentially unamiable; it would ill
become one whom he always treated with the utmost
kindness to say or think anything of the kind. But his
amiability was not superficial, effusive, exuberant; it
seldom reached that boiling-point which we call geniality;

[1] See article by Julius Elias in *Die neue Rundschau*, December,
1906, p. 1461.

and for that very reason Thomas Stockmann became the
most genial of his characters. He may be called Ibsen's
Colonel Newcome. We have seen from the letter to
Hegel (p. 7) that the poet regarded him with much the
same ironic affection which Thackeray must have felt for
that other Thomas who, amid many differences, had the
same simple-minded, large-hearted, child-like nature.

In technical quality, *An Enemy of the People* is wholly
admirable. We have only to compare it with *Pillars of
Society*, the last play in which Ibsen had painted a broad
satiric picture of the life of a Norwegian town, to feel how
great an advance he had made in the intervening five
years. In naturalness of exposition, suppleness of development, and what may be called general untheatri-
cality of treatment, the later play has every possible advantage over the earlier. In one point only can it be said
that Ibsen has allowed a touch of artificiality to creep in.
In order to render the peripetia of the third act more
striking, he has made Hovstad, Billing, and Aslaksen, in
the earlier scenes, unnaturally inapprehensive of the sacrifices implied in Stockmann's scheme of reform. It is
scarcely credible that they should be so free and emphatic
in their offers of support to the Doctor's agitation, before
they have made the smallest inquiry as to what it is likely
to cost the town. They think, it may be said, that the
shareholders of the Baths will have to bear the whole expense; but surely some misgivings could not but cross
their minds as to whether the shareholders would be
prepared to do so.

AN ENEMY OF THE PEOPLE
(1882)

CHARACTERS

DOCTOR THOMAS STOCKMANN, *medical officer of the Baths.*
MRS. STOCKMANN, *his wife.*
PETRA, *their daughter, a teacher.*
EILIF
MORTEN ⎫ *their sons, thirteen and ten years old respectively.*
PETER STOCKMANN, *the doctor's elder brother, Burgomaster[1] and chief of police, chairman of the Baths Committee, etc.*
MORTEN KIIL,[2] *master tanner, Mrs. Stockmann's adoptive-father.*
HOVSTAD, *editor of the "People's Messenger."*
BILLING, *on the staff of the paper.*
HORSTER, *a ship's captain.*
ASLAKSEN, *a printer.*

Participants in a meeting of citizens: all sorts and conditions of men, some women, and a band of schoolboys.

The action passes in a town on the South Coast of Norway.

[1] "Burgomaster" is the most convenient substitute for "Byfogd," but "Town Clerk" would perhaps be more nearly equivalent. It is impossible to find exact counterparts in English for the different grades of the Norwegian bureaucracy.
[2] Pronounce: *Keel.*

AN ENEMY OF THE PEOPLE

PLAY IN FIVE ACTS

═══════

ACT FIRST

Evening. DR. STOCKMANN'S *sitting-room; simply but neatly decorated and furnished. In the wall to the right are two doors, the further one leading to the hall, the nearer one to the Doctor's study. In the opposite wall, facing the hall door, a door leading to the other rooms of the house. Against the middle of this wall stands the stove; further forward a sofa with a mirror above it, and in front of it an oval table with a cover. On the table a lighted lamp, with a shade. In the back wall an open door leading to the dining-room, in which is seen a supper-table, with a lamp on it.*

BILLING *is seated at the supper-table, with a napkin under his chin.* MRS. STOCKMANN *is standing by the table and placing before him a dish with a large joint of roast beef. The other seats round the table are empty; the table is in disorder, as after a meal.*

MRS. STOCKMANN.

If you come an hour late, Mr. Billing, you must put up with a cold supper.

BILLING.

[*Eating.*]   It is excellent—really first rate.

15

MRS. STOCKMANN.

You know how Stockmann insists on regular meal-hours——

BILLING.

Oh, I don't mind at all. I almost think I enjoy my supper more when I can sit down to it like this, alone and undisturbed.

MRS. STOCKMANN.

Oh, well, if you enjoy it—— [*Listening in the direction of the hall.*] I believe this is Mr. Hovstad coming too.

BILLING.

Very likely.

BURGOMASTER STOCKMANN *enters, wearing an overcoat and an official gold-laced cap, and carrying a stick.*

BURGOMASTER.

Good evening, sister-in-law.

MRS. STOCKMANN.

[*Coming forward into the sitting-room.*] Oh, good evening; is it you? It is good of you to look in.

BURGOMASTER.

I was just passing, and so—— [*Looks towards the drawing-room.*] Ah, I see you have company.

MRS. STOCKMANN.

[*Rather embarrassed.*] Oh no, not at all; it's the merest chance. [*Hurriedly.*] Won't you sit down and have a little supper?

BURGOMASTER.

I ? No, thank you. Good gracious! hot meat in the evening! That wouldn't suit my digestion.

MRS. STOCKMANN.

Oh, for once in a way——

BURGOMASTER.

No, no,—much obliged to you. I stick to tea and bread and butter. It's more wholesome in the long run —and rather more economical, too.

MRS. STOCKMANN.

[*Smiling.*] You mustn't think Thomas and I are mere spendthrifts, either.

BURGOMASTER.

You are not, sister-in-law; far be it from me to say that. [*Pointing to the Doctor's study.*] Is he not at home?

MRS. STOCKMANN.

No, he has gone for a little turn after supper—with the boys.

BURGOMASTER.

I wonder if that is a good thing to do? [*Listening.*] There he is, no doubt.

MRS. STOCKMANN.

No, that is not he. [*A knock.*] Come in!

HOVSTAD *enters from the hall.*

MRS. STOCKMANN.

Ah, it's Mr. Hovstad——

HOVSTAD.

You must excuse me; I was detained at the printer's. Good evening, Burgomaster.

BURGOMASTER.

[*Bowing rather stiffly.*]   Mr. Hovstad?   You come on business, I presume?

HOVSTAD.

Partly.   About an article for the paper.

BURGOMASTER.

So I supposed.   I hear my brother is an extremely prolific contributor to the *People's Messenger*.

HOVSTAD.

Yes, when he wants to unburden his mind on one thing or another, he gives the *Messenger* the benefit.

MRS. STOCKMANN.

[*To* HOVSTAD.]   But will you not——?   [*Points to the dining-room.*]

BURGOMASTER.

Well, well, I am far from blaming him for writing for the class of readers he finds most in sympathy with him. And, personally, I have no reason to bear your paper any ill-will, Mr. Hovstad.

HOVSTAD.

No, I should think not.

BURGOMASTER.

One may say, on the whole, that a fine spirit of mutual tolerance prevails in our town—an excellent public spirit.   And that is because we have a great common interest to hold us together—an interest in which all right-minded citizens are equally concerned——

HOVSTAD.

Yes—the Baths.

BURGOMASTER.

Just so.   We have our magnificent new Baths.   Mark my words!   The whole life of the town will centre around the Baths, Mr. Hovstad.   There can be no doubt of it!

MRS. STOCKMANN.

That is just what Thomas says.

BURGOMASTER.

How marvellously the place has developed, even in this couple of years!   Money has come into circulation, and brought life and movement with it.   Houses and ground-rents rise in value every day.

HOVSTAD.

And there are fewer people out of work.

BURGOMASTER.

That is true.   There is a gratifying diminution in the burden imposed on the well-to-do classes by the poor-rates; and they will be still further lightened if only we have a really good summer this year—a rush of visitors— plenty of invalids, to give the Baths a reputation.

HOVSTAD.

I hear there is every prospect of that.

BURGOMASTER.

Things look most promising.   Inquiries about apartments and so forth keep on pouring in.

HOVSTAD.

Then the Doctor's paper will come in very opportunely.

BURGOMASTER.

Has he been writing again?

HOVSTAD.

This is a thing he wrote in the winter; enlarging on the virtues of the Baths, and on the excellent sanitary conditions of the town.   But at that time I held it over.

BURGOMASTER.

Ah—I suppose there was something not quite judicious about it?

HOVSTAD.

Not at all.   But I thought it better to keep it till the spring, when people are beginning to look about them, and think of their summer quarters——

BURGOMASTER.

You were right, quite right, Mr. Hovstad.

MRS. STOCKMANN.

Yes, Thomas is really indefatigable where the Baths are concerned.

BURGOMASTER.

It is his duty as one of the staff.

HOVSTAD.

And of course he was really their creator.

BURGOMASTER.

Was he? Indeed! I gather that certain persons are of that opinion. But I should have thought that I, too, had a modest share in that undertaking.

MRS. STOCKMANN.

Yes, that is what Thomas is always saying.

HOVSTAD.

No one dreams of denying it, Burgomaster. You set the thing going, and put it on a practical basis; everybody knows that. I only meant that the original idea was the Doctor's.

BURGOMASTER.

Yes, my brother has certainly had ideas enough in his time—worse luck! But when it comes to realising them, Mr. Hovstad, we want men of another stamp. I should have thought that in this house at any rate——

MRS. STOCKMANN.

Why, my dear brother-in-law——

HOVSTAD.

Burgomaster, how can you——?

MRS. STOCKMANN.

Do go in and have some supper, Mr. Hovstad; my husband is sure to be home directly.

HOVSTAD.

Thanks; just a mouthful, perhaps.

[*He goes into the dining-room.*

BURGOMASTER.

[*Speaking in a low voice.*]   It is extraordinary how people who spring direct from the peasant class never can get over their want of tact.

MRS. STOCKMANN.

But why should you care?   Surely you and Thomas can share the honour, like brothers.

BURGOMASTER.

Yes, one would suppose so; but it seems a share of the honour is not enough for some persons.

MRS. STOCKMANN.

What nonsense!   You and Thomas always get on so well together.   [*Listening.*]   There, I think I hear him.

[*Goes and opens the door to the hall.*

DR. STOCKMANN.

[*Laughing and talking loudly, without.*] Here's another visitor for you, Katrina. Isn't it capital, eh? Come in, Captain Horster. Hang your coat on that peg. What! you don't wear an overcoat? Fancy, Katrina, I caught him in the street, and I could hardly get him to come in.

CAPTAIN HORSTER *enters and bows to* MRS. STOCKMANN.

DR. STOCKMANN.

[*In the doorway.*] In with you, boys. They're famishing again! Come along, Captain Horster; you must try our roast beef——

[*He forces* HORSTER *into the dining-room.* EILIF *and* MORTEN *follow them.*

MRS. STOCKMANN.

But, Thomas, don't you see——

DR. STOCKMANN.

[*Turning round in the doorway.*] Oh, is that you, Peter! [*Goes up to him and holds out his hand.*] Now this is really capital.

BURGOMASTER.

Unfortunately, I have only a moment to spare——

DR. STOCKMANN.

Nonsense! We shall have some toddy in a minute. You're not forgetting the toddy, Katrina?

MRS. STOCKMANN.

Of course not; the water's boiling.
[*She goes into the dining-room.*

BURGOMASTER.

Toddy too——!

DR. STOCKMANN.

Yes; sit down, and let's make ourselves comfortable.

BURGOMASTER.

Thanks; I never join in drinking parties.

DR. STOCKMANN.

But this isn't a party.

BURGOMASTER.

I don't know what else—— [*Looks towards the dining-room.*] It's extraordinary how they can get through all that food.

DR. STOCKMANN.

[*Rubbing his hands.*] Yes, doesn't it do one good to see young people eat? Always hungry! That's as it should be. They need good, solid meat to put stamina into them! It is they that have got to whip up the ferment of the future, Peter.

BURGOMASTER.

May I ask what there is to be "whipped up," as you call it?

DR. STOCKMANN.

You'll have to ask the young people that—when the time comes. We shan't see it, of course. Two old fogies like you and me——

BURGOMASTER.

Come, come! Surely that is a very extraordinary expression to use——

DR. STOCKMANN.

Oh, you mustn't mind my nonsense, Peter. I'm in such glorious spirits, you see. I feel so unspeakably happy in the midst of all this growing, germinating life. Isn't it a marvellous time we live in! It seems as though a whole new world were springing up around us.

BURGOMASTER.

Do you really think so?

DR. STOCKMANN.

Of course, you can't see it as clearly as I do. You have passed your life in the midst of it all; and that deadens the impression. But I who had to vegetate all those years in that little hole in the north, hardly ever seeing a soul that could speak a stimulating word to me— all this affects me as if I had suddenly dropped into the heart of some teeming metropolis.

BURGOMASTER.

Well, metropolis——

DR. STOCKMANN.

Oh, I know well enough that things are on a small scale here, compared with many other places. But

there's life here—there's promise—there's an infinity of
things to work and strive for; and that is the main point.
[*Calling.*]   Katrina, haven't there been any letters?

MRS. STOCKMANN.

[*In the dining-room.*]   No, none at all.

DR. STOCKMANN.

And then a good income, Peter!   That's a thing one
learns to appreciate when one has lived on starvation
wages——

BURGOMASTER.

Good heavens——!

DR. STOCKMANN.

Oh yes, I can tell you we often had hard times of it
up there.   And now we can live like princes!   To-day,
for example, we had roast beef for dinner; and we've
had some of it for supper too.   Won't you have some?
Come along—just look at it, at any rate——

BURGOMASTER.

No, no; certainly not——

DR. STOCKMANN.

Well then, look here—do you see we've bought a
table-cover?

BURGOMASTER.

Yes, so I observed.

DR. STOCKMANN.

Dr. Stockmann.

And a lamp-shade, too. Do you see? Katrina has been saving up for them. They make the room look comfortable, don't they? Come over here. No, no, no, not there. So—yes! Now you see how it concentrates the light——. I really think it has quite an artistic effect. Eh?

Burgomaster.

Yes, when one can afford such luxuries——

Dr. Stockmann.

Oh, I can afford it now. Katrina says I make almost as much as we spend.

Burgomaster.

Ah—almost!

Dr. Stockmann.

Besides, a man of science must live in some style. Why, I believe a mere sheriff [1] spends much more a year than I do.

Burgomaster.

Yes, I should think so! A member of the superior magistracy——

Dr. Stockmann.

Well then, even a common shipowner! A man of that sort will get through many times as much——

Burgomaster.

That is natural, in your relative positions.

[1] *Amtmand*, the chief magistrate of an *Amt* or county; consequently a high dignitary in the official hierarchy.

DR. STOCKMANN.

And after all, Peter, I really don't squander any
money. But I can't deny myself the delight of having
people about me. I m u s t have them. After living so
long out of the world, I find it a necessity of life to have
bright, cheerful, freedom-loving, hard-working young fellows around me—and that's what they are, all of them,
that are sitting there eating so heartily. I wish you knew
more of Hovstad——

BURGOMASTER.

Ah, that reminds me—Hovstad was telling me that he
is going to publish another article of yours.

DR. STOCKMANN.

An article of mine?

BURGOMASTER.

Yes, about the Baths. An article you wrote last winter.

DR. STOCKMANN.

Oh, that one! But I don't want that to appear for the
present.

BURGOMASTER.

Why not? It seems to me this is the very time for it.

DR. STOCKMANN.

Very likely—under ordinary circumstances——
[*Crosses the room.*

BURGOMASTER.

[*Following him with his eyes.*] And what is unusual in the circumstances now?

DR. STOCKMANN.

[*Standing still.*] The fact is, Peter, I really cannot tell you just now; not this evening, at all events. There may prove to be a great deal that is unusual in the circumstances. On the other hand, there may be nothing at all. Very likely it's only my fancy.

BURGOMASTER.

Upon my word, you are very enigmatical. Is there anything in the wind? Anything I am to be kept in the dark about? I should think, as Chairman of the Bath Committee——

DR. STOCKMANN.

And I should think that I—— Well, well, don't let us get our backs up, Peter.

BURGOMASTER.

God forbid! I am not in the habit of "getting my ack up," as you express it. But I must absolutely insist that all arrangements shall be made and carried out in a businesslike manner, and through the properly constituted authorities. I cannot be a party to crooked or underhand courses.

DR. STOCKMANN.

Have *I* ever been given to crooked or underhand courses?

BURGOMASTER.

At any rate you have an ingrained propensity to taking your own course.   And that, in a well-ordered community, is almost as inadmissible.   The individual must subordinate himself to society, or, more precisely, to the authorities whose business it is to watch over the welfare of society.

DR. STOCKMANN.

Maybe.   But what the devil has that to do with me?

BURGOMASTER.

Why this is the very thing, my dear Thomas, that it seems you will never learn.   But take care; you will have to pay for it—sooner or later.   Now I have warned you.   Good-bye.

DR. STOCKMANN.

Are you stark mad?   You're on a totally wrong track——

BURGOMASTER.

I am not often on the wrong track.   Moreover, I must protest against——   [*Bowing towards dining-room.*] Good-bye, sister-in-law; good-day to you, gentlemen.

[*He goes.*

MRS. STOCKMANN.

[*Entering the sitting-room.*]   Has he gone?

DR. STOCKMANN.

Yes, and in a fine temper, too.

MRS. STOCKMANN.

Why, my dear Thomas, what have you been doing to him now?

DR. STOCKMANN.

Nothing at all. He can't possibly expect me to account to him for everything—before the time comes.

MRS. STOCKMANN.

What have you to account to him for?

DR. STOCKMANN.

H'm;—never mind about that, Katrina.—It's very odd the postman doesn't come.

[HOVSTAD, BILLING and HORSTER *have risen from table and come forward into the sitting-room.* EILIF *and* MORTEN *presently follow.*

BILLING.

[*Stretching himself.*] Ah! Strike me dead if one doesn't feel a new man after such a meal.

HOVSTAD.

The Burgomaster didn't seem in the best of tempers this evening.

DR. STOCKMANN.

That's his stomach. He has a very poor digestion.

HOVSTAD.

I fancy it's the staff of the *Messenger* he finds it hardest to stomach.

MRS. STOCKMANN.

I thought you got on well enough with him.

HOVSTAD.

Oh, yes; but it's only a sort of armistice between us.

BILLING.

That's it!   That word sums up the situation.

DR. STOCKMANN.

We must remember that Peter is a lonely bachelor, poor devil!   He has no home to be happy in; only business, business.   And then all that cursëd weak tea he goes and pours down his throat!   Now then, chairs round the table, boys!   Katrina, shan't we have the toddy now?

MRS. STOCKMANN.

[*Going towards the dining-room.*]   I am just getting it.

DR. STOCKMANN.

And you, Captain Horster, sit beside me on the sofa. So rare a guest as you——.   Sit down, gentlemen, sit down.
[*The men sit round the table;* MRS. STOCKMANN *brings in a tray with kettle, glasses, decanters, etc.*

MRS. STOCKMANN.

Here you have it: here's arrak, and this is rum, and this cognac.   Now, help yourselves.

DR. STOCKMANN.

[*Taking a glass.*] So we will. [*While the toddy is being mixed.*] And now out with the cigars. Eilif, I think you know where the box is. And Morten, you may fetch my pipe. [*The boys go into the room on the right.*] I have a suspicion that Eilif sneaks a cigar now and then, but I pretend not to notice. [*Calls.*] And my smoking-cap, Morten! Katrina, can't you tell him where I left it. Ah, he's got it. [*The boys bring in the things.*] Now, friends, help yourselves. I stick to my pipe, you know;—this one has been on many a stormy journey with me, up there in the north. [*They clink glasses.*] Your health! Ah, I can tell you it's better fun to sit cosily here, safe from wind and weather.

MRS. STOCKMANN.

[*Who sits knitting.*] Do you sail soon, Captain Horster?

HORSTER.

I hope to be ready for a start by next week.

MRS. STOCKMANN.

And you're going to America?

HORSTER.

Yes, that's the intention.

BILLING.

But then you'll miss the election of the new Town Council.

HORSTER.

Is there to be an election again?

BILLING.

Didn't you know?

HORSTER.

No, I don't trouble myself about those things.

BILLING.

But I suppose you take an interest in public affairs?

HORSTER.

No, I don't understand anything about them.

BILLING.

All the same, one ought at least to vote.

HORSTER.

Even those who don't understand anything about it?

BILLING.

Understand? Why, what do you mean by that? Society is like a ship: every man must put his hand to the helm.

HORSTER.

That may be all right on shore; but at sea it wouldn't do at all.

HOVSTAD.

It's remarkable how little sailors care about public affairs as a rule.

BILLING.

Most extraordinary.

DR. STOCKMANN.

Sailors are like birds of passage; they are at home both in the south and in the north. So it behoves the rest of us to be all the more energetic, Mr. Hovstad. Will there be anything of public interest in the *People's Messenger* to-morrow?

HOVSTAD.

Nothing of local interest. But the day after to-morrow I think of printing your article——

DR. STOCKMANN.

Oh confound it, that article! No, you'll have to hold it over.

HOVSTAD.

Really? We happen to have plenty of space, and I should say this was the very time for it——

DR. STOCKMANN.

Yes, yes, you may be right; but you must hold it over all the same. I shall explain to you by-and-by.

PETRA, *wearing a hat and cloak, and with a number of exercise-books under her arm, enters from the hall.*

PETRA.

Good evening.

DR. STOCKMANN.

Good evening, Petra. Is that you?
[*General greetings.* PETRA *puts her cloak, hat, and books on a chair by the door.*

PETRA.

Here you all are, enjoying yourselves, while I've been out slaving.

DR. STOCKMANN.

Well then, you come and enjoy yourself too.

BILLING.

May I mix you a little——?

PETRA.

[*Coming towards the table.*] Thank you, I'd rather help myself—you always make it too strong.   By the way, father, I have a letter for you.
[*Goes to the chair where her things are lying.*

DR. STOCKMANN.

A letter!   From whom?

PETRA.

[*Searching in the pocket of her cloak.*]   I got it from the postman just as I was going out——

DR. STOCKMANN.

[*Rising and going towards her.*]   And you only bring it me now?

PETRA.

I really hadn't time to run up again.   Here it is.

DR. STOCKMANN.

[*Seizing the letter.*]   Let me see, let me see, child. [*Reads the address.*]   Yes; this is it——!

MRS. STOCKMANN.

Is it the one you have been so anxious about, Thomas?

DR. STOCKMANN.

Yes it is. I must go at once. Where shall I find a light, Katrina? Is there no lamp in my study again!

MRS. STOCKMANN.

Yes—the lamp is lighted. It's on the writing-table.

DR. STOCKMANN.

Good, good. Excuse me one moment——
[*He goes into the room on the right.*

PETRA.

What can it be, mother?

MRS. STOCKMANN.

I don't know. For the last few days he has been continually on the look-out for the postman.

BILLING.

Probably a country patient——

PETRA.

Poor father! He'll soon have far too much to do. [*Mixes her toddy.*] Ah, this will taste good!

HOVSTAD.

Have you been teaching in the night school as well to-day?

PETRA.

[*Sipping from her glass.*]   Two hours.

BILLING.

And four hours in the morning at the institute——

PETRA.

[*Sitting down by the table.*]   Five hours.

MRS. STOCKMANN.

And I see you have exercises to correct this evening.

PETRA.

Yes, a heap of them.

HORSTER.

It seems to me you have plenty to do, too.

PETRA.

Yes; but I like it.   You feel so delightfully tired after it.

BILLING.

Do you like that?

PETRA.

Yes, for then you sleep so well.

MORTEN.

I say, Petra, you must be a great sinner.

PETRA.

A sinner?

MORTEN.

Yes, if you work so hard. Mr. Rörlund [1] says work is a punishment for our sins.

EILIF.

[*Contemptuously.*] Bosh! What a silly you are, to believe such stuff as that.

MRS. STOCKMANN.

Come come, Eilif.

BILLING.

[*Laughing.*] Capital, capital!

HOVSTAD.

Should you not like to work so hard, Morten?

MORTEN.

No, I shouldn't.

HOVSTAD.

Then what will you do with yourself in the world?

MORTEN.

I should like to be a Viking.

EILIF.

But then you'd have to be a heathen.

MORTEN.

Well, so I would.

[1] See *Pillars of Society.*

BILLING.

There I agree with you, Morten! I say just the same thing.

MRS. STOCKMANN.

[*Making a sign to him.*] No, no, Mr. Billing, I'm sure you don't.

BILLING.

Strike me dead but I do, though. I am a heathen, and I'm proud of it. You'll see we shall all be heathens soon.

MORTEN.

And shall we be able to do anything we like then?

BILLING.

Well, you see, Morten——

MRS. STOCKMANN.

Now run away, boys; I'm sure you have lessons to prepare for to-morrow.

EILIF.

You might let me stay just a little longer——

MRS. STOCKMANN.

No, you must go too. Be off, both of you.
  [*The boys say good-night and go into the room on the
    left.*

HOVSTAD.

Do you really think it can hurt the boys to hear these things?

MRS. STOCKMANN.

Well, I don't know; I don't like it.

PETRA.

Really, mother, I think you are quite wrong there.

MRS. STOCKMANN.

Perhaps. But I don't like it—not here, at home.

PETRA.

There's no end of hypocrisy both at home and at school. At home you must hold your tongue, and at school you have to stand up and tell lies to the children.

HORSTER.

Have you to tell lies?

PETRA.

Yes; do you think we don't have to tell them many and many a thing we don't believe ourselves?

BILLING.

Ah, that's too true.

PETRA.

If only I could afford it, I should start a school myself, and things should be very different there.

BILLING.

Oh, afford it——!

HORSTER.

If you really think of doing t h a t, Miss Stockmann, I shall be delighted to let you have a room at my place. You know my father's old house is nearly empty; there's a great big dining-room on the ground floor——

PETRA.

[*Laughing.*] Oh, thank you very much—but I'm afraid it won't come to anything.

HOVSTAD.

No, I fancy Miss Petra is more likely to go over to journalism. By the way, have you had time to look into the English novel you promised to translate for us?

PETRA.

Not yet. But you shall have it in good time.

DR. STOCKMANN *enters from his room, with the letter open in his hand.*

DR. STOCKMANN.

[*Flourishing the letter.*] Here's news, I can tell you, that will waken up the town!

BILLING.

News?

MRS. STOCKMANN.

What news?

DR. STOCKMANN.

A great discovery, Katrina!

HOVSTAD.

Indeed?

MRS. STOCKMANN.

Made by you?

DR. STOCKMANN.

Precisely—by me! [*Walks up and down.*] N o w let
them go on accusing me of fads and crack-brained notions. But they won't dare to! Ha-ha! I tell you they
won't dare!

PETRA.

Do tell us what it is, father.

DR. STOCKMANN.

Well, well, give me time, and you shall hear all about
it. If only I had Peter here now! This just shows how
we men can go about forming judgments like the blindest
moles——

HOVSTAD.

What do you mean, Doctor?

DR. STOCKMANN.

[*Stopping beside the table.*] Isn't it the general opinion
that our town is a healthy place?

HOVSTAD.

Of course.

DR. STOCKMANN.

A quite exceptionally healthy place, indeed—a place
to be warmly recommended, both to invalids and people in health——

MRS. STOCKMANN.

My dear Thomas——

DR. STOCKMANN.

And assuredly we haven't failed to recommend and belaud it.   I've sung its praises again and again, both in the *Messenger* and in pamphlets——

HOVSTAD.

Well, what then?

DR. STOCKMANN.

These Baths, that we have called the pulse of the town, its vital nerve, and—and the devil knows what else——

BILLING.

"Our city's palpitating heart," I once ventured to call them in a convivial moment——

DR. STOCKMANN.

Yes, I daresay.   Well—do you know what they really are, these mighty, magnificent, belauded Baths, that have cost so much money—do you know what they are?

HOVSTAD.

No, what are they?

MRS. STOCKMANN.

Do tell us.

DR. STOCKMANN.

Simply a pestiferous hole.

PETRA.

The Baths, father?

MRS. STOCKMANN.

[*At the same time.*]   Our Baths!

HOVSTAD.

[*Also at the same time.*]   But, Doctor——!

BILLING.

Oh, it's incredible!

DR. STOCKMANN.

I tell you the whole place is a poisonous whited-sepul-
chre; noxious in the highest degree!   All that filth up
there in the Mill Dale—the stuff that smells so horribly—
taints the water in the feed-pipes of the Pump-Room;
and the same accursëd poisonous refuse oozes out by the
beach——

HOVSTAD.

Where the sea-baths are?

DR. STOCKMANN.

Exactly.

HOVSTAD.

But how are you so sure of all this, Doctor?

DR. STOCKMANN.

I've investigated the whole thing as conscientiously as
possible.   I've long had my suspicions about it.   Last

year we had some extraordinary cases of illness among
the patients—both typhoid and gastric attacks——

MRS. STOCKMANN.

Yes, I remember.

DR. STOCKMANN.

We thought at the time that the visitors had brought
the infection with them; but afterwards—last winter—I
began to question that.   So I set about testing the water
as well as I could.

MRS. STOCKMANN.

It was t h a t you were working so hard at!

DR. STOCKMANN.

Yes, you may well say I've worked, Katrina.   But
here, you know, I hadn't the necessary scientific appli-
ances; so I sent samples both of our drinking-water and
of our sea-water to the University, for exact analysis by
a chemist.

HOVSTAD.

And you have received his report?

DR. STOCKMANN.

[Showing letter.]   Here it is!   And it proves beyond
dispute the presence of putrefying organic matter in the
water—millions of infusoria.   It's absolutely pernicious
to health, whether used internally or externally.

MRS. STOCKMANN.

What a blessing you found it out in time.

DR. STOCKMANN.

Yes, you may well say that.

HOVSTAD.

And what do you intend to do now, Doctor?

DR. STOCKMANN.

Why, to set things right, of course.

HOVSTAD.

You think it can be done, then?

DR. STOCKMANN.

It m u s t be done.   Else the whole Baths are useless, ruined.   But there's no fear.   I am quite clear as to what is required.

MRS. STOCKMANN.

But, my dear Thomas, why should you have made such a secret of all this?

DR. STOCKMANN.

Would you have had me rush all over the town and chatter about it, before I was quite certain?   No, thank you; I'm not so mad as that.

PETRA.

But to us at home——

DR. STOCKMANN.

I couldn't say a word to a living soul.   But to-morrow you may look in at the Badger's——

MRS. STOCKMANN.

Oh, Thomas!

DR. STOCKMANN.

Well well, at your grandfather's. The old fellow w i l l be astonished! He thinks I'm not quite right in my head—yes, and plenty of others think the same, I've noticed. But now these good people shall see—yes, they shall see now! [*Walks up and down rubbing his hands.*] What a stir there will be in the town, Katrina! Just think of it! All the water-pipes will have to be relaid.

HOVSTAD.

[*Rising.*] All the water-pipes——?

DR. STOCKMANN.

Why, of course. The intake is too low down; it must be moved much higher up.

PETRA.

So you were right, after all.

DR. STOCKMANN.

Yes, do you remember, Petra? I wrote against it when they were beginning the works. But no one would listen to me then. Now, you may be sure, I shall give them my full broadside—for of course I've prepared a statement for the Directors; it has been lying ready a whole week; I've only been waiting for this report. [*Points to letter.*] But now they shall have it at once. [*Goes into his room and returns with a MS. in his hand.*] See! Four closely-written sheets! And I'll enclose the

report.   A newspaper, Katrina!   Get me something to
wrap them up in.   There—that's it.   Give it to—to—
[*Stamps.*]—what the devil's her name?   Give it to the
girl, I mean, and tell her to take it at once to the Burgomaster.

> [Mrs. Stockmann *goes out with the packet through
> the dining-room.*

Petra.

What do you think Uncle Peter will say, father?

Dr. Stockmann.

What should he say?   He can't possibly be otherwise
than pleased that so important a fact has been brought
to light.

Hovstad.

I suppose you will let me put a short announcement
of your discovery in the *Messenger.*

Dr. Stockmann.

Yes, I shall be much obliged if you will.

Hovstad.

It is highly desirable that the public should know about
it as soon as possible.

Dr. Stockmann.

Yes, certainly.

Mrs. Stockmann.

[*Returning.*]   She's gone with it.

BILLING.

Strike me dead if you won't be the first man in the town, Doctor!

DR. STOCKMANN.

[*Walks up and down in high glee.*] Oh, nonsense! After all, I have done no more than my duty. I've been a lucky treasure-hunter, that's all. But all the same——

BILLING.

Hovstad, don't you think the town ought to get up a torchlight procession in honour of Dr. Stockmann?

HOVSTAD.

I shall certainly propose it.

BILLING.

And I'll talk it over with Aslaksen.

DR. STOCKMANN.

No, my dear friends; let all such claptrap alone. I won't hear of anything of the sort. And if the Directors should want to raise my salary, I won't accept it. I tell you, Katrina, I will not accept it.

MRS. STOCKMANN.

You are quite right, Thomas.

PETRA.

[*Raising her glass.*] Your health, father!

HOVSTAD *and* BILLING.

Your health, your health, Doctor!

HORSTER.

[*Clinking glasses with the* DOCTOR.]   I hope you may
have nothing but joy of your discovery.

DR. STOCKMANN.

Thanks, thanks, my dear friends! I can't tell you
how happy I am—! Oh, what a blessing it is to feel
that you have deserved well of your native town and
your fellow citizens.   Hurrah, Katrina!

[*He puts both his arms round her neck, and whirls
her round with him.* MRS. STOCKMANN *screams
and struggles.   A burst of laughter, applause, and
cheers for the* DOCTOR.   *The boys thrust their heads
in at the door.*

ACT SECOND

The Doctor's *sitting-room. The dining-room door is closed. Morning.*

MRS. STOCKMANN.

[*Enters from the dining-room with a sealed letter in her hand, goes to the foremost door on the right, and peeps in.*] Are you there, Thomas?

DR. STOCKMANN.

[*Within.*] Yes, I have just come in. [*Enters.*] What is it?

MRS. STOCKMANN.

A letter from your brother. [*Hands it to him.*

DR. STOCKMANN.

Aha, let us see. [*Opens the envelope and reads.*] "The MS. sent me is returned herewith——" [*Reads on, mumbling to himself.*] H'm——

MRS. STOCKMANN.

Well, what does he say?

DR. STOCKMANN.

[*Putting the paper in his pocket.*] Nothing; only that he'll come up himself about midday.

52

MRS. STOCKMANN.

Then be sure you remember to stay at home.

DR. STOCKMANN.

Oh, I can easily manage that; I've finished my morning's visits.

MRS. STOCKMANN.

I am very curious to know how he takes it.

DR. STOCKMANN.

You'll see he won't be over-pleased that it is I that have made the discovery, and not he himself.

MRS. STOCKMANN.

Ah, that's just what I'm afraid of.

DR. STOCKMANN.

Of course at bottom he'll be glad.   But still—Peter is damnably unwilling that any one but himself should do anything for the good of the town.

MRS. STOCKMANN.

Do you know, Thomas, I think you might stretch a point, and share the honour with him.   Couldn't it appear that it was he that put you on the track——?

DR. STOCKMANN.

By all means, for aught I care.   If only I can get things put straight——

Old MORTEN KIIL *puts his head in at the hall door,*
and asks slyly:

MORTEN KIIL.

Is it—is it true?

MRS. STOCKMANN.

[*Going towards him.*] Father—is that you?

DR. STOCKMANN.

Hallo, father-in-law! Good morning, good morning.

MRS. STOCKMANN.

Do come in.

MORTEN KIIL.

Yes, if it's true; if not, I'm off again.

DR. STOCKMANN.

If what is true?

MORTEN KIIL.

This crazy business about the water-works. Now is it true?

DR. STOCKMANN.

Why, of course it is. But how came y o u to hear of it?

MORTEN KIIL.

[*Coming in.*] Petra looked in on her way to the school——

DR. STOCKMANN.

Oh, did she?

MORTEN KIIL.

Ay ay—and she told me—. I thought she was only making game of me; but that's not like Petra either.

DR. STOCKMANN.

No, indeed; how could you think so?

MORTEN KIIL.

Oh, you can never be sure of anybody. You may be
made a fool of before you know where you are. So it is
true, after all?

DR. STOCKMANN.

Most certainly it is. Do sit down, father-in-law.
[*Forces him down on the sofa.*] Now isn't it a real blessing for the town——?

MORTEN KIIL.

[*Suppressing his laughter.*] A blessing for the town?

DR. STOCKMANN.

Yes, that I made this discovery in time——

MORTEN KIIL.

[*As before.*] Ay, ay, ay!—Well, I could never have
believed that you would play monkey-tricks with your
very own brother.

DR. STOCKMANN.

Monkey-tricks!

MRS. STOCKMANN.

Why, father dear——

MORTEN KIIL.

[*Resting his hands and chin on the top of his stick
and blinking slyly at the* DOCTOR.] What was it again?

Wasn't it that some animals had got into the water-pipes?

DR. STOCKMANN.

Yes; infusorial animals.

MORTEN KIIL.

And any number of these animals had got in, Petra said—whole swarms of them.

DR. STOCKMANN.

Certainly; hundreds of thousands.

MORTEN KIIL.

But no one can see them—isn't that it?

DR. STOCKMANN.

Quite right; no one can see them.

MORTEN KIIL.

[*With a quiet, chuckling laugh.*]   I'll be damned if that isn't the best thing I've heard of you yet.

DR. STOCKMANN.

What do you mean?

MORTEN KIIL.

But you'll never in this world make the Burgomaster take in anything of the sort.

DR. STOCKMANN.

Well, that we shall see.

MORTEN KIIL.

Do you really think he'll be so crazy?

DR. STOCKMANN.

I hope the whole town will be so crazy.

MORTEN KIIL.

The whole town! Well, I don't say but it may. But it serves them right; it'll teach them a lesson. They wanted to be so much cleverer than we old fellows. They hounded me out of the Town Council. Yes; I tell you they hounded me out like a dog, that they did. But now it's their turn. Just you keep up the game with them, Stockmann.

DR. STOCKMANN.

Yes, but, father-in-law——

MORTEN KIIL.

Keep it up, I say. [*Rising.*] If you can make the Burgomaster and his gang eat humble pie, I'll give a hundred crowns straight away to the poor.

DR. STOCKMANN.

Come, that's good of you.

MORTEN KIIL.

Of course I've little enough to throw away; but if you can manage that, I shall certainly remember the poor at Christmas-time, to the tune of fifty crowns.

HOVSTAD *enters from hall.*

HOVSTAD.

Good morning! [*Pausing*.] Oh! I beg your pardon——

DR. STOCKMANN.

Not at all.   Come in, come in.

MORTEN KIIL.

[*Chuckling again*.]   He!   Is he in it too?

HOVSTAD.

What do you mean?

DR. STOCKMANN.

Yes, of course he is.

MORTEN KIIL.

I might have known it!   It's to go into the papers. Ah, you're the one, Stockmann!   Do you two lay your heads together; I'm off.

DR. STOCKMANN.

Oh no; don't go yet, father-in-law.

MORTEN KIIL.

No, I'm off now.   Play them all the monkey-tricks you can think of.   Deuce take me but you shan't lose by it.   [*He goes*, MRS. STOCKMANN *accompanying him*.

DR. STOCKMANN.

[*Laughing*.]   What do you think—?   The old fellow doesn't believe a word of all this about the water-works.

HOVSTAD.

Was that what he——?

DR. STOCKMANN.

Yes; that was what we were talking about. And I daresay you have come on the same business?

HOVSTAD.

Yes. Have you a moment to spare, Doctor?

DR. STOCKMANN.

As many as you like, my dear fellow.

HOVSTAD.

Have you heard anything from the Burgomaster?

DR. STOCKMANN.

Not yet. He'll be here presently.

HOVSTAD.

I have been thinking the matter over since last evening.

DR. STOCKMANN.

Well?

HOVSTAD.

To you, as a doctor and a man of science, this business of the water-works appears an isolated affair. I daresay it hasn't occurred to you that a good many other things are bound up with it?

DR. STOCKMANN.

Indeed! In what way? Let us sit down, my dear fellow.—No; there, on the sofa.

[HOVSTAD *sits on sofa; the* DOCTOR *in an easy-chair on the other side of the table.*

DR. STOCKMANN.

Well, so you think——?

HOVSTAD.

You said yesterday that the water is polluted by impurities in the soil.

DR. STOCKMANN.

Yes, undoubtedly; the mischief comes from that poisonous swamp up in the Mill Dale.

HOVSTAD.

Excuse me, Doctor, but I think it comes from a very different swamp.

DR. STOCKMANN.

What swamp may that be?

HOVSTAD.

The swamp in which our whole municipal life is rotting.

DR. STOCKMANN.

The devil, Mr. Hovstad! What notion is this you've got hold of?

HOVSTAD.

All the affairs of the town have gradually drifted into the hands of a pack of bureaucrats——

DR. STOCKMANN.

Come now, they're not all bureaucrats.

HOVSTAD.

No; but those who are not are the friends and adherents of those who are.   We are entirely under the thumb of a ring of wealthy men, men of old family and position in the town.

DR. STOCKMANN.

Yes, but they are also men of ability and insight.

HOVSTAD.

Did they show ability and insight when they laid the water-pipes where they are?

DR. STOCKMANN.

No; that, of course, was a piece of stupidity.   But that will be set right now.

HOVSTAD.

Do you think it will go so smoothly?

DR. STOCKMANN.

Well, smoothly or not, it will have to be done.

HOVSTAD.

Yes, if the press exerts its influence.

DR. STOCKMANN.

Not at all necessary, my dear fellow; I am sure my brother——

HOVSTAD.

Excuse me, Doctor, but I must tell you that I think of taking the matter up.

DR. STOCKMANN.

In the paper?

HOVSTAD.

Yes. When I took over the *People's Messenger*, I was determined to break up the ring of obstinate old block-heads who held everything in their hands.

DR. STOCKMANN.

But you told me yourself what came of it. You nearly ruined the paper.

HOVSTAD.

Yes, at that time we had to draw in our horns, that's true enough. The whole Bath scheme might have fallen through if these men had been sent about their business. But now the Baths are an accomplished fact, and we can get on without these august personages.

DR. STOCKMANN.

Get on without them, yes; but still we owe them a great deal.

HOVSTAD.

The debt shall be duly acknowledged. But a journalist of my democratic tendencies cannot let such an

opportunity slip through his fingers.   We must explode
the tradition of official infallibility.   That rubbish must
be got rid of, like every other superstition.

DR. STOCKMANN.

There I am with you with all my heart, Mr. Hovstad.
If it's a superstition, away with it!

HOVSTAD.

I should be sorry to attack the Burgomaster, as he is
your brother.   But I know you think with me—the truth
before all other considerations.

DR. STOCKMANN.

Why, of course. [*Vehemently.*] But still—! but still——!

HOVSTAD.

You mustn't think ill of me.   I am neither more self-
interested nor more ambitious than other men.

DR. STOCKMANN.

Why, my dear fellow—who says you are?

HOVSTAD.

I come of humble folk, as you know; and I have had
ample opportunities of seeing what the lower classes
really require.   And that is to have a share in the direction of public affairs, Doctor.   That is what develops
ability and knowledge and self-respect——

DR. STOCKMANN.

I understand that perfectly.

HOVSTAD.

Yes; and I think a journalist incurs a heavy responsibility if he lets slip a chance of helping to emancipate the downtrodden masses. I know well enough that our oligarchy will denounce me as an agitator, and so forth; but what do I care? If only my conscience is clear, I——

DR. STOCKMANN.

Just so, just so, my dear Mr. Hovstad. But still—deuce take it——! [*A knock at the door.*] Come in!

ASLAKSEN, *the printer, appears at the door leading to the hall. He is humbly but respectably dressed in black, wears a white necktie, slightly crumpled, and has a silk hat and gloves in his hand.*

ASLAKSEN.

[*Bowing.*] I beg pardon, Doctor, for making so bold——

DR. STOCKMANN.

[*Rising.*] Hallo! If it isn't Mr. Aslaksen!

ASLAKSEN.

Yes, it's me, Doctor.

HOVSTAD.

[*Rising.*] Is it me you want, Aslaksen?

ASLAKSEN.

No, not at all. I didn't know you were here. No, it's the Doctor himself——

DR. STOCKMANN.

Well, what can I do for you?

ASLAKSEN.

Is it true, what Mr. Billing tells me, that you're going to get us a better set of water-works?

DR. STOCKMANN.

Yes, for the Baths.

ASLAKSEN.

Of course, of course. Then I just looked in to say that I'll back up the movement with all my might.

HOVSTAD.

[*To the* DOCTOR.]   You see!

DR. STOCKMANN.

I'm sure I thank you heartily; but——

ASLAKSEN.

You may find it no such bad thing to have us small middle-class men at your back.   We form what you may call a compact majority in the town—when we really make up our minds, that's to say.   And it's always well to have the majority with you, Doctor.

DR. STOCKMANN.

No doubt, no doubt; but I can't conceive that any special measures will be necessary in this case.   I should think in so clear and straightforward a matter——

ASLAKSEN.

Yes, but all the same, it can do no harm. I know the
local authorities very well—the powers that be are not
over ready to adopt suggestions from outsiders. So I
think it wouldn't be amiss if we made some sort of a
demonstration.

HOVSTAD.

Precisely my opinion.

DR. STOCKMANN.

A demonstration, you say?   But in what way would
you demonstrate?

ASLAKSEN.

Of course with great moderation, Doctor. I always
insist upon moderation; for moderation is a citizen's first
virtue—at least that's my way of thinking.

DR. STOCKMANN.

We all know that, Mr. Aslaksen.

ASLAKSEN.

Yes, I think my moderation is generally recognised.
And this affair of the water-works is very important for
us small middle-class men. The Baths bid fair to become, as you might say, a little gold-mine for the town.
We shall all have to live by the Baths, especially we house-
owners. So we want to support the Baths all we can;
and as I am Chairman of the House-owners' Association——

DR. STOCKMANN.

Well——?

ASLAKSEN.

And as I'm an active worker for the Temperance[1] Society—of course you know, Doctor, that I'm a temperance man?

DR. STOCKMANN.

To be sure, to be sure.

ASLAKSEN.

Well, you'll understand that I come in contact with a great many people. And as I'm known to be a prudent and law-abiding citizen, as you yourself remarked, Doctor, I have certain influence in the town, and hold some power in my hands—though I say it that shouldn't.

DR. STOCKMANN.

I know that very well, Mr. Aslaksen.

ASLAKSEN.

Well then, you see—it would be easy for me to get up an address, if it came to a pinch.

DR. STOCKMANN.

An address?

ASLAKSEN.

Yes, a kind of vote of thanks to you, from the citizens of the town, for your action in a matter of such general concern. Of course it will have to be drawn up with all fitting moderation, so as to give no offence to the authori-

---

[1] The word "mådehold," in Norwegian, means both "moderation" and "temperance."

ties and parties in power.   But so long as we're careful
about that, no one can take it ill, I should think.

HOVSTAD.

Well, even if they didn't particularly like it——

ASLAKSEN.

No, no, no; no offence to the powers that be, Mr. Hovstad.   No opposition to people that can take it out of us
again so easily.   I've had enough of that in my time; no
good ever comes of it.   But no one can object to the free
but temperate expression of a citizen's opinion.

DR. STOCKMANN.

[*Shaking his hand.*]   I can't tell you, my dear Mr.
Aslaksen, how heartily it delights me to find so much
support among my fellow townsmen.   I'm so happy—so
happy!   Come, you'll have a glass of sherry?   Eh?

ASLAKSEN.

No, thank you; I never touch spirituous liquors.

DR. STOCKMANN.

Well, then, a glass of beer—what do you say to that?

ASLAKSEN.

Thanks, not that either, Doctor.   I never take anything so early in the day.   And now I'll be off round the
town, and talk to some of the house-owners, and prepare
public opinion.

DR. STOCKMANN.

It's extremely kind of you, Mr. Aslaksen; but I really cannot get it into my head that all these preparations are necessary. The affair seems to me so simple and self-evident.

ASLAKSEN.

The authorities always move slowly, Doctor—God forbid I should blame them for it——

HOVSTAD.

We'll stir them up in the paper to-morrow, Aslaksen.

ASLAKSEN.

No violence, Mr. Hovstad. Proceed with moderation, or you'll do nothing with them. Take my advice; I've picked up experience in the school of life.—And now I'll say good morning, Doctor. You know now that at least you have us small middle-class men behind you, solid as a wall. You have the compact majority on your side, Doctor.

DR. STOCKMANN.

Many thanks, my dear Mr. Aslaksen. [*Holds out his hand.*] Good-bye, good-bye.

ASLAKSEN.

Are you coming to the office, Mr. Hovstad?

HOVSTAD.

I shall come on presently. I have still one or two things to arrange.

ASLAKSEN.

Very well.
  [*Bows and goes.*   DR. STOCKMANN *accompanies him
  into the hall.*

HOVSTAD.

[*As the* DOCTOR *re-enters.*]   Well, what do you say to
that, Doctor?   Don't you think it is high time we should
give all this weak-kneed, half-hearted cowardice a good
shaking-up?

DR. STOCKMANN.

Are you speaking of Aslaksen?

HOVSTAD.

Yes, I am.   He's a decent enough fellow, but he's one
of those who are sunk in the swamp.   And most people
here are just like him; they are for ever wavering and
wobbling from side to side; what with scruples and misgivings, they never dare advance a step.

DR. STOCKMANN.

Yes, but Aslaksen seems to me thoroughly well-inten-
tioned.

HOVSTAD.

There is one thing I value more than good intentions,
and that is an attitude of manly self-reliance.

DR. STOCKMANN.

There I am quite with you.

HOVSTAD.

So I am going to seize this opportunity, and try whether I can't for once put a little grit into their good intentions. The worship of authority must be rooted up in this town. This gross, inexcusable blunder of the water-works must be brought home clearly to every voter.

DR. STOCKMANN.

Very well. If you think it's for the good of the community, so be it; but not till I have spoken to my brother.

HOVSTAD.

At all events, I shall be writing my leader in the meantime. And if the Burgomaster won't take the matter up——

DR. STOCKMANN.

But how can you conceive his refusing?

HOVSTAD.

Oh, it's not inconceivable. And then——

DR. STOCKMANN.

Well then, I promise you—; look here—in that case you may print my paper—put it in just as it is.

HOVSTAD.

May I? Is that a promise?

DR. STOCKMANN.

[*Handing him the manuscript.*] There it is; take it with you. You may as well read it in any case; you can return it to me afterwards.

HOVSTAD.

Very good; I shall do so.   And now, good-bye, Doctor.

DR. STOCKMANN.

Good-bye, good-bye.   You'll see it will all go smoothly,
Mr. Hovstad—as smoothly as possible.

HOVSTAD.

H'm—we shall see.
[*Bows and goes out through the hall.*

DR. STOCKMANN.

[*Going to the dining-room door and looking in.*]   Katrina!   Hallo! are you back, Petra?

PETRA.

[*Entering.*]   Yes, I've just got back from school.

MRS. STOCKMANN.

[*Entering.*]   Hasn't he been here yet?

DR. STOCKMANN.

Peter?   No; but I have been having a long talk with
Hovstad.   He's quite enthusiastic about my discovery.
It turns out to be of much wider import than I thought at
first.   So he has placed his paper at my disposal, if I
should require it.

MRS. STOCKMANN.

Do you think you will?

DR. STOCKMANN.

Not I! But at the same time, one cannot but be
proud to know that the enlightened, independent press
is on one's side. And what do you think? I have had
a visit from the Chairman of the House-owners' Association too.

MRS. STOCKMANN.

Really? What did he want?

DR. STOCKMANN.

To assure me of his support. They will all stand by
me at a pinch. Katrina, do you know what I have behind me?

MRS. STOCKMANN.

Behind you? No. What have you behind you?

DR. STOCKMANN.

The compact majority!

MRS. STOCKMANN.

Oh! Is that good for you, Thomas?

DR. STOCKMANN.

Yes, indeed; I should think it w a s good. [*Rubbing
his hands as he walks up and down.*] Great God! what
a delight it is to feel oneself in such brotherly unison with
one's fellow townsmen?

PETRA.

And to do so much that's good and useful, father!

DR. STOCKMANN.

And all for one's native town, too!

MRS. STOCKMANN.

There's the bell.

DR. STOCKMANN.

That must be he.   [*Knock at the door.*]   Come in!
   Enter BURGOMASTER STOCKMANN *from the hall.*

BURGOMASTER.

Good morning.

DR. STOCKMANN.

I'm glad to see you, Peter.

MRS. STOCKMANN.

Good morning, brother-in-law.   How are you?

BURGOMASTER.

Oh, thanks, so-so.   [*To the* DOCTOR.]   Yesterday evening, after office hours, I received from you a dissertation
upon the state of the water at the Baths.

DR. STOCKMANN.

Yes.   Have you read it?

BURGOMASTER.

I have

DR. STOCKMANN.

And what do you think of the affair?

BURGOMASTER.

H'm—   [*With a sidelong glance.*

MRS. STOCKMANN.

Come, Petra.

[*She and* PETRA *go into the room on the left.*

BURGOMASTER.

[*After a pause.*]   Was it necessary to make all these investigations behind my back?

DR. STOCKMANN.

Yes, till I was absolutely certain, I——

BURGOMASTER.

And are you absolutely certain now?

DR. STOCKMANN.

My paper must surely have convinced you of that.

BURGOMASTER.

Is it your intention to submit this statement to the
Board of Directors, as a sort of official document?

DR. STOCKMANN.

Of course.   Something must be done in the matter,
and that promptly.

BURGOMASTER.

As usual, you use very strong expressions in your statement.   Amongst other things, you say that what we offer
our visitors is a slow poison.

Dr. Stockmann.

Why, Peter, what else can it be called? Only think—poisoned water both internally and externally! And that to poor invalids who come to us in all confidence, and pay us handsomely to cure them!

Burgomaster.

And then you announce as your conclusion that we must build a sewer to carry off the alleged impurities from the Mill Dale, and must re-lay all the water-pipes.

Dr. Stockmann.

Yes. Can you suggest any other plan?—I know of none.

Burgomaster.

I found a pretext for looking in at the town engineer's this morning, and—in a half-jesting way—I mentioned these alterations as things we might possibly have to consider, at some future time.

Dr. Stockmann.

At some future time!

Burgomaster.

Of course he smiled at what he thought my extravagance. Have you taken the trouble to think what your proposed alterations would cost? From what the engineer said, I gathered that the expenses would probably amount up to several hundred thousand crowns.

Dr. Stockmann.

So much as that?

BURGOMASTER.

Yes. But that is not the worst. The work would take at least two years.

DR. STOCKMANN.

Two years! Do you mean to say two whole years?

BURGOMASTER.

At least. And what are we to do with the Baths in the meanwhile? Are we to close them? We should have no alternative. Do you think any one would come here, if it got abroad that the water was pestilential?

DR. STOCKMANN.

But, Peter, that's precisely what it is.

BURGOMASTER.

And all this now, just now, when the Baths are doing so well! Neighbouring towns, too, are not without their claims to rank as health-resorts. Do you think they would not at once set to work to divert the full stream of visitors to themselves? Undoubtedly they would; and we should be left stranded. We should probably have to give up the whole costly undertaking; and so you would have ruined your native town.

DR. STOCKMANN.

I—ruined——!

BURGOMASTER.

It is only through the Baths that the town has any future worth speaking of. You surely know that as well as I do.

DR. STOCKMANN.

Then what do you think should be done?

BURGOMASTER.

I have not succeeded in convincing myself that the condition of the water at the Baths is as serious as your statement represents.

DR. STOCKMANN.

I tell you it's if anything worse—or will be in the summer, when the hot weather sets in.

BURGOMASTER.

I repeat that I believe you exaggerate greatly. A competent physician should know what measures to take— he should be able to obviate deleterious influences, and to counteract them in case they should make themselves unmistakably felt.

DR. STOCKMANN.

Indeed—?   And then—?

BURGOMASTER.

The existing water-works are, once for all, a fact, and must naturally be treated as such.   But when the time comes, the Directors will probably not be indisposed to consider whether it may not be possible, without unreasonable pecuniary sacrifices, to introduce certain improvements.

DR. STOCKMANN.

And do you imagine I could ever be a party to such dishonesty?

BURGOMASTER.

Dishonesty?

DR. STOCKMANN.

Yes, it would be dishonesty—a fraud, a lie, an absolute
crime against the public, against society as a whole!

BURGOMASTER.

I have not, as I before remarked, been able to convince
myself that there is really any such imminent danger.

DR. STOCKMANN.

You have! You must have! I know that my demonstration is absolutely clear and convincing. And you understand it perfectly, Peter, only you won't admit it. It
was you who insisted that both the Bath-buildings and
the water-works should be placed where they now are;
and it's t h a t—it's that damned blunder that you won't
confess. Pshaw! Do you think I don't see through you?

BURGOMASTER.

And even if it were so? If I do watch over my reputation with a certain anxiety, I do it for the good of
the town. Without moral authority I cannot guide and
direct affairs in the way I consider most conducive to
the general welfare. Therefore—and on various other
grounds—it is of great moment to me that your statement should not be submitted to the Board of Directors.
It must be kept back, for the good of the community.
Later on I will bring up the matter for discussion, and
we will do the best we can, quietly; but not a word, not a
whisper, of this unfortunate business must come to the
public ears.

DR. STOCKMANN.

But it can't be prevented now, my dear Peter.

BURGOMASTER.

It must and shall be prevented.

DR. STOCKMANN.

It can't be, I tell you; far too many people know about it already.

BURGOMASTER.

Know about it!   Who?   Surely not those fellows on the *People's Messenger*——?

DR. STOCKMANN.

Oh yes; they know.   The liberal, independent press will take good care that you do your duty.

BURGOMASTER.

[*After a short pause.*]   You are an amazingly reckless man, Thomas.   Have not you reflected what the consequences of this may be to yourself?

DR. STOCKMANN.

Consequences?—Consequences to me?

BURGOMASTER.

Yes—to you and yours.

DR. STOCKMANN.

What the devil do you mean?

BURGOMASTER.

I believe I have always shown myself ready and willing to lend you a helping hand.

DR. STOCKMANN.

Yes, you have, and I thank you for it.

BURGOMASTER.

I ask for no thanks. Indeed, I was in some measure forced to act as I did—for my own sake. I always hoped I should be able to keep you a little in check, if I helped to improve your pecuniary position.

DR. STOCKMANN.

What! So it was only for your own sake——!

BURGOMASTER.

In a measure, I say. It is painful for a man in an official position, when his nearest relative goes and compromises himself time after time.

DR. STOCKMANN.

And you think I do that?

BURGOMASTER.

Yes, unfortunately, you do, without knowing it. Yours is a turbulent, unruly, rebellious spirit. And then you have an unhappy propensity for rushing into print upon every possible and impossible occasion. You no sooner hit upon an idea than you must needs write a newspaper article or a whole pamphlet about it.

DR. STOCKMANN.

Isn't it a citizen's duty, when he has conceived a new idea, to communicate it to the public!

BURGOMASTER.

Oh, the public has no need for new ideas.   The public gets on best with the good old recognised ideas it has already.

DR. STOCKMANN.

You say that right out!

BURGOMASTER.

Yes, I must speak frankly to you for once.   Hitherto I have tried to avoid it, for I know how irritable you are; but now I must tell you the truth, Thomas   You have no conception how much you injure yourself by your officiousness.   You complain of the authorities, ay, of the Government itself—you cry them down and maintain that you have been slighted, persecuted.   But what else can you expect, with your impossible disposition?

DR. STOCKMANN.

Oh, indeed!   So I am impossible, am I?

BURGOMASTER.

Yes, Thomas, you are an impossible man to work with. I know that from experience.   You have no consideration for any one or any thing; you seem quite to forget that you have me to thank for your position as medical officer of the Baths——

DR. STOCKMANN.

It was mine by right! Mine, and no one else's! I was the first to discover the town's capabilities as a watering-place; I saw them, and, at that time, I alone. For years I fought single-handed for this idea of mine; I wrote and wrote——

BURGOMASTER.

No doubt; but then the right time had not come. Of course, in that out-of-the-world corner, you could not judge of that. As soon as the propitious moment arrived, I—and others—took the matter in hand——

DR. STOCKMANN.

Yes, and you went and bungled the whole of my glorious plan. Oh, we see now what a set of wiseacres you were!

BURGOMASTER.

All *I* can see is that you are again seeking an outlet for your pugnacity. You want to make an onslaught on your superiors—that is an old habit of yours. You cannot endure any authority over you; you look askance at any one who holds a higher post than your own; you regard him as a personal enemy—and then you care nothing what kind of weapon you use against him. But now I have shown you how much is at stake for the town, and consequently for me too. And therefore I warn you, Thomas, that I am inexorable in the demand I am about to make of you!

DR. STOCKMANN.

What demand?

BURGOMASTER.

As you have not had the sense to refrain from chatter-ing to outsiders about this delicate business, which should have been kept an official secret, of course it cannot now be hushed up.   All sorts of rumours will get abroad, and evil-disposed persons will invent all sorts of additions to them.   It will therefore be necessary for you publicly to contradict these rumours.

DR. STOCKMANN.

I!   How?   I don't understand you?

BURGOMASTER.

We expect that, after further investigation, you will come to the conclusion that the affair is not nearly so serious or pressing as you had at first imagined.

DR. STOCKMANN.

Aha!   So you expect that?

BURGOMASTER.

Furthermore, we expect you to express your confidence that the Board of Directors will thoroughly and conscien-tiously carry out all measures for the remedying of any possible defects.

DR. STOCKMANN.

Yes, but that you'll never be able to do, so long as you go on tinkering and patching.   I tell you that, Peter; and it's my deepest, sincerest conviction——

BURGOMASTER.

As an official, you have no right to hold any individual conviction.

DR. STOCKMANN.

[*Starting.*] No right to——?

BURGOMASTER.

As an official, I say. In your private capacity, of course, it is another matter. But as a subordinate official of the Baths, you have no right to express any conviction at issue with that of your superiors.

DR. STOCKMANN.

This is too much! I, a doctor, a man of science, have no right to——!

BURGOMASTER.

The matter in question is not a purely scientific one; it is a complex affair; it has both a technical and an economic side.

DR. STOCKMANN.

What the devil do I care what it is! I will be free to speak my mind upon any subject under the sun!

BURGOMASTER.

As you please—so long as it does not concern the Baths. With them we forbid you to meddle.

DR. STOCKMANN.

[*Shouts.*] You forbid——! You! A set of——

BURGOMASTER.

I forbid it—*I*, your chief; and when I issue an order, you have simply to obey.

DR. STOCKMANN.

[*Controlling himself.*] Upon my word, Peter, if you weren't my brother——

PETRA.

[*Tears open the door.*] Father, you shan't submit to this!

MRS. STOCKMANN.

[*Following her.*] Petra, Petra!

BURGOMASTER.

Ah! So we have been listening!

MRS. STOCKMANN.

The partition is so thin, we couldn't help——

PETRA.

I stood and listened on purpose.

BURGOMASTER.

Well, on the whole, I am not sorry——

DR. STOCKMANN.

[*Coming nearer to him.*] You spoke to me of forbidding and obeying——

BURGOMASTER.

You have forced me to adopt that tone.

DR. STOCKMANN.

And am I to give myself the lie, in a public declaration?

BURGOMASTER.

We consider it absolutely necessary that you should issue a statement in the terms indicated.

DR. STOCKMANN.

And if I do not obey?

BURGOMASTER.

Then we shall ourselves put forth a statement to reassure the public.

DR. STOCKMANN.

Well and good; then I shall write against you. I shall stick to my point and prove that *I* am right, and you wrong. And what will you do then?

BURGOMASTER.

Then I shall be unable to prevent your dismissal.

DR. STOCKMANN.

What——!

PETRA.

Father! Dismissal!

MRS. STOCKMANN.

Dismissal!

BURGOMASTER.

Your dismissal from the Baths. I shall be compelled to move that notice be given you at once, and that you have henceforth no connection whatever with the Baths.

DR. STOCKMANN.

You would dare to do that!

BURGOMASTER.

It is you who are playing the daring game.

PETRA.

Uncle, this is a shameful way to treat a man like father!

MRS. STOCKMANN.

Do be quiet, Petra!

BURGOMASTER.

[*Looking at* PETRA.]   Aha!   We have opinions of our own already, eh?   To be sure, to be sure!   [*To* MRS. STOCKMANN.]   Sister-in-law, you are presumably the most rational member of this household.   Use all your influence with your husband; try to make him realise what all this will involve both for his family——

DR. STOCKMANN.

My family concerns myself alone!

BURGOMASTER.

——both for his family, I say, and for the town **he** lives in.

DR. STOCKMANN.

It is I that have the real good of the town at heart!
I want to lay bare the evils that, sooner or later, must
come to light. Ah! You shall see whether I love my
native town.

BURGOMASTER.

You, who, in your blind obstinacy, want to cut off the
town's chief source of prosperity!

DR. STOCKMANN.

That source is poisoned, man! Are you mad? We
live by trafficking in filth and corruption! The whole
of our flourishing social life is rooted in a lie!

BURGOMASTER.

Idle fancies—or worse. The man who scatters broad-
cast such offensive insinuations against his native place
must be an enemy of society.

DR. STOCKMANN.

[*Going towards him.*] You dare to——!

MRS. STOCKMANN.

[*Throwing herself between them.*] Thomas!

PETRA.

[*Seizing her father's arm.*] Keep calm, father!

BURGOMASTER.

I will not expose myself to violence. You have had
your warning now. Reflect upon what is due to yourself and to your family. Good-bye.   [*He goes.*

DR. STOCKMANN.

[*Walking up and down.*] And I must put up with such treatment! In my own house, Katrina! What do you say to that!

MRS. STOCKMANN.

Indeed, it's a shame and a disgrace, Thomas——

PETRA.

Oh, if I could only get hold of uncle——!

DR. STOCKMANN.

It's my own fault. I ought to have stood up against them long ago—to have shown my teeth—and used them too!—And to be called an enemy of society! Me! I won't bear it; by Heaven, I won't!

MRS. STOCKMANN.

But my dear Thomas, after all, your brother has the power——

DR. STOCKMANN.

Yes, but I have the right.

MRS. STOCKMANN.

Ah yes, right, right! What good does it do to have the right, if you haven't any might?

PETRA.

Oh, mother—how can you talk so?

DR. STOCKMANN.

What! No good, in a free community, to have right
on your side? What an absurd idea, Katrina! And
besides—haven't I the free and independent press before
me—and the compact majority at my back? That is
might enough, I should think!

MRS. STOCKMANN.

Why, good heavens, Thomas! you're surely not thinking of——?

DR. STOCKMANN.

What am I not thinking of?

MRS. STOCKMANN.

——of setting yourself up against your brother, I
mean.

DR. STOCKMANN.

What the devil would you have me do, if not stick to
what is right and true?

PETRA.

Yes, that's what I should like to know?

MRS. STOCKMANN.

But it will be of no earthly use. If they won't, they
won't.

DR. STOCKMANN.

Ho-ho, Katrina! just wait a while, and you shall see
whether I can fight my battles to the end.

MRS. STOCKMANN.

Yes, to the end of getting your dismissal; that is what will happen.

DR. STOCKMANN.

Well then, I shall at any rate have done my duty towards the public, towards society—I who am called an enemy of society!

MRS. STOCKMANN.

But towards your family, Thomas? Towards us at home? Do you think t h a t is doing your duty towards those who are dependent on you?

PETRA.

Oh, mother, don't always think first of us.

MRS. STOCKMANN.

Yes, it's easy for you to talk; you can stand alone if need be.—But remember the boys, Thomas; and think a little of yourself too, and of me——

DR. STOCKMANN.

You're surely out of your senses, Katrina! If I were to be such a pitiful coward as to knuckle under to this Peter and his confounded crew—should I ever have another happy hour in all my life?

MRS. STOCKMANN.

I don't know about that; but God preserve us from the happiness we shall all of us have if you persist in defying them. There you will be again, with nothing to

live on, with no regular income. I should have thought
we had had enough of that in the old days. Remember
them, Thomas; think of what it all means.

DR. STOCKMANN.

[*Struggling with himself and clenching his hands.*]
And this is what these jacks-in-office can bring upon a
free and honest man! Isn't it revolting, Katrina?

MRS. STOCKMANN.

Yes, no doubt they are treating you shamefully. But
God knows there's plenty of injustice one must just submit to in this world.—Here are the boys, Thomas. Look
at them! What is to become of them? Oh no, no! you
can never have the heart——

EILIF *and* MORTEN, *with school-books, have meanwhile
entered.*

DR. STOCKMANN.

The boys——! [*With a sudden access of firmness and
decision.*] Never, though the whole earth should crum-
ble, will I bow my neck beneath the yoke.
[*Goes towards his room.*

MRS. STOCKMANN.

[*Following him.*] Thomas—what are you going to do?

DR. STOCKMANN.

[*At the door.*] I must have the right to look my boys
in the face when they have grown into free men.
[*Goes into his room.*

MRS. STOCKMANN.

[*Bursts into tears.*]   Ah, God help us all!

PETRA.

Father is true to the core.   He will never give in!
[*The boys ask wonderingly what it all means;* PETRA
signs to them to be quiet.

ACT THIRD

The Editor's Room of the " People's Messenger." In the
background, to the left, an entrance-door; to the right
another door, with glass panes, through which can
be seen the composing-room. A door in the right-
hand wall. In the middle of the room a large table
covered with papers, newspapers, and books. In
front, on the left, a window, and by it a desk with a
high stool. A couple of arm-chairs beside the table;
some other chairs along the walls. The room is dingy
and cheerless, the furniture shabby, the arm-chairs
dirty and torn. In the composing-room are seen a
few compositors at work; further back, a hand-press
in operation.

Hovstad *is seated at the desk, writing. Presently* Billing
enters from the right, with the Doctor's *manuscript*
in his hand.

BILLING.

Well, I must say——!

HOVSTAD.

[*Writing.*]   Have you read it through?

BILLING.

[*Laying the MS. on the desk.*]   Yes, I should think I
had.

HOVSTAD.

Don't you think the Doctor comes out strong?

BILLING.

Strong! Why, strike me dead if he isn't crushing! Every word falls like a—well, like a sledge-hammer.

HOVSTAD.

Yes, but these fellows won't collapse at the first blow.

BILLING.

True enough; but we'll keep on hammering away, blow after blow, till the whole officialdom comes crashing down. As I sat in there reading that article, I seemed to hear the revolution thundering afar.

HOVSTAD.

[*Turning round.*] Hush! Don't let Aslaksen hear that.

BILLING.

[*In a lower voice.*] Aslaksen's a white-livered, cowardly fellow, without a spark of manhood in him. But this time you'll surely carry your point? Eh? You'll print the Doctor's paper?

HOVSTAD.

Yes, if only the Burgomaster doesn't give in——

BILLING.

That would be deuced annoying.

HOVSTAD.

Well, whatever happens, fortunately we can turn the situation to account. If the Burgomaster won't agree to the Doctor's proposal, he'll have all the small middle-class down upon him—all the House-owners' Association, and the rest of them. And if he does agree to it, he'll fall out with the whole crew of big shareholders in the Baths, who have hitherto been his main support——

BILLING.

Yes, of course; for no doubt they'll have to fork out a lot of money——

HOVSTAD.

You may take your oath of that. And then, don't you see, when the ring is broken up, we'll din it into the public day by day that the Burgomaster is incompetent in every respect, and that all responsible positions in the town, the whole municipal government in short, must be entrusted to men of liberal ideas.

BILLING.

Strike me dead if that isn't the square truth! I see it—I see it: we are on the eve of a revolution!

[*A knock at the door.*

HOVSTAD.

Hush! [*Calls.*] Come in!

DR. STOCKMANN *enters from the back, left.*

HOVSTAD.

[*Going towards him.*] Ah, here is the Doctor. Well?

DR. STOCKMANN.

Print away, Mr. Hovstad!

HOVSTAD.

So it has come to that?

BILLING.

Hurrah!

DR. STOCKMANN.

Print away, I tell you.   To be sure it has come to that.
Since they will have it so, they must.   War is declared,
Mr. Billing!

BILLING.

War to the knife, say I!   War to the death, Doctor!

DR. STOCKMANN.

This article is only the beginning.   I have four or five
others sketched out in my head already.   But where do
you keep Aslaksen?

BILLING.

[*Calling into the printing-room.*]   Aslaksen! just come
here a moment.

HOVSTAD.

Four or five more articles, eh?   On the same subject?

DR. STOCKMANN.

Oh no—not at all, my dear fellow.   No; they will deal
with quite different matters.   But they're all of a piece
with the water-works and sewer question.   One thing
leads to another.   It's just like beginning to pick at an
old house, don't you know?

BILLING.

Strike me dead, but that's true! You feel you can't leave off till you've pulled the whole lumber-heap to pieces.

ASLAKSEN.

[*Enters from the printing-room.*] Pulled to pieces! Surely the Doctor isn't thinking of pulling the Baths to pieces?

HOVSTAD.

Not at all. Don't be alarmed.

DR. STOCKMANN.

No, we were talking of something quite different. Well, what do you think of my article, Mr. Hovstad?

HOVSTAD.

I think it's simply a masterpiece——

DR. STOCKMANN.

Yes, isn't it? I'm glad you think so—very glad.

HOVSTAD.

It's so clear and to the point. One doesn't in the least need to be a specialist to understand the gist of it. I am certain every intelligent man will be on your side.

ASLAKSEN.

And all the prudent ones too, I hope?

BILLING.

Both the prudent and imprudent—in fact, almost the whole town.

ASLAKSEN.

Then I suppose we may venture to print it.

DR. STOCKMANN.

I should think so!

HOVSTAD.

It shall go in to-morrow.

DR. STOCKMANN.

Yes, plague take it, not a day must be lost.   Look here, Mr. Aslaksen, this is what I wanted to ask you: won't you take personal charge of the article?

ASLAKSEN.

Certainly I will.

DR. STOCKMANN.

Be as careful as if it were gold. No printers' errors; every word is important. I shall look in again presently; perhaps you'll be able to let me see a proof.—Ah! I can't tell you how I long to have the thing in print—to see it launched——

BILLING.

Yes, like a thunderbolt!

DR. STOCKMANN.

——and submitted to the judgment of every intelligent citizen.   Oh, you have no idea what I have had to put up with to-day. I've been threatened with all sorts of things. I was to be robbed of my clearest rights as a human being——

BILLING.

What! Your rights as a human being!

DR. STOCKMANN.

——I was to humble myself, and eat the dust; I was to set my personal interests above my deepest, holiest convictions——

BILLING.

Strike me dead, but that's too outrageous!

HOVSTAD.

Oh, what can you expect from that quarter?

DR. STOCKMANN.

But they shall find they were mistaken in me; they shall learn that in black and white, I promise them! I shall throw myself into the breach every day in the *Messenger*, bombard them with one explosive article after another——

ASLAKSEN.

Yes, but look here——

BILLING.

Hurrah! It's war! War!

DR. STOCKMANN.

I shall smite them to the earth, I shall crush them, I shall level their entrenchments to the ground in the eyes of all right-thinking men! That's what I shall do!

ASLAKSEN.

But above all things be temperate, Doctor; bombard with moderation——

BILLING.

Not at all, not at all! Don't spare the dynamite!

DR. STOCKMANN.

[*Going on imperturbably.*] For now it's no mere question of water-works and sewers, you see. No, the whole community must be purged, disinfected——

BILLING.

T h e r e sounds the word of salvation!

DR. STOCKMANN.

All the old bunglers must be sent packing, you understand. And that in every possible department! Such endless vistas have opened out before me to-day. I am not quite clear about everything yet, but I shall see my way presently. It's young and vigorous standard-bearers we must look for, my friends; we must have new captains at all the outposts.

BILLING.

Hear, hear!

DR. STOCKMANN.

And if only we hold together, it will go so smoothly, so smoothly! The whole revolution will glide off the stocks just like a ship. Don't you think so?

HOVSTAD.

For my part, I believe we have now every prospect of placing our municipal affairs in the right hands.

ASLAKSEN.

And if only we proceed with moderation, I really don't think there can be any danger.

DR. STOCKMANN.

Who the devil cares whether there's danger or not! What I do, I do in the name of truth and for conscience' sake.

HOVSTAD.

You are a man to be backed up, Doctor.

ASLAKSEN.

Yes, there's no doubt the Doctor is a true friend to the town; he's what I call a friend of society.

BILLING.

Strike me dead if Dr. Stockmann isn't a Friend of the People, Aslaksen!

ASLAKSEN.

I have no doubt the House-owners' Association will soon adopt that expression.

Dr. Stockmann.

[*Shaking their hands, deeply moved.*]   Thanks, thanks, my dear, faithful friends; it does me good to hear you. My respected brother called me something very different. Never mind!   Trust me to pay him back with interest! But I must be off now to see a poor devil of a patient.   I shall look in again, though.   Be sure you look after the article, Mr. Aslaksen; and, whatever you do, don't leave out any of my notes of exclamation!   Rather put in a few more!   Well, good-bye for the present, good-bye, good-bye.

    [*Mutual salutations while they accompany him to the door.   He goes out.*

Hovstad.

He will be invaluable to us.

Aslaksen.

Yes, so long as he confines himself to this matter of the Baths.   But if he goes further, it will scarcely be advisable to follow him.

Hovstad.

H'm—that entirely depends on——

Billing.

You're always so confoundedly timid, Aslaksen.

Aslaksen.

Timid?   Yes, when it's a question of attacking local authorities, I a m timid, Mr. Billing; I have learnt caution in the school of experience, let me tell you. But start me on the higher politics, confront me with the Government itself, and then see if I'm timid.

BILLING.

No, you're not; but that's just where your inconsistency comes in.

ASLAKSEN.

The fact is, I am keenly alive to my responsibilities. If you attack the Government, you at least do society no harm; for the men attacked don't care a straw, you see— they stay where they are all the same. But l o c a l authorities can be turned out; and then we might get some incompetent set into power, to the irreparable injury both of house-owners and other people.

HOVSTAD.

But the education of citizens by self-government—do you never think of t h a t?

ASLAKSEN.

When a man has solid interests to protect, he can't think of everything, Mr. Hovstad.

HOVSTAD.

Then I hope I may never have solid interests to protect.

BILLING.

Hear, hear!

ASLAKSEN.

[*Smiling.*] H'm! [*Points to the desk.*] Governor Stensgård[1] sat in that editorial chair before you.

BILLING.

[*Spitting.*] Pooh! A turncoat like that!

HOVSTAD.

I am no weathercock—and never will be.

ASLAKSEN.

A politician should never be too sure of anything on
earth, Mr. Hovstad. And as for you, Mr. Billing, you
ought to take in a reef or two, I should say, now that you
are applying for the secretaryship to the Town Council.

BILLING.

I——!

HOVSTAD.

Is that so, Billing?

BILLING.

Well, yes—but, deuce take it, you understand, I'm
only doing it to spite their high-mightinesses.

ASLAKSEN.

Well, that has nothing to do with me. But if I am to
be accused of cowardice and inconsistency, I should just

---

[1] It will be remembered that Aslaksen figures in *The League of
Youth*, of which Stensgård is the central character. Stensgård, we
see, has justified Lundestad's prophecy by attaining the high ad-
ministrative dignity of "Stiftamtmand," here roughly translated
"Governor."

like to point out t h i s : My political record is open to
every one. I have not changed at all, except in becoming more moderate. My heart still belongs to the people; but I don't deny that my reason inclines somewhat
towards the authorities—the local ones, I mean.

[*Goes into the printing-room.*

BILLING.

Don't you think we should try to get rid of him, Hovstad?

HOVSTAD.

Do you know of any one else that will pay for our
paper and printing?

BILLING.

What a confounded nuisance it is to have no capital!

HOVSTAD.

[*Sitting down by the desk.*] Yes, if we only had
that——

BILLING.

Suppose you applied to Dr. Stockmann?

HOVSTAD.

[*Turning over his papers.*] What would be the good?
He hasn't a rap.

BILLING.

No; but he has a good man behind him—old Morten
Kiil—"The Badger," as they call him.

HOVSTAD.

[*Writing.*]   Are you so sure he has money?

BILLING.

Yes, strike me dead if he hasn't!   And part of it must certainly go to Stockmann's family.   He's bound to provide for—for the children at any rate.

HOVSTAD.

[*Half turning.*]   Are you counting on t h a t?

BILLING.

Counting?   How should I be counting on it?

HOVSTAD.

Best not!   And that secretaryship you shouldn't count on either; for I can assure you you won't get it.

BILLING.

Do you think I don't know that?   A refusal is the very thing I want.   Such a rebuff fires the spirit of opposition in you, gives you a fresh supply of gall, as it were; and that's just what you need in a god-forsaken hole like this, where anything really stimulating so seldom happens.

HOVSTAD.

[*Writing.*]   Yes, yes.

BILLING.

Well—they shall soon hear from me!—Now I'll go and write the appeal to the House-owners' Association.

[*Goes into the room on the right.*

HOVSTAD.

[*Sits at his desk, biting his penholder, and says slowly:*] H'm—so that's the way of it.—[*A knock at the door.*] Come in.

PETRA *enters from the back, left.*

HOVSTAD.

[*Rising.*] What! Is it you? Here?

PETRA.

Yes; please excuse me——

HOVSTAD.

[*Offering her an arm-chair.*] Won't you sit down?

PETRA.

No, thanks; I must go again directly.

HOVSTAD.

Perhaps you bring a message from your father——?

PETRA.

No, I have come on my own account. [*Takes a book from the pocket of her cloak.*] Here is that English story.

HOVSTAD.

Why have you brought it back?

PETRA.

Because I won't translate it.

HOVSTAD.

But you promised——

PETRA.

Yes; but then I hadn't read it. I suppose you have not read it either?

HOVSTAD.

No; you know I can't read English; but——

PETRA.

Exactly; and that's why I wanted to tell you that you must find something else. [*Putting the book on the table.*] This will never do for the *Messenger*.

HOVSTAD.

Why not?

PETRA.

Because it flies in the face of all your convictions.

HOVSTAD.

Well, for that matter——

PETRA.

You don't understand me. It makes out that a supernatural power looks after the so-called good people in this world, and turns everything to their advantage at last; while all the so-called bad people are punished.

HOVSTAD.

Yes, but that's all right. That's the very thing the public like.

PETRA.

And would y o u supply the public with such stuff?
You don't believe a word of it yourself. You know well
enough that things do not really happen like that.

HOVSTAD.

Of course not; but an editor can't always do as he
likes. He has often to humour people's fancies in minor
matters. After all, politics is the chief thing in life—at
any rate for a newspaper; and if I want the people to
follow me along the path of emancipation and progress,
I mustn't scare them away. If they find a moral story
like this down in the cellar,[1] they are all the more ready
to take in what we tell them above—they feel themselves
safer.

PETRA.

For shame! You're not such a hypocrite as to set
traps like that for your readers. You're not a spider.

HOVSTAD.

[*Smiling.*] Thanks for your good opinion. It's true
that the idea is Billing's, not mine.

PETRA.

Mr. Billing's!

HOVSTAD.

Yes, at least he was talking in that strain the other
day. It was Billing that was so anxious to get the story
into the paper; I don't even know the book.

[1] The reference is to the continental feuilleton at the foot of the
page.

PETRA.

But how can Mr. Billing, with his advanced views——

HOVSTAD.

Well, Billing is many-sided. He's applying for the secretaryship to the Town Council, I hear.

PETRA.

I don't believe that, Mr. Hovstad. How could he descend to such a thing?

HOVSTAD.

That you must ask h i m .

PETRA.

I could never have thought it of Billing!

HOVSTAD.

[*Looking more closely at her.*] No? Is it such a surprise to you?

PETRA.

Yes. And yet—perhaps not. Oh, I don't know——

HOVSTAD.

We journalists are not worth much, Miss Petra.

PETRA.

Do you really say that?

HOVSTAD.

I think so, now and then.

PETRA.

Yes, in the little every-day squabbles—that I can understand. But now that you have taken up a great cause——

HOVSTAD.

You mean this affair of your father's?

PETRA.

Of course. I should think you must feel yourself worth more than the general run of people now.

HOVSTAD.

Yes, to-day I do feel something of the sort.

PETRA.

Yes, surely you must. Oh, it's a glorious career you have chosen! To be the pioneer of unrecognised truths and new and daring ways of thought!—even, if that were all, to stand forth fearlessly in support of an injured man——

HOVSTAD.

Especially when the injured man is—I hardly know how to put it——

PETRA.

You mean when he is so upright and true?

HOVSTAD.

[*In a low voice.*] I mean—especially when he is your father.

PETRA.

[*Suddenly taken aback.*]   T h a t ?

HOVSTAD.

Yes, Petra—Miss Petra.

PETRA.

So that is your chief thought, is it?   Not the cause
itself?   Not the truth?   Not father's great, warm heart?

HOVSTAD.

Oh, that too, of course.

PETRA.

No, thank you; you said too much that time, Mr. Hovstad.   Now I shall never trust you again, in anything.

HOVSTAD.

Can you be so hard on me because it's mainly for
your sake——?

PETRA.

What I blame you for is that you have not acted
straightforwardly towards father.   You have talked to
him as if you cared only for the truth and the good of
the community.   You have trifled with both father and
me.   You are not the man you pretended to be.   And
that I will never forgive you—never.

HOVSTAD.

You shouldn't say that so bitterly, Miss Petra—least
of all now.

PETRA.

Why not now?

HOVSTAD.

Because your father cannot do without my help.

PETRA.

[*Measuring him from head to foot.*]   So you are capable of t h a t, too?   Oh, shame!

HOVSTAD.

No, no.   I spoke without thinking.   You mustn't believe that of me.

PETRA.

I know what to believe.   Good-bye.

ASLAKSEN *enters from printing-room, hurriedly and mysteriously.*

ASLAKSEN.

What do you think, Mr. Hovstad—[*Seeing* PETRA.] Ow, that's awkward——

PETRA.

Well, there is the book.   You must give it to some one else.   [*Going towards the main door.*

HOVSTAD.

[*Following her.*]   But, Miss Petra——

PETRA.

Good-bye.   [*She goes.*

ASLAKSEN.

I say, Mr. Hovstad!

HOVSTAD.

Well well; what is it?

ASLAKSEN.

The Burgomaster's out there, in the printing-office.

HOVSTAD.

The Burgomaster?

ASLAKSEN.

Yes. He wants to speak to you; he came in by the back way—he didn't want to be seen, you understand.

HOVSTAD.

What can be the meaning of this? Stop, I'll go myself——

[*Goes towards the printing-room, opens the door, bows and invites the* BURGOMASTER *to enter.*

HOVSTAD.

Keep a look-out, Aslaksen, that no one——

ASLAKSEN.

I understand.   [*Goes into the printing-room.*

BURGOMASTER.

You didn't expect to see me here, Mr. Hovstad.

HOVSTAD.

No, I cannot say that I did.

BURGOMASTER.

[*Looking about him.*] You are very comfortably installed here—capital quarters.

HOVSTAD.

Oh——

BURGOMASTER.

And here have I come, without with your leave or by your leave, to take up your time——

HOVSTAD.

You are very welcome, Burgomaster; I am at your service. Let me take your cap and stick. [*He does so, and puts them on a chair.*] And won't you be seated?

BURGOMASTER.

[*Sitting down by the table.*] Thanks. [HOVSTAD *also sits by the table.*] I have been much—very much worried to-day, Mr. Hovstad.

HOVSTAD.

Really? Well, I suppose with all your various duties, Burgomaster——

BURGOMASTER.

It is the Doctor that has been causing me annoyance to-day.

HOVSTAD.

Indeed! The Doctor?

BURGOMASTER.

He has written a sort of memorandum to the Directors about some alleged shortcomings in the Baths.

HOVSTAD.

Has he really?

BURGOMASTER.

Yes; hasn't he told you? I thought he said——

HOVSTAD.

Oh yes, by-the-bye, he did mention something——

ASLAKSEN.

[*From the printing-office.*] I've just come for the manuscript——

HOVSTAD.

[*In a tone of vexation.*] Oh!—there it is on the desk.

ASLAKSEN.

[*Finding it.*] All right.

BURGOMASTER.

Why, t h a t is the very thing——

ASLAKSEN.

Yes, this is the Doctor's article, Burgomaster.

HOVSTAD.

Oh, is t h a t what you were speaking of?

BURGOMASTER.

Precisely.   What do you think of it?

HOVSTAD.

I have no technical knowledge of the matter, and I've only glanced through it.

BURGOMASTER.

And yet you are going to print it!

HOVSTAD.

I can't very well refuse a signed communication——

ASLAKSEN.

I have nothing to do with the editing of the paper, Burgomaster——

BURGOMASTER.

Of course not.

ASLAKSEN.

I merely print what is placed in my hands.

BURGOMASTER.

Quite right, quite right.

ASLAKSEN.

So I must——   [*Goes towards the printing-room.*

BURGOMASTER.

No, stop a moment, Mr. Aslaksen.   With your permission, Mr. Hovstad——

HOVSTAD.

By all means, Burgomaster.

BURGOMASTER.

You are a discreet and thoughtful man, Mr. Aslaksen.

ASLAKSEN.

I am glad you think so, Burgomaster.

BURGOMASTER.

And a man of very wide influence.

ASLAKSEN.

Well—chiefly among the lower middle-class.

BURGOMASTER.

The small taxpayers form the majority—here as everywhere.

ASLAKSEN.

That's very true.

BURGOMASTER.

And I have no doubt that you know the general feeling among them.   Am I right?

ASLAKSEN.

Yes, I think I may say that I do, Burgomaster.

BURGOMASTER.

Well—since our townsfolk of the poorer class appear to be so heroically eager to make sacrifices——

ASLAKSEN.

How so?

HOVSTAD.

Sacrifices?

BURGOMASTER.

It is a pleasing evidence of public spirit—a most pleasing evidence. I admit it is more than I should quite have expected. But, of course, you know public feeling better than I do.

ASLAKSEN.

Yes but, Burgomaster——

BURGOMASTER.

And assuredly it is no small sacrifice the town will have to make.

HOVSTAD.

The town?

ASLAKSEN.

But I don't understand—— It's the Baths——

BURGOMASTER.

At a rough provisional estimate, the alterations the Doctor thinks desirable will come to two or three hundred thousand crowns.

ASLAKSEN.

That's a lot of money; but——

BURGOMASTER.

Of course we shall be obliged to raise a municipal loan.

HOVSTAD.

[*Rising.*]   You surely can't mean that the town——?

ASLAKSEN.

Would you come upon the rates?   Upon the scanty savings of the lower middle-class?

BURGOMASTER.

Why, my dear Mr. Aslaksen, where else are the funds to come from?

ASLAKSEN.

The proprietors of the Baths must see to that.

BURGOMASTER.

The proprietors are not in a position to go to any further expense.

ASLAKSEN.

Are you quite sure of that, Burgomaster?

BURGOMASTER.

I have positive information.   So if these extensive alterations are called for, the town itself will have to bear the cost.

ASLAKSEN.

Oh, plague take it all—I beg your pardon!—but this is quite another matter, Mr. Hovstad.

HOVSTAD.

Yes, it certainly is.

BURGOMASTER.

The worst of it is, that we shall be obliged to close the establishment for a couple of years.

HOVSTAD.

To close it? Completely?

ASLAKSEN.

For two years!

BURGOMASTER.

Yes, the work will require that time—at least.

ASLAKSEN.

But, damn it all! we can't stand that, Burgomaster. What are we house-owners to live on in the meantime?

BURGOMASTER.

It's extremely difficult to say, Mr. Aslaksen. But what would you have us do? Do you think a single visitor will come here if we go about making them fancy that the water is poisoned, that the place is pestilential, that the whole town——

ASLAKSEN.

And it's all nothing but fancy?

BURGOMASTER.

With the best will in the world, I have failed to convince myself that it is anything else.

ASLAKSEN.

In that case it's simply inexcusable of Dr. Stockmann
—I beg your pardon, Burgomaster, but——

BURGOMASTER.

I'm sorry to say you are only speaking the truth, Mr.
Aslaksen. Unfortunately, my brother has always been
noted for his rashness.

ASLAKSEN.

And yet you want to back him up in this, Mr. Hovstad!

HOVSTAD.

But who could possibly imagine that——?

BURGOMASTER.

I have drawn up a short statement of the facts, as they
appear from a sober-minded standpoint; and I have inti-
mated that any drawbacks that may possibly exist can
no doubt be remedied by measures compatible with the
finances of the Baths.

HOVSTAD.

Have you the article with you, Burgomaster?

BURGOMASTER.

[*Feeling in his pockets.*]   Yes; I brought it with me, in
case you——

ASLAKSEN.

[*Quickly.*]   Plague take it, there he is!

BURGOMASTER.

Who ?   My brother ?

HOVSTAD.

Where ? where ?

ASLAKSEN.

He's coming through the composing-room.

BURGOMASTER.

Most unfortunate!   I don't want to meet him here, and yet there are several things I want to talk to you about.

HOVSTAD.

[*Pointing to the door on the right.*]   Go in there for a moment.

BURGOMASTER.

But——?

HOVSTAD.

You'll find nobody but Billing there.

ASLAKSEN.

Quick, quick, Burgomaster; he's just coming.

BURGOMASTER.

Very well, then.   But try to get rid of him quickly.
[*He goes out by the door on the right, which* ASLAKSEN *opens, and closes behind him.*

HOVSTAD.

Pretend to be busy, Aslaksen.

[*He sits down and writes.* ASLAKSEN *turns over a heap of newspapers on a chair, right.*

DR. STOCKMANN.

[*Entering from the composing-room.*]   Here I am, back again.   [*Puts down his hat and stick.*

HOVSTAD.

[*Writing.*]   Already, Doctor?   Make haste with what we were speaking of, Aslaksen.   We've no time to lose to-day.

DR. STOCKMANN.

[*To* ASLAKSEN.]   No proof yet, I hear.

ASLAKSEN.

[*Without turning round.*]   No; how could you expect it?

DR. STOCKMANN.

Of course not; but you understand my impatience. I can have no rest or peace until I see the thing in print.

HOVSTAD.

H'm; it will take a good while yet.   Don't you think so, Aslaksen?

ASLAKSEN.
I'm afraid it will.

DR. STOCKMANN.

All right, all right, my good friend; then I shall look in again.   I'll look in twice if necessary.   With so much at stake—the welfare of the whole town—one mustn't grudge a little trouble. [*Is on the point of going but stops and comes back.*] Oh, by the way—there's one other thing I must speak to you about.

Hovstad.

Excuse me; wouldn't some other time——?

Dr. Stockmann.

I can tell you in two words. You see it's this: when people read my article in the paper to-morrow, and find I have spent the whole winter working quietly for the good of the town——

Hovstad.

Yes but, Doctor——

Dr. Stockmann.

I know what you're going to say. You don't think it was a bit more than my duty—my simple duty as a citizen. Of course I know that, as well as you do. But you see, my fellow townsmen—good Lord! the poor souls think so much of me——

Aslaksen.

Yes, the townspeople have hitherto thought very highly of you, Doctor.

Dr. Stockmann.

That's exactly why I'm afraid that—. What I wanted to say was this: when all this comes to them—especially to the poorer classes—as a summons to take the affairs of the town into their own hands for the future——

HOVSTAD.

[*Rising.*]   H'm, Doctor, I won't conceal from you——

DR. STOCKMANN.

Aha! I thought there was something brewing! But I won't hear of it. If they are getting up anything of that sort——

HOVSTAD.

Of what sort?

DR. STOCKMANN.

Well, anything of any sort—a procession with banners, or a banquet, or a subscription for a testimonial, or whatever it may be—you must give me your solemn promise to put a stop to it. And you too, Mr. Aslaksen; do you hear?

HOVSTAD.

Excuse me, Doctor; we may as well tell you the whole truth first as last——

MRS. STOCKMANN *enters from the back, left.*

MRS. STOCKMANN.

[*Seeing the* DOCTOR.]   Ah! just as I thought!

HOVSTAD.

[*Going towards her.*]   Mrs. Stockmann, too?

DR. STOCKMANN.

What the devil do y o u want here, Katrina?

MRS. STOCKMANN.

You know very well what I want.

HOVSTAD.

Won't you sit down? Or perhaps——

MRS. STOCKMANN.

Thanks, please don't trouble. And you must forgive my following my husband here; remember, I am the mother of three children.

DR. STOCKMANN.

Stuff and nonsense! We all know that well enough.

MRS. STOCKMANN.

Well, it doesn't look as if you thought very much about your wife and children to-day, or you wouldn't be so ready to plunge us all into ruin.

DR. STOCKMANN.

Are you quite mad, Katrina! Has a man with a wife and children no right to proclaim the truth? Has he no right to be an active and useful citizen? Has he no right to do his duty by the town he lives in?

MRS. STOCKMANN.

Everything in moderation, Thomas!

ASLAKSEN.

That's just what I say. Moderation in everything.

Mrs. Stockmann.

You are doing us a great wrong, Mr. Hovstad, in enticing my husband away from house and home, and befooling him in this way.

Hovstad.

I am not befooling any one——

Dr. Stockmann.

Befooling! Do you think I should let myself be befooled?

Mrs. Stockmann.

Yes, that's just what you do. I know very well that you are the cleverest man in the town; but you're very easily made a fool of, Thomas. [*To* Hovstad.] Remember that he loses his post at the Baths if you print what he has written——

Aslaksen.

What!

Hovstad.

Well now, really, Doctor——

Dr. Stockmann.

[*Laughing.*] Ha ha! just let them try—! No no, my dear, they'll think twice about that. I have the compact majority behind me, you see!

Mrs. Stockmann.

That's just the misfortune, that you should have such a horrid thing behind you.

DR. STOCKMANN.

Nonsense, Katrina;—you go home and look after your house, and let me take care of society. How can you be in such a fright when you see me so confident and happy? [*Rubbing his hands and walking up and down.*] Truth and the People must win the day; you may be perfectly sure of that. Oh! I can see all our free-souled citizens standing shoulder to shoulder like a conquering army——! [*Stopping by a chair.*] Why, what the devil is t h a t?

ASLAKSEN.

[*Looking at it.*] Oh Lord!

HOVSTAD.

[*The same.*] H'm—

DR. STOCKMANN.

Why, here's the top-knot of authority!
[*He takes the* BURGOMASTER'S *official cap carefully between the tips of his fingers and holds it up.*

MRS. STOCKMANN.

The Burgomaster's cap!

DR. STOCKMANN.

And here's the staff of office, too! But how in the devil's name did they——?

HOVSTAD.

Well then——

DR. STOCKMANN.

Ah, I understand! He has been here to talk you over. Ha, ha! He reckoned without his host that time! And when he caught sight of me in the printing-room— [*Bursts out laughing*]—he took to his heels, eh, Mr. Aslaksen?

ASLAKSEN.

[*Hurriedly.*] Exactly; he took to his heels, Doctor.

DR. STOCKMANN.

Made off without his stick and——. No, t h a t won't do! Peter never left anything behind him. But where the devil have you stowed him? Ah—in here, of course. Now you shall see, Katrina!

MRS. STOCKMANN.

Thomas—I implore you——!

ASLAKSEN.

Take care, Doctor!
[DR. STOCKMANN *has put on the* BURGOMASTER'S *cap and grasped his stick; he now goes up to the door, throws it open, and makes a military salute.*

The BURGOMASTER *enters, red with anger. Behind him comes* BILLING.

BURGOMASTER.

What is the meaning of these antics?

DR. STOCKMANN.

Respect, my good Peter! Now, it's I that am in power in this town.   [*He struts up and down.*

MRS. STOCKMANN.

[*Almost in tears.*] Oh, Thomas!

BURGOMASTER.

[*Following him.*] Give me my cap and stick!

DR. STOCKMANN.

[*As before.*] You may be Chief of Police, but I am Burgomaster. I am master of the whole town I tell you!

BURGOMASTER.

Put down my cap, I say. Remember it is an official cap, as by law prescribed!

DR. STOCKMANN.

Pshaw! Do you think the awakening lion of the democracy will let itself be scared by a gold-laced cap? There's to be a revolution in the town to-morrow, let me tell you. You threatened me with dismissal; but now *I* dismiss y o u —dismiss you from all your offices of trust—. You think I can't do it?—Oh, yes, I can! I have the irresistible forces of society on my side. Hovstad and Billing will thunder in the *People's Messenger*, and Aslaksen will take the field at the head of the House-owners' Association——

ASLAKSEN.

No, Doctor, I shall not.

DR. STOCKMANN.

Why, of course you will——

BURGOMASTER.

Aha! Perhaps Mr. Hovstad would like to join the agitation after all?

HOVSTAD.

No, Burgomaster.

ASLAKSEN.

No, Mr. Hovstad isn't such a fool as to ruin both himself and the paper for the sake of a delusion.

DR. STOCKMANN.

[*Looking about him.*]   What does all this mean?

HOVSTAD.

You have presented your case in a false light, Doctor; therefore I am unable to give you my support.

BILLING.

And after what the Burgomaster has been so kind as to explain to me, I——

DR. STOCKMANN.

In a false light! Well, I am responsible for that.   Just you print my article, and I promise you I shall prove it up to the hilt.

HOVSTAD.

I shall not print it.   I cannot, and will not, and dare not print it.

DR. STOCKMANN.

You dare not?   What nonsense is this?   You are editor; and I suppose it's the editor that controls a paper.

ASLAKSEN.

No, it's the subscribers, Doctor.

BURGOMASTER.

Fortunately.

ASLAKSEN.

It's public opinion, the enlightened majority, the house-owners and all the rest. It's t h e y who control a paper.

DR. STOCKMANN.

[*Calmly.*]   And all these powers I have against me?

ASLAKSEN.

Yes, you have.   It would mean absolute ruin for the town if your article were inserted.

DR. STOCKMANN.

So t h a t is the way of it!

BURGOMASTER.

My hat and stick!
    [DR. STOCKMANN *takes off the cap and lays it on the table along with the stick.*

BURGOMASTER.

[*Taking them both.*]   Your term of office has come to an untimely end.

DR. STOCKMANN.

The end is not yet.   [*To* HOVSTAD.]   So you are quite determined not to print my article in the *Messenger?*

HOVSTAD.

Quite; for the sake of your family, if for no other reason.

MRS. STOCKMANN.

Oh, be kind enough to leave his family out of the question, Mr. Hovstad.

BURGOMASTER.

[*Takes a manuscript from his pocket.*] When this appears, the public will be in possession of all necessary information; it is an authentic statement. I place it in your hands.

HOVSTAD.

[*Taking the MS.*] Good. It shall appear in due course.

DR. STOCKMANN.

And not mine! You imagine you can kill me and the truth by a conspiracy of silence! But it won't be so easy as you think. Mr. Aslaksen, will you be good enough to print my article at once, as a pamphlet? I'll pay for it myself, and be my own publisher. I'll have four hundred copies—no, five—six hundred.

ASLAKSEN.

No. If you offered me its weight in gold, I dare not lend my press to such a purpose, Doctor. I daren't fly in the face of public opinion. You won't get it printed anywhere in the whole town.

DR. STOCKMANN.

Then give it me back.

HOVSTAD.

[*Handing him the MS.*]   By all means.

DR. STOCKMANN.

[*Taking up his hat and cane.*]   It shall be made public all the same.   I shall read it at a great mass meeting; all my fellow citizens shall hear the voice of truth!

BURGOMASTER.

Not a single society in the town would let you their hall for such a purpose.

ASLAKSEN.

Not one, I'm quite certain.

BILLING.

No, strike me dead if they would!

MRS. STOCKMANN.

That would be too disgraceful!   Why do they turn against you like this, every one of them?

DR. STOCKMANN.

[*Irritated.*]   I'll tell you why.   It's because in this town all the men are old women—like you.   They all think of nothing but their families, not of the general good.

MRS. STOCKMANN.

[*Taking his arm.*]   Then I'll show them that an—an old woman can be a man for once in a way.   For n o w I'll stand by you, Thomas.

DR. STOCKMANN.

Bravely said, Katrina! I swear by my soul and conscience the truth shall out! If they won't let me a hall, I'll hire a drum and march through the town with it; and I'll read my paper at every street corner.

BURGOMASTER.

You can scarcely be such a raving lunatic as that?

DR. STOCKMANN.

I am.

ASLAKSEN.

You would not get a single man in the whole town to go with you.

BILLING.

No, strike me dead if you would!

MRS. STOCKMANN.

Don't give in, Thomas. I'll ask the boys to go with you.

DR. STOCKMANN.

That's a splendid idea!

MRS. STOCKMANN.

Morten will be delighted; and Eilif will go too, I daresay.

DR. STOCKMANN.

Yes, and so will Petra! And you yourself, Katrina!

MRS. STOCKMANN.

No no, not I.   But I'll stand at the window and watch you—that I will.

DR. STOCKMANN.

[*Throwing his arms about her and kissing her.*]   Thank you for that!   Now, my good sirs, we're ready for the fight!   Now we shall see whether your despicable tactics can stop the mouth of the patriot who wants to purge society!

>   [*He and his wife go out together by the door in the back, left.*

BURGOMASTER.

[*Shaking his head dubiously.*]   Now he has turned h e r head too!

ACT FOURTH

A large old-fashioned room in CAPTAIN HORSTER'S *house.
An open folding-door in the background leads to an
anteroom. In the wall on the left are three windows.
About the middle of the opposite wall is a platform,
and on it a small table, two candles, a water-bottle
and glass, and a bell. For the rest, the room is lighted
by sconces placed between the windows. In front, on
the left, is a table with a candle on it, and by it a
chair. In front, to the right, a door, and near it a few
chairs.*

*Large assemblage of all classes of townsfolk. In the crowd
are a few women and schoolboys. More and more people gradually stream in from the back until the room
is quite full.*

FIRST CITIZEN.

[*To another standing near him.*] So you're here too,
Lamstad?

SECOND CITIZEN.

I never miss a public meeting.

A BYSTANDER.

I suppose you've brought your whistle?

SECOND CITIZEN.

Of course I have; haven't you?

THIRD CITIZEN.

I should think so. And Skipper Evensen said he'd bring a thumping big horn.

SECOND CITIZEN.

He's a good 'un, is Evensen! [*Laughter in the group.*

A FOURTH CITIZEN.

[*Joining them.*] I say, what's it all about? What's going on here to-night?

SECOND CITIZEN.

Why, it's Dr. Stockmann that's going to lecture against the Burgomaster.

FOURTH CITIZEN.

But the Burgomaster's his brother.

FIRST CITIZEN.

That makes no difference. Dr. Stockmann's not afraid of him.

THIRD CITIZEN.

But he's all wrong; the *People's Messenger* says so.

SECOND CITIZEN.

Yes, he must be wrong this time; for neither the House-owners' Association nor the Citizens' Club would let him have a hall.

FIRST CITIZEN.

They wouldn't even lend him the hall at the Baths.

SECOND CITIZEN.

No, you may be sure they wouldn't.

A MAN.

[*In another group.*]   Now, who's the one to follow in this business, eh?

ANOTHER MAN.

[*In the same group.*]   Just keep your eye on Aslaksen, and do as he does.

BILLING.

[*With a portfolio under his arm, makes his way through the crowd.*]   Excuse me, gentlemen.   Will you allow me to pass?   I'm here to report for the *People's Messenger.* Many thanks.   [*Sits by the table on the left.*

A WORKING-MAN.

Who's he?

ANOTHER WORKING-MAN.

Don't you know him?   It's that fellow Billing, that writes for Aslaksen's paper.

CAPTAIN HORSTER *enters by the door in front on the right, escorting* MRS. STOCKMANN *and* PETRA.   EILIF *and* MORTEN *follow them.*

HORSTER.

This is where I thought you might sit; you can so easily slip out if anything should happen.

MRS. STOCKMANN.

Do you think there will be any disturbance?

HORSTER.

One can never tell—with such a crowd. But there's no occasion for anxiety.

MRS. STOCKMANN.

[*Sitting down.*] How kind it was of you to offer Stockmann this room.

HORSTER.

Since no one else would, I——

PETRA.

[*Who has also seated herself.*] And it was brave too, Captain Horster.

HORSTER.

Oh, I don't see where the bravery comes in.

HOVSTAD *and* ASLAKSEN *enter at the same moment, but make their way through the crowd separately.*

ASLAKSEN.

[*Going up to* HORSTER.] Hasn't the Doctor come yet?

HORSTER.

He's waiting in there.
[*A movement at the door in the background.*

HOVSTAD.

[*To* BILLING.] There's the Burgomaster! Look!

BILLING.

Yes, strike me dead if he hasn't put in an appearance after all!

BURGOMASTER STOCKMANN *makes his way blandly through the meeting, bowing politely to both sides, and takes his stand by the wall on the left. Soon afterwards,* DR. STOCKMANN *enters by the door on the right. He wears a black frockcoat and white necktie. Faint applause, met by a subdued hissing. Then silence.*

DR. STOCKMANN.

[*In a low tone.*]   How do you feel, Katrina?

MRS. STOCKMANN.

Quite comfortable, thank you.   [*In a low voice.*]   Now do keep your temper, Thomas.

DR. STOCKMANN.

Oh, I shall keep myself well in hand.   [*Looks at his watch, ascends the platform, and bows.*]   It's a quarter past the hour, so I shall begin——   [*Takes out his MS.*

ASLAKSEN.

But surely a chairman must be elected first.

DR. STOCKMANN.

No, that's not at all necessary.

SEVERAL GENTLEMEN.

[*Shouting.*]   Yes, yes.

BURGOMASTER.

I should certainly say that a chairman ought to be elected.

DR. STOCKMANN.

But I've called this meeting to give a lecture, Peter!

BURGOMASTER.

Dr. Stockmann's lecture may possibly lead to differences of opinion.

SEVERAL VOICES IN THE CROWD.

A chairman!   A chairman!

HOVSTAD.

The general voice of the meeting seems to be for a chairman!

DR. STOCKMANN.

[*Controlling himself.*]   Very well then; let the meeting have its way.

ASLAKSEN.

Will not the Burgomaster take the chair?

THREE GENTLEMEN.

[*Clapping.*]   Bravo!   Bravo!

BURGOMASTER.

For reasons you will easily understand, I must decline. But, fortunately, we have among us one whom I think we

can all accept.   I allude to the president of the House-
owners' Association, Mr. Aslaksen.

MANY VOICES.

Yes, yes!   Bravo Aslaksen!   Hurrah for Aslaksen!
[DR. STOCKMANN *takes his MS. and descends from
the platform.*

ASLAKSEN.

Since my fellow citizens repose this trust in me, I cannot refuse——
[*Applause and cheers.* ASLAKSEN *ascends the platform.*

BILLING.

[*Writing.*]   So—"Mr. Aslaksen was elected by ac-
clamation——"

ASLAKSEN.

And now, as I have been called to the chair, I take
the liberty of saying a few brief words.   I am a quiet,
peace-loving man; I am in favour of discreet moderation,
and of—and of moderate discretion.   Every one who
knows me, knows that.

MANY VOICES.

Yes, yes, Aslaksen!

ASLAKSEN.

I have learnt in the school of life and of experience
that moderation is the virtue in which the individual citizen finds his best advantage——

BURGOMASTER.

Hear, hear!

ASLAKSEN.

——and it is discretion and moderation, too, that best
serve the community.   I could therefore suggest to our
respected fellow citizen, who has called this meeting, that
he should endeavour to keep within the bounds of moderation.

A MAN.

[*By the door.*] Three cheers for the Temperance
Society!

A VOICE.

Go to the devil!

VOICES.

Hush! hush!

ASLAKSEN.

No interruptions, gentlemen!—Does any one wish to
offer any observations?

BURGOMASTER.

Mr. Chairman!

ASLAKSEN.

Burgomaster Stockmann will address the meeting.

BURGOMASTER.

On account of my close relationship—of which you
are probably aware—to the present medical officer of
the Baths, I should have preferred not to speak here
this evening.   But my position as chairman of the Baths,

and my care for the vital interests of this town, force
me to move a resolution. I may doubtless assume that
not a single citizen here present thinks it desirable that
untrustworthy and exaggerated statements should get
abroad as to the sanitary condition of the Baths and of
our town.

MANY VOICES.

No, no, no!   Certainly not!   We protest!

BURGOMASTER.

I therefore beg to move, "That this meeting declines
to hear the proposed lecture or speech on the subject by
the medical officer of the Baths."

DR. STOCKMANN.

[*Flaring up.*]   Declines to hear——!   What do you
mean ?

MRS. STOCKMANN.

[*Coughing.*]   H'm! h'm!

DR. STOCKMANN.

[*Controlling himself.*]   So I am not to be heard ?

BURGOMASTER.

In my statement in the *People's Messenger* I have
made the public acquainted with the essential facts, so
that all well-disposed citizens can easily form their own
judgment.   From that statement it will be seen that the
medical officer's proposal—besides amounting to a vote
of censure upon the leading men of the town—at bottom

only means saddling the ratepayers with an unnecessary outlay of at least a hundred thousand crowns.

[*Sounds of protest and some hissing.*

ASLAKSEN.

[*Ringing the bell.*] Order, gentlemen! I must beg leave to support the Burgomaster's resolution. I quite agree with him that there is something beneath the surface of the Doctor's agitation. In all his talk about the Baths, it is really a revolution he is aiming at; he wants to effect a redistribution of power. No one doubts the excellence of Dr. Stockmann's intentions—of course there cannot be two opinions as to that. I, too, am in favour of self-government by the people, if only it doesn't cost the ratepayers too much. But in this case it would do so; and therefore I'll be hanged if—excuse me—in short, I cannot go with Dr. Stockmann upon this occasion. You can buy even gold too dear; that's my opinion.

[*Loud applause on all sides.*

HOVSTAD.

I, too feel bound to explain my attitude. Dr. Stockmann's agitation seemed at first to find favour in several quarters, and I supported it as impartially as I could. But it presently appeared that we had been misled by a false representation of the facts——

DR. STOCKMANN.

False——!

HOVSTAD.

Well then, an untrustworthy representation. This the Burgomaster's report has proved. I trust no one here present doubts my liberal principles; the attitude of the *Messenger* on all great political questions is well known to you all.   But I have learned from men of judgment and experience that in purely local matters a paper must observe a certain amount of caution.

Aslaksen.

I entirely agree with the speaker.

Hovstad.

And in the matter under discussion it is quite evident that Dr. Stockmann has public opinion against him. But, gentlemen, what is an editor's clearest and most imperative duty?   Is it not to work in harmony with his readers?   Has he not in some sort received a tacit mandate to further assiduously and unweariedly the interests of his constituents?   Or am I mistaken in this?

Many Voices.

No, no, no!   Hovstad is right!

Hovstad.

It has cost me a bitter struggle to break with a man in whose house I have of late been a frequent guest—with a man who, up to this day, has enjoyed the unqualified goodwill of his fellow citizens—with a man whose only, or, at any rate, whose chief fault is that he consults his heart rather than his head.

A Few Scattered Voices.

That's true!   Hurrah for Dr. Stockmann!

Beerbohm Tree as Dr. Stockmann in " An Enemy of
the People "

HOVSTAD.

But my duty towards the community has constrained me to break with him. Then, too, there is another consideration that impels me to oppose him, and, if possible, to block the ill-omened path upon which he is entering: consideration for his family——

DR. STOCKMANN.

Keep to the water-works and sewers!

HOVSTAD.

——consideration for his wife and his unprotected[1] children.

MORTEN.

Is that us, mother?

MRS. STOCKMANN.

Hush!

ASLAKSEN.

I will now put the Burgomaster's resolution to the vote.

DR. STOCKMANN.

You need not. I have no intention of saying anything this evening of all the filth at the Baths. No! You shall hear something quite different.

BURGOMASTER.

[*Half aloud.*] What next, I wonder?

[1] Literally, "unprovided-for."

A Drunken Man.

[*At the main entrance.*] I'm a ratepayer, so I've a right to my opinion! And it's my full, firm, incomprehensible opinion that——

Several Voices.

Silence up there!

Others.

He's drunk!   Turn him out!
> [*The drunken man is turned out.*

Dr. Stockmann.

Can I speak?

Aslaksen.

[*Ringing the bell.*] Dr. Stockmann will address the meeting.

Dr. Stockmann.

A few days ago, I should have liked to see any one venture upon such an attempt to gag me as has been made here to-night! I would have fought like a lion for my sacred rights! But now I care little enough; for now I have more important things to speak of.
> [*The people crowd closer round him.   Morten Kiil comes in sight among the bystanders.*

Dr. Stockmann.

[*Continuing.*] I have been pondering a great many things during these last days—thinking such a multitude of thoughts, that at last my head was positively in a whirl——

BURGOMASTER.

[*Coughing.*]   H'm——!

DR. STOCKMANN.

But presently things seemed to straighten themselves out, and I saw them clearly in all their bearings.   That is why I stand here this evening.   I am about to make great revelations, my fellow citizens!   I am going to announce to you a far-reaching discovery, beside which the trifling fact that our water-works are poisoned, and that our health-resort is built on pestilential ground, sinks into insignificance.

MANY VOICES.

[*Shouting.*]   Don't speak about the Baths!   We won't listen to that!   No more of that!

DR. STOCKMANN.

I have said I would speak of the great discovery I have made within the last few days—the discovery that all our sources of spiritual life are poisoned, and that our whole society rests upon a pestilential basis of falsehood.

SEVERAL VOICES.

[*In astonishment and half aloud.*]   What's he saying?

BURGOMASTER.

Such an insinuation——!

ASLAKSEN.

[*With his hand on the bell.*]   I must call upon the speaker to moderate his expressions.

DR. STOCKMANN.

I have loved my native town as dearly as any man can love the home of his childhood. I was young when I left our town, and distance, homesickness and memory threw, as it were, a glamour over the place and its people.

> [*Some applause and cries of approval.*

DR. STOCKMANN.

Then for years I was imprisoned in a horrible hole, far away in the north. As I went about among the people scattered here and there over the stony wilderness, it seemed to me, many a time, that it would have been better for these poor famishing creatures to have had a cattle-doctor to attend them, instead of a man like me.

> [*Murmurs in the room.*

BILLING.

[*Laying down his pen.*] Strike me dead if I've ever heard——!

HOVSTAD.

What an insult to an estimable peasantry!

DR. STOCKMANN.

Wait a moment!—I don't think any one can reproach me with forgetting my native town up there. I sat brooding like an eider duck, and what I hatched was—the plan of the Baths.

> [*Applause and expressions of dissent.*

DR. STOCKMANN.

And when, at last, fate ordered things so happily that I could come home again—then, fellow citizens, it seemed to me that I hadn't another desire in the world. Yes, one desire I had: an eager, constant, burning desire to be of service to my birthplace, and to its people.

BURGOMASTER.

[*Gazing into vacancy.*] A strange method to select——!

DR. STOCKMANN.

So I went about revelling in my happy illusions. But yesterday morning—no, it was really two nights ago—my mind's eyes were opened wide, and the first thing I saw was the colossal stupidity of the authorities——

[*Noise, cries, and laughter.* MRS. STOCKMANN *coughs repeatedly.*

BURGOMASTER.

Mr. Chairman!

ASLAKSEN.

[*Ringing his bell.*] In virtue of my position——!

DR. STOCKMANN.

It's petty to catch me up on a word, Mr. Aslaksen! I only mean that I became alive to the extraordinary muddle our leading men had been guilty of, down at the Baths. I cannot for the life of me abide leading men —I've seen enough of them in my time. They are like goats in a young plantation: they do harm at every point; they block the path of a free man wherever he turns— and I should be glad if we could exterminate them like other noxious animals—— [*Uproar in the room.*

BURGOMASTER.

Mr. Chairman, are such expressions permissible?

ASLAKSEN.

[*With his hand on the bell.*] Dr. Stockmann——

DR. STOCKMANN.

I can't conceive how it is that I have only now seen through these gentry; for haven't I had a magnificent example before my eyes here every day—my brother Peter—slow of understanding, tenacious in prejudice——
    [*Laughter, noise, and whistling.* MRS. STOCKMANN *coughs.* ASLAKSEN *rings violently.*

THE DRUNKEN MAN.

[*Who has come in again.*] Is it me you're alluding to? Sure enough, my name's Petersen; but devil take me if——

ANGRY VOICES.

Out with that drunken man! Turn him out!
                [*The man is again turned out.*

BURGOMASTER.

Who is that person?

A BYSTANDER.

I don't know him, Burgomaster.

ANOTHER.

He doesn't belong to the town.

A THIRD.

I believe he's a timber-dealer from——
                [*The rest is inaudible.*

ASLAKSEN.

The man was evidently intoxicated.—Continue, Dr.
Stockmann; but pray endeavour to be moderate.

DR. STOCKMANN.

Well, fellow citizens, I shall say no more about our
leading men. If any one imagines, from what I have
just said, that it's these gentlemen I want to make short
work of to-night, he is mistaken—altogether mistaken.
For I cherish the comfortable conviction that these lag-
gards, these relics of a decaying order of thought, are
diligently cutting their own throats. They need no doctor to hasten their end. And it is not people of t h a t
sort that constitute the real danger to society; it is not
they who are most active in poisoning the sources of our
spiritual life and making a plague-spot of the ground
beneath our feet; it is not t h e y who are the most
dangerous enemies of truth and freedom in our society.

CRIES FROM ALL SIDES.

Who, then? Who is it? Name, name!

DR. STOCKMANN.

Yes, you may be sure I shall name them! For t h i s
is the great discovery I made yesterday: [*In a louder
tone.*] The most dangerous foe to truth and freedom in
our midst is the compact majority. Yes, it's the confounded, compact, liberal majority—that, and nothing
else! There, I've told you.

> [*Immense disturbance in the room. Most of the au-
> dience are shouting, stamping, and whistling.
> Several elderly gentlemen exchange furtive glances*

and seem to be enjoying the scene. MRS. STOCK-
MANN *rises in alarm.* EILIF *and* MORTEN *ad-*
vance threateningly towards the schoolboys, who
are making noises. ASLAKSEN *rings the bell and*
calls for order. HOVSTAD *and* BILLING *both speak,*
but nothing can be heard. At last quiet is restored.

ASLAKSEN.

I must request the speaker to withdraw his ill-consid-
ered expressions.

DR. STOCKMANN.

Never, Mr. Aslaksen! For it's this very majority that
robs me of my freedom, and wants to forbid me to speak
the truth.

HOVSTAD.

The majority always has right on its side.

BILLING.

Yes, and truth too, strike me dead!

DR. STOCKMANN.

The majority never has right on its side. Never I
say! That is one of the social lies that a free, thinking
man is bound to rebel against. Who make up the majority in any given country? Is it the wise men or the
fools? I think we must agree that the fools are in a
terrible, overwhelming majority, all the wide world over
But how in the devil's name can it ever be right for the
fools to rule over the wise men?   [*Uproar and yells.*

DR. STOCKMANN.

Yes, yes, you can shout me down, but you cannot gainsay me. The majority has m i g h t —unhappily—but r i g h t it has not. It is I, and the few, the individuals, that are in the right. The minority is always right.

[Renewed uproar.

HOVSTAD.

Ha ha! Dr. Stockmann has turned aristocrat since the day before yesterday!

DR. STOCKMANN.

I have said that I have no words to waste on the little, narrow-chested, short-winded crew that lie in our wake. Pulsating life has nothing more to do with them. I am speaking of the few, the individuals among us, who have made all the new, germinating truths their own. These men stand, as it were, at the outposts, so far in the van that the compact majority has not yet reached them— and t h e r e they fight for truths that are too lately born into the world's consciousness to have won over the majority.

HOVSTAD.

So the Doctor's a revolutionist now!

DR. STOCKMANN.

Yes, by Heaven, I am, Mr. Hovstad! I am going to revolt against the lie that truth belongs exclusively to the majority. What sort of truths do the majority rally round? Truths so stricken in years that they are sinking into decrepitude. When a truth is so old as that, gentlemen, it's in a fair way to become a lie.

[Laughter and jeers.

Dr. Stockmann.

Yes, yes, you may believe me or not, as you please; but truths are by no means the wiry Methusalehs some people think them. A normally-constituted truth lives— let us say—as a rule, seventeen or eighteen years; at the outside twenty; very seldom more. And truths so patriarchal as that are always shockingly emaciated; yet it's not till then that the majority takes them up and recommends them to society as wholesome food. I can assure you there's not much nutriment in that sort of fare; you may take my word as a doctor for that. All these majority-truths are like last year's salt pork; they're like rancid, mouldy ham, producing all the moral scurvy that devastates society.

Aslaksen.

It seems to me that the honourable speaker is wandering rather far from the subject.

Burgomaster.

I beg to endorse the Chairman's remark.

Dr. Stockmann.

Why you're surely mad, Peter! I'm keeping as closely to my text as I possibly can; for my text is precisely this —that the masses, the majority, this devil's own compact majority—it's that, I say, that's poisoning the sources of our spiritual life, and making a plague-spot of the ground beneath our feet.

Hovstad.

And you make this charge against the great, independent majority, just because they have the sense to accept only certain and acknowledged truths?

Dr. Stockmann.

Ah, my dear Mr. Hovstad, don't talk about certain truths! The truths acknowledged by the masses, the multitude, were certain truths to the vanguard in our grandfathers' days. We, the vanguard of to-day, don't acknowledge them any longer; and I don't believe there exists any other certain truth but this—that no society can live a healthy life upon truths so old and marrowless.

Hovstad.

But instead of all this vague talk, suppose you were to give us some specimens of these old marrowless truths that we are living upon.

[*Approval from several quarters.*

Dr. Stockmann.

Oh, I could give you no end of samples from the rubbish-heap; but, for the present, I shall keep to one acknowledged truth, which is a hideous lie at bottom, but which Mr. Hovstad, and the *Messenger*, and all adherents of the *Messenger*, live on all the same.

Hovstad.

And that is——?

Dr. Stockmann.

That is the doctrine you have inherited from your forefathers, and go on thoughtlessly proclaiming far and wide—the doctrine that the multitude, the vulgar herd, the masses, are the pith of the people—that they a r e the people—that the common man, the ignorant, undeveloped member of society, has the same right to sanction and to condemn, to counsel and to govern, as the intellectually distinguished few.

BILLING.

Well, now, strike me dead——!

HOVSTAD.

[*Shouting at the same time.*]   Citizens, please note this!

ANGRY VOICES.

Ho-ho!   Aren't we the people?   Is it only the grand folks that are to govern?

A WORKING MAN.

Out with the fellow that talks like that!

OTHERS.

Turn him out!

A CITIZEN.

[*Shouting.*]   Blow your horn, Evensen.
   [*The deep notes of a horn are heard; whistling, and terrific noise in the room.*

DR. STOCKMANN.

[*When the noise has somewhat subsided.*]   Now do be reasonable!   Can't you bear even for once in a way to hear the voice of truth?   I don't ask you all to agree with me on the instant.   But I certainly should have expected Mr. Hovstad to back me up, as soon as he had collected himself a bit.   Mr. Hovstad sets up to be a free-thinker——

SEVERAL VOICES.

[*Subdued and wondering.*] Freethinker, did he say? What? Mr. Hovstad a freethinker?

HOVSTAD.

[*Shouting.*] Prove it, Dr. Stockmann. When have I said so in print?

DR. STOCKMANN.

[*Reflecting.*] No, upon my soul, you're right there; you've never had the frankness to do that. Well, well, I won't put you on the rack, Mr. Hovstad. Let me be the freethinker then. And now I'll make it clear to you all, and on scientific grounds too, that the *Messenger* is leading you shamefully by the nose, when it tells you that you, the masses, the crowd, are the true pith of the people. I tell you that's only a newspaper lie. The masses are nothing but the raw material that must be fashioned into a People.

[*Murmurs, laughter, and disturbance in the room.*

DR. STOCKMANN.

Is it not so with all other living creatures? What a difference between a cultivated and an uncultivated breed of animals! Just look at a common barn-door hen. What meat do you get from such a skinny carcase? Not much, I can tell you! And what sort of eggs does she lay? A decent crow or raven can lay nearly as good. Then take a cultivated Spanish or Japanese hen, or take a fine pheasant or turkey—ah! then you'll see the difference! And now look at the dog, our near relation. Think first of an ordinary vulgar cur—I mean one of those wretched, ragged, plebeian mongrels that

haunt the gutters, and soil the sidewalks.   Then place
such a mongrel by the side of a poodle-dog, descended
through many generations from an aristocratic stock,
who have lived on delicate food, and heard harmonious
voices and music.   Do you think the brain of the poodle
isn't very differently developed from that of the mongrel?
Yes, you may be sure it is!   It's well-bred poodle-pups
like this that jugglers train to perform the most marvellous tricks.   A common peasant-cur could never learn
anything of the sort—not if he tried till doomsday.

[*Noise and laughter are heard all round.*

A Citizen.

[*Shouting.*]   Do you want to make dogs of us now?

Another Man.

We're not animals, Doctor!

Dr. Stockmann.

Yes, on my soul, but we a r e animals, my good sir!
We're one and all of us animals, whether we like it or
not.   But truly there are few enough aristocratic animals
among us.   Oh, there's a terrible difference between
poodle-men and mongrel-men!   And the ridiculous part
of it is, that Mr. Hovstad quite agrees with me so long
as it's four-legged animals we're talking of——

Hovstad.

Oh, beasts are only beasts.

Dr. Stockmann.

Well and good—but no sooner do I apply the law to
two-legged animals, than Mr. Hovstad stops short; then

he daren't hold his own opinions, or think out his own thoughts; then he turns the whole principle upside down, and proclaims in the *People's Messenger* that the barn-door hen and the gutter-mongrel are precisely the finest specimens in the menagerie. But that's always the way, so long as the commonness still lingers in your system, and you haven't worked your way up to spiritual distinction.

HOVSTAD.

I make no pretence to any sort of distinction. I come of simple peasant folk, and I am proud that my root should lie deep down among the common people, who are here being insulted.

WORKMEN.

Hurrah for Hovstad. Hurrah! hurrah!

DR. STOCKMANN.

The sort of common people I am speaking of are not found among the lower classes alone; they crawl and swarm all around us—up to the very summits of society. Just look at your own smug, respectable Burgomaster! Why, my brother Peter belongs as clearly to the common people as any man that walks on two legs——

[*Laughter and hisses.*

BURGOMASTER.

I protest against such personalities.

DR. STOCKMANN.

[*Imperturbably.*] ——and that not because, like myself, he's descended from a good-for-nothing old pirate from Pomerania, or thereabouts—for that's our ancestry——

BURGOMASTER.

An absurd tradition! Utterly groundless.

DR. STOCKMANN.

——but he is so because he thinks the thoughts and holds the opinions of his official superiors. Men who do that, belong, intellectually-speaking, to the common people; and that is why my distinguished brother Peter is at bottom so undistinguished,—and consequently so illiberal.

BURGOMASTER.

Mr. Chairman——!

HOVSTAD.

So that the distinguished people in this country are the Liberals? That's quite a new light on the subject.

[*Laughter.*

DR. STOCKMANN.

Yes, that is part of my new discovery. And this, too, follows: that liberality of thought is almost precisely the same thing as morality. Therefore I say it's absolutely unpardonable of the *Messenger* to proclaim, day out, day in, the false doctrine that it's the masses, the multitude, the compact majority, that monopolise liberality and morality,—and that vice and corruption and all sorts of spiritual uncleanness ooze out of culture, as all that filth oozes down to the Baths from the Mill Dale tanworks! [*Noise and interruptions.*

DR. STOCKMANN.

[*Goes on imperturbably, smiling in his eagerness.*] And yet this same *Messenger* can preach about elevating the masses and the multitude to a higher level of well-being! Why, deuce take it, if the *Messenger's* own doctrine holds good, the elevation of the masses would simply mean hurling them straight to perdition! But, happily, the notion that culture demoralises is nothing but an old traditional lie. No it's stupidity, poverty, the ugliness of life, that do the devil's work! In a house that isn't aired and swept every day—my wife maintains that the floors ought to be scrubbed too, but perhaps that is going too far;—well,—in such a house, I say, within two or three years, people lose the power of thinking or acting morally. Lack of oxygen enervates the conscience. And there seems to be precious little oxygen in many and many a house in this town, since the whole compact majority is unscrupulous enough to want to found its future upon a quagmire of lies and fraud.

ASLAKSEN.

I cannot allow so gross an insult to be levelled against a whole community.

A GENTLEMAN.

I move that the Chairman order the speaker to sit down.

EAGER VOICES.

Yes, yes! That's right! Sit down! Sit down!

DR. STOCKMANN.

[*Flaring up.*] Then I shall proclaim the truth at every street corner! I shall write to newspapers in other towns! The whole country shall know how matters stand here!

HOVSTAD.

It almost seems as if the Doctor's object were to ruin the town.

DR. STOCKMANN.

Yes, so well do I love my native town that I would rather ruin it than see it flourishing upon a lie.

ASLAKSEN.

That's plain speaking.

[*Noise and whistling.* MRS. STOCKMANN *coughs in vain; the* DOCTOR *no longer heeds her.*

HOVSTAD.

[*Shouting amid the tumult.*] The man who would ruin a whole community must be an enemy to his fellow citizens!

DR. STOCKMANN.

[*With growing excitement.*] What does it matter if a lying community is ruined! Let it be levelled to the ground, say I! All men who live upon a lie ought to be exterminated like vermin! You'll end by poisoning the whole country; you'll bring it to such a pass that the whole country will deserve to perish. And if ever it comes to that, I shall say, from the bottom of my heart: Perish the country! Perish all its people!

A MAN.

[*In the crowd.*] Why, he talks like a regular enemy of the people!

BILLING.

Strike me dead but there spoke the people's voice!

THE WHOLE ASSEMBLY.

[*Shouting.*]   Yes! yes! yes!   He's an enemy of the people!   He hates his country!   He hates the whole people!

ASLAKSEN.

Both as a citizen of this town and as a human being, I am deeply shocked at what it has been my lot to hear to-night.   Dr. Stockmann has unmasked himself in a manner I should never have dreamt of.   I must reluctantly subscribe to the opinion just expressed by some estimable citizens; and I think we ought to formulate this opinion in a resolution.   I therefore beg to move, "That this meeting declares the medical officer of the Baths, Dr. Thomas Stockmann, to be an enemy of the people."

[*Thunders of applause and cheers.   Many form a circle round the* DOCTOR *and hoot at him.*   MRS. STOCKMANN *and* PETRA *have risen.*   MORTEN *and* EILIF *fight the other schoolboys, who have also been hooting.   Some grown-up persons separate them.*

DR. STOCKMANN.

[*To the people hooting.*]   Ah, fools that you are!   I tell you that——

ASLAKSEN.

[*Ringing.*]   The Doctor is out of order in speaking. A formal vote must be taken; but out of consideration for personal feelings, it will be taken in writing and without names.   Have you any blank paper, Mr. Billing?

BILLING.

Here's both blue and white paper——

ASLAKSEN.

Capital; that will save time. Cut it up into slips. That's it. [*To the meeting.*] Blue means no, white means aye. I myself will go round and collect the votes.
[*The* BURGOMASTER *leaves the room.* ASLAKSEN *and a few others go round with pieces of paper in hats.*

A GENTLEMAN.

[*To* HOVSTAD.] What can be the matter with the Doctor? What does it all mean?

HOVSTAD.

Why, you know what a hare-brained creature he is.

ANOTHER GENTLEMAN.

[*To* BILLING.] I say, you're often at his house. Have you ever noticed if the fellow drinks?

BILLING

Strike me dead if I know what to say. The toddy's always on the table when any one looks in.

A THIRD GENTLEMAN.

No, I should rather say he went off his head at times.

FIRST GENTLEMAN.

I wonder if there's madness in the family?

BILLING.

I shouldn't be surprised.

A FOURTH GENTLEMAN.

No, it's pure malice. He wants to be revenged for something or other.

BILLING.

He was certainly talking about a rise in his salary the other day; but he didn't get it.

ALL THE GENTLEMEN.

[*Together*.]   Aha! That explains everything.

THE DRUNKEN MAN.

[*In the crowd*.]   I want a blue one, I do! And I'll have a white one too.

SEVERAL PEOPLE.

There's the tipsy man again! Turn him out.

MORTEN KIIL.

[*Approaching the* DOCTOR.]   Well, Stockmann, you see now what such monkey-tricks lead to?

DR. STOCKMANN.

I have done my duty.

MORTEN KIIL.

What was that you said about the Mill Dale tanneries?

DR. STOCKMANN.

You heard what I said—that all the filth comes from them.

MORTEN KIIL.

From my tannery as well?

DR. STOCKMANN.

I'm sorry to say yours is the worst of all.

MORTEN KIIL.

Are you going to put t h a t in the papers, too?

DR. STOCKMANN.

I can't gloze anything over.

MORTEN KIIL.

This may cost you dear, Stockmann!   [*He goes out.*

A FAT GENTLEMAN.

[*Goes up to* HORSTER, *without bowing to the ladies.*] Well, Captain, so you lend your house to enemies of the people.

HORSTER.

I suppose I can do as I please with my own property, Sir.

THE GENTLEMAN.

Then of course you can have no objection if I follow your example?

HORSTER.

What do you mean, Sir?

THE GENTLEMAN.

You shall hear from me to-morrow.

[*Turns away and goes out.*

PETRA.

Wasn't that the owner of your ship, Captain Horster?

HORSTER.

Yes, that was Mr. Vik.

ASLAKSEN.

[*With the voting papers in his hands, ascends the plat-form and rings.*] Gentlemen! I have now to announce the result of the vote. All the voters, with one exception——

A YOUNG GENTLEMAN.

That's the tipsy man!

ASLAKSEN.

With the exception of one intoxicated person, this meeting of citizens unanimously declares the medical officer of the Baths, Dr. Thomas Stockmann, to be an enemy of the people. [*Cheers and applause.*] Three cheers for our fine old municipality! [*Cheers.*] Three cheers for our able and energetic Burgomaster, who has so loyally set family prejudice aside! [*Cheers.*] The meeting is dissolved. [*He descends.*

BILLING.

Three cheers for the Chairman!

ALL.

Hurrah for Aslaksen!

DR. STOCKMANN.

My hat and coat, Petra.   Captain, have you room for passengers to the new world?

HORSTER.

For you and yours, Doctor, we'll make room.

DR. STOCKMANN.

[*While* PETRA *helps him to put on his coat.*]   Good. Come Katrina, come boys!

> [*He gives his wife his arm.*

MRS. STOCKMANN.

[*In a low voice.*]   Thomas, dear, let us go out by the back way.

DR. STOCKMANN.

No back ways, Katrina!   [*In a loud voice.*]   You shall hear from the enemy of the people, before he shakes the dust from his feet!   I am not so forbearing as a certain person; I don't say: I forgive you, for you know not what you do.

ASLAKSEN.

[*Shouts.*]   That is a blasphemous comparison, Dr. Stockmann!

BILLING.

Strike me——! This is more than a serious man can stand!

A COARSE VOICE.

And he threatens us into the bargain!

ANGRY CRIES.

Let's smash his windows! Duck him in the fiord!

A MAN.

[*In the crowd.*] Blow your horn, Evensen! Blow, man, blow!
> [*Horn-blowing, whistling, and wild shouting. The* DOCTOR, *with his family, goes towards the door.* HORSTER *clears the way for them.*

ALL.

[*Yelling after them as they go out.*] Enemy of the people! Enemy of the people! Enemy of the people!

BILLING.

Strike me dead if I'd care to drink toddy at Stockmann's to-night!
> [*The people throng towards the door; the shouting is taken up by others outside; from the street are heard cries of "Enemy of the people! Enemy of the people!"*

ACT FIFTH

DR. STOCKMANN'S *Study. Bookshelves and glass cases with various collections along the walls. In the back, a door leading to the hall; in front, on the left, a door to the sitting-room. In the wall to the right are two windows, all the panes of which are smashed. In the middle of the room is the* DOCTOR'S *writing-table, covered with books and papers. The room is in disorder. It is forenoon.*

DR. STOCKMANN, *in dressing-gown, slippers, and skullcap, is bending down and raking with an umbrella under one of the cabinets; at last he rakes out a stone.*

DR. STOCKMANN.

[*Speaking through the sitting-room doorway.*] Katrina, I've found another!

MRS. STOCKMANN.

[*In the sitting-room.*] Oh, I'm sure you'll find plenty more.

DR. STOCKMANN.

[*Placing the stone on a pile of others on the table.*] I shall keep these stones as sacred relics. Eilif and Morten shall see them every day, and when I die they shall be heirlooms. [*Raking under the bookcase.*] Hasn't— what the devil is her name?—the girl—hasn't she been for the glazier yet?

MRS. STOCKMANN.

[*Coming in.*] Yes, but he said he didn't know whether he would be able to come to-day.

DR. STOCKMANN.

I believe, if the truth were told, he daren't come.

MRS. STOCKMANN.

Well, Randina, too, had an idea he was afraid to come, because of the neighbours. [*Speaks through the sitting-room doorway.*] What is it, Randina?—Very well. [*Goes out, and returns immediately.*] Here is a letter for you, Thomas.

DR. STOCKMANN.

Let me see. [*Opens the letter and reads.*] Aha!

MRS. STOCKMANN.

Who is it from?

DR. STOCKMANN.

From the landlord. He gives us notice.

MRS. STOCKMANN.

Is it possible? He is such a nice man——

DR. STOCKMANN.

[*Looking at the letter.*] He daren't do otherwise, he says. He is very unwilling to do it; but he daren't do otherwise—on account of his fellow citizens—out of respect for public opinion—is in a dependent position—doesn't dare to offend certain influential men——

MRS. STOCKMANN.

There, you see, Thomas.

DR. STOCKMANN.

Yes, yes, I see well enough; they are all cowards, every one of them, in this town; no one dares do anything for fear of all the rest. [*Throws the letter on the table*.] But it's all the same to us, Katrina. We will shape our course for the new world, and then——

MRS. STOCKMANN.

But are you sure this idea of going abroad is altogether wise, Thomas?

DR. STOCKMANN.

Would you have me stay here, where they have pilloried me as an enemy of the people, branded me, smashed my windows! And look here, Katrina, they've torn a hole in my black trousers, too.

MRS. STOCKMANN.

Oh dear; and these are the best you have!

DR. STOCKMANN.

A man should never put on his best trousers when he goes out to battle for freedom and truth. Well, I don't care so much about the trousers; them you can always patch up for me. But that the mob, the rabble, should dare to attack me as if they were my equals—t h a t is what I can't, for the life of me, stomach!

MRS. STOCKMANN.

Yes, they have behaved abominably to you here, Thomas; but is that any reason for leaving the country altogether?

DR. STOCKMANN.

Do you think the plebeians aren't just as insolent in other towns? Oh yes, they are, my dear; it's six of one and half a dozen of the other. Well, never mind; let the curs yelp; t h a t ' s not the worst; the worst is that every one, all over the country, is the slave of his party. Not that I suppose—very likely it's no better in the free West either; the compact majority, and enlightened public opinion, and all the other devil's trash is rampant there too. But you see the conditions are larger there than here; they may kill you, but they don't slow-torture you; they don't screw up a free soul in a vice, as they do at home here. And then, if need be, you can keep out of it all. [*Walks up and down.*] If I only knew of any primeval forest, or a little South Sea island to be sold cheap——

MRS. STOCKMANN.

Yes, but the boys, Thomas.

DR. STOCKMANN.

[*Comes to a standstill.*] What an extraordinary woman you are, Katrina! Would you rather have the boys grow up in such a society as ours? Why, you could see for yourself yesterday evening that one half of the population is stark mad, and if the other half hasn't lost its wits, that's only because they are brute beasts who haven't any wits to lose.

MRS. STOCKMANN.

But really, my dear Thomas, you do say such imprudent things.

DR. STOCKMANN.

What! Isn't it the truth that I tell them? Don't they turn all ideas upside down? Don't they stir up right and wrong into one hotch-potch? Don't they call lies everything that I know to be the truth? But the maddest thing of all is to see crowds of grown men, calling themselves Liberals, go about persuading themselves and others that they are friends of freedom! Did you ever hear anything like it, Katrina?

MRS. STOCKMANN.

Yes, yes, no doubt. But——

PETRA *enters from the sitting-room.*

MRS. STOCKMANN.

Back from school already?

PETRA.

Yes; I have been dismissed.

MRS. STOCKMANN.

Dismissed?

DR. STOCKMANN.

You too!

PETRA.

Mrs. Busk gave me notice, and so I thought it best to leave there and then.

DR. STOCKMANN.

You did perfectly right!

MRS. STOCKMANN.

Who could have thought Mrs. Busk was such a bad woman!

PETRA.

Oh mother, Mrs. Busk isn't bad at all; I saw clearly how sorry she was. But she dared not do otherwise, she said; and so I am dismissed.

DR. STOCKMANN.

[*Laughing and rubbing his hands.*] She dared not do otherwise—just like the rest! Oh, it's delicious.

MRS. STOCKMANN.

Oh well, after that frightful scene last night——

PETRA.

It wasn't only that. What do you think, father——?

DR. STOCKMANN.

Well?

PETRA.

Mrs. Busk showed me no fewer than three letters she had received this morning——

DR. STOCKMANN.

Anonymous, of course?

PETRA.

Yes.

DR. STOCKMANN.

They never dare give their names, Katrina!

PETRA.

And two of them stated that a gentleman who is often at our house said at the club last night that I held extremely advanced opinions upon various things——

DR. STOCKMANN.

Of course you didn't deny it.

PETRA.

Of course not.   You know Mrs. Busk herself is pretty advanced in her opinions when we're alone together; but now that this has come out about me, she dared not keep me on.

MRS. STOCKMANN.

Some one that is often at our house, too.   There, you see, Thomas, what comes of all your hospitality.

DR. STOCKMANN.

We won't live any longer in such a pig-sty!   Pack up as quickly as you can, Katrina; let's get away—the sooner the better.

MRS. STOCKMANN.

Hush!   I think there is some one in the passage.   See who it is, Petra.

PETRA.

[*Opening the door.*] Oh, is it you, Captain Horster? Please come in.

HORSTER.

[*From the hall.*] Good morning. I thought I might just look in and ask how you are.

DR. STOCKMANN.

[*Shaking his hand.*] Thanks; that's very good of you.

MRS. STOCKMANN.

And thank you for helping us through the crowd last night, Captain Horster.

PETRA.

How did you ever get home again?

HORSTER.

Oh, that was all right. I am tolerably able-bodied, you know; and those fellows' bark is worse than their bite.

DR. STOCKMANN.

Yes, isn't it extraordinary, this piggish cowardice? Come here, and let me show you something! Look, here are all the stones they threw in at us. Only look at them! Upon my soul there aren't more than two decent-sized lumps in the whole heap; the rest are nothing but pebbles—mere gravel. They stood down there, and yelled, and swore they'd half kill me;—but as for really doing it—no, there's mighty little fear of t h a t in this town!

HORSTER.

You may thank your stars for that this time, Doctor.

DR. STOCKMANN.

So I do, of course.   But it's depressing all the same; for if ever it should come to a serious national struggle, you may be sure public opinion would be for taking to its heels, and the compact majority would scamper for their lives like a flock of sheep, Captain Horster.   T h a t is what's so melancholy to think of; it grieves me to the heart.—But deuce take it—it's foolish of me to feel anything of the sort!   They have called me an enemy of the people; well then, let me b e an enemy of the people!

MRS. STOCKMANN.

That you'll never be, Thomas.

DR. STOCKMANN.

You'd better not take your oath of it, Katrina.   A bad name may act like a pin-scratch in the lung.   And that confounded word—I can't get rid of it; it has sunk deep into my heart; and there it lies gnawing and sucking like an acid.   And no magnesia can cure me.

PETRA.

Pooh; you should only laugh at them, father.

HORSTER.

People will think differently yet, Doctor.

MRS. STOCKMANN.

Yes, Thomas, that's as certain as that you are standing here.

DR. STOCKMANN.

Yes, perhaps, when it is too late.   Well, as they make their bed so they must lie!   Let them go on wallowing here in their pig-sty, and learn to repent having driven a patriot into exile.   When do you sail, Captain Horster?

HORSTER.

Well—that's really what I came to speak to you about——

DR. STOCKMANN.

What?   Anything wrong with the ship?

HORSTER.

No; but the fact is, I shan't be sailing in her.

PETRA.

Surely you have not been dismissed?

HORSTER.

[*Smiling.*]   Yes, I have.

PETRA.

You too!

MRS. STOCKMANN.

There, you see, Thomas.

DR. STOCKMANN.

And for the truth's sake! Oh, if I could possibly have imagined such a thing——

HORSTER.

You mustn't be troubled about this; I shall soon find a berth with some other company, elsewhere.

DR. STOCKMANN.

And this is that man Vik! A wealthy man, independent of every one! Faugh!

HORSTER.

Oh, for that matter, he's a very well-meaning man. He said himself he would gladly have kept me on if only he dared——

DR. STOCKMANN.

But he didn't dare? Of course not!

HORSTER.

It's not so easy, he said, when you belong to a party——

DR. STOCKMANN.

My gentleman has hit it there! A party is like a sausage-machine; it grinds all the brains together in one mash; and that's why we see nothing but porridge-heads and pulp-heads all around!

MRS. STOCKMANN.

Now really, Thomas!

PETRA.

[*To* HORSTER.] If only you hadn't seen us home, perhaps it would not have come to this.

HORSTER.

I don't regret it.

PETRA.

[*Gives him her hand.*] Thank you for that!

HORSTER.

[*To* DR. STOCKMANN.] And then, too, I wanted to tell you this: if you are really determined to go abroad, I've thought of another way——

DR. STOCKMANN.

That's good—if only we can get off quickly——

MRS. STOCKMANN.

Hush! Isn't that a knock?

PETRA.

I believe it is uncle.

DR. STOCKMANN.

Aha! [*Calls.*] Come in!

MRS. STOCKMANN.

My dear Thomas, now do promise me——

The BURGOMASTER *enters from the hall.*

BURGOMASTER.

[*In the doorway.*] Oh, you are engaged.   Then I'd better——

DR. STOCKMANN.

No no; come in.

BURGOMASTER.

But I wanted to speak to you alone.

MRS. STOCKMANN.

We can go into the sitting-room.

HORSTER.

And I shall look in again presently.

DR. STOCKMANN.

No no; go with the ladies, Captain Horster; I must hear more about——

HORSTER.

All right, then I'll wait.
   [*He follows* MRS. STOCKMANN *and* PETRA *into the sitting-room.   The* BURGOMASTER *says nothing, but casts glances at the windows.*

DR. STOCKMANN.

I daresay you find it rather draughty here to-day? Put on your cap.

BURGOMASTER.

Thanks, if I may.   [*Does so.*]   I fancy I caught cold yesterday evening.   I stood there shivering——

DR. STOCKMANN.

Really.   On my soul, now, I found it quite warm enough.

BURGOMASTER.

I regret that it was not in my power to prevent these nocturnal excesses.

DR. STOCKMANN.

Have you anything else in particular to say to me?

BURGOMASTER.

[*Producing a large letter.*]   I have this document for you from the Directors of the Baths.

DR. STOCKMANN.

My dismissal?

BURGOMASTER.

Yes; dated from to-day.   [*Places the letter on the table.*] We are very sorry—but frankly, we dared not do otherwise, on account of public opinion.

DR. STOCKMANN.

[*Smiling.*]   Dared not?   I've heard that phrase already to-day.

BURGOMASTER.

I beg you to realise your position clearly.   For the future, you cannot count upon any sort of practice in the town.

DR. STOCKMANN.

Devil take the practice! But how can you be so sure of that?

BURGOMASTER.

The House-owners' Association is sending round a circular from house to house, in which all well-disposed citizens are called upon not to employ you; and I dare swear that not a single head of a family will venture to refuse his signature; he simply d a r e not.

DR. STOCKMANN.

Well well; I don't doubt that. But what then?

BURGOMASTER.

If I might advise, I would suggest that you should leave the town for a time——

·DR. STOCKMANN.

Yes, I've had some such idea in my mind already.

BURGOMASTER.

Good. And when you have had six months or so for mature deliberation, if you could make up your mind to acknowledge your error, with a few words of regret——

DR. STOCKMANN.

I might perhaps be reinstated, you think?

BURGOMASTER.

Perhaps it's not quite out of the question.

DR. STOCKMANN.

Yes, but how about public opinion? You daren't, on account of public opinion.

BURGOMASTER.

Opinion is extremely variable. And, to speak candidly, it is of the greatest importance for us to have such an admission under your own hand.

DR. STOCKMANN.

Yes, I daresay it would be mightily convenient for you! But you remember what I've said to you before about such foxes' tricks!

BURGOMASTER.

At that time your position was infinitely more favourable; at that time you thought you had the whole town at your back——

DR. STOCKMANN.

Yes, and now I have the whole town o n my back—— [*Flaring up.*] But no—not if I had the devil and his dam on my back—! Never—never, I tell you!

BURGOMASTER.

The father of a family has no right[1] to act as you are doing. You have no right to do it, Thomas.

---

[1] "Has no right" represents the Norwegian "tör ikke"—the phrase which, elsewhere in this scene, is translated "dare not." The latter rendering should perhaps have been adhered to throughout; but in this passage the Norwegian words convey a shade of meaning which is best represented by "has no right."

DR. STOCKMANN.

I have no right!   There's only one thing in the world that a free man has no right to do; and do you know what that is?

BURGOMASTER.

No.

DR. STOCKMANN.

Of course not; but *I* will tell you.   A free man has no right to wallow in filth like a cur; he has no right to act so that he ought to spit in his own face!

BURGOMASTER.

That sounds extremely plausible; and if there were not another explanation of your obstinacy—but we all know there is——

DR. STOCKMANN.

What do you mean by that?

BURGOMASTER.

You understand well enough.   But as your brother, and as a man who knows the world, I warn you not to build too confidently upon prospects and expectations that may very likely come to nothing.

DR. STOCKMANN.

Why, what on earth are you driving at?

BURGOMASTER.

Do you really want me to believe that you are ignorant of the terms of old Morten Kiil's will?

Dr. Stockmann.

I know that the little he has is to go to a home for old and needy artisans.   But what has that got to do with me?

Burgomaster.

To begin with, "the little he has" is no trifle.   Morten Kiil is a tolerably wealthy man.

Dr. Stockmann.

I have never had the least notion of that!

Burgomaster.

H'm—really?   Then I suppose you have no notion that a not inconsiderable part of his fortune is to go to your children, you and your wife having a life-interest in it.   Has he not told you that?

Dr. Stockmann.

No, I'll be hanged if he has!   On the contrary, he has done nothing but grumble about being so preposterously over-taxed.   But are you really sure of this, Peter?

Burgomaster.

I have it from a thoroughly trustworthy source.

Dr. Stockmann.

Why, good heavens, then Katrina's provided for—and the children too!   Oh, I must tell her——[*Calls.*]   Katrina, Katrina!

BURGOMASTER.

[*Holding him back.*]   Hush! don't say anything about it yet.

MRS. STOCKMANN.

[*Opening the door.*]   What is it?

DR. STOCKMANN.

Nothing my dear; go in again.
[MRS. STOCKMANN *closes the door.*

DR. STOCKMANN.

[*Pacing up and down.*]   Provided for!   Only think— all of them provided for!   And for life!   After all, it's a grand thing to feel yourself secure!

BURGOMASTER.

Yes, but that is just what you are not.   Morten Kiil can revoke his will any day or hour he chooses.

DR. STOCKMANN.

But he won't, my good Peter.   The Badger is only too delighted to see me fall foul of you and your wiseacre friends.

BURGOMASTER.

[*Starts and looks searchingly at him.*]   Aha!   That throws a new light o n a good many things.

DR. STOCKMANN.

What things?

BURGOMASTER.

So the whole affair has been a carefully-concocted intrigue. Your recklessly violent onslaught—in the name of truth—upon the leading men of the town——

DR. STOCKMANN.

Well, what of it?

BURGOMASTER.

It was nothing but a preconcerted requital for that vindictive old Morten Kiil's will.

DR. STOCKMANN.

[*Almost speechless.*] Peter—you are the most abominable plebeian I have ever known in all my born days.

BURGOMASTER.

All is over between us. Your dismissal is irrevocable —for now we have a weapon against you. [*He goes out.*

DR. STOCKMANN.

Shame! shame! shame! [*Calls.*] Katrina! The floor must be scrubbed after him! Tell her to come here with a pail—what's her name? confound it—the girl with the smudge on her nose——

MRS. STOCKMANN.

[*In the sitting-room doorway.*] Hush, hush! Thomas!

PETRA.

[*Also in the doorway.*] Father, here's grandfather; he wants to know if he can speak to you alone.

DR. STOCKMANN.

Yes, of course he can. [*By the door.*]   Come in, father-in-law.

MORTEN KIIL *enters.*   DR. STOCKMANN *closes the door behind him.*

DR. STOCKMANN.

Well, what is it?   Sit down.

MORTEN KIIL.

I won't sit down. [*Looking about him.*] It looks cheerful here to-day, Stockmann.

DR. STOCKMANN.

Yes, don't you think so?

MORTEN KIIL.

Sure enough. And you've plenty of fresh air too; you've got your fill of that oxygen you were talking about yesterday.   You must have a rare good conscience to-day, I should think.

DR. STOCKMANN.

Yes, I have.

MORTEN KIIL.

So I should suppose.   [*Tapping himself on the breast.*] But do you know what *I* have got here?

DR. STOCKMANN.

A good conscience too, I hope.

MORTEN KIIL.

Pooh! No; something far better than that.
[*Takes out a large pocket-book, opens it, and shows*
STOCKMANN *a bundle of papers.*

DR. STOCKMANN.

[*Looking at him in astonishment.*] Shares in the Baths!

MORTEN KIIL.

They weren't difficult to get to-day.

DR. STOCKMANN.

And you've gone and bought these up——?

MORTEN KIIL.

All I had the money to pay for.

DR. STOCKMANN.

Why, my dear sir,—just when things are in such a
desperate way at the Baths——

MORTEN KIIL.

If you behave like a reasonable being, you can soon
set the Baths all right again.

DR. STOCKMANN.

Well, you can see for yourself I'm doing all I can.
But the people of this town are mad!

MORTEN KIIL.

You said yesterday that the worst filth came from my tannery.   Now, if that's true, then my grandfather, and my father before me, and I myself, have for ever so many years been poisoning the town with filth, like three destroying angels.   Do you think I'm going to sit quiet under such a reproach?

DR. STOCKMANN.

Unfortunately, you can't help it.

MORTEN KIIL.

No, thank you.   I hold fast to my good name.   I've heard that people call me "the Badger."   A badger's a sort of a pig, I know; but I'm determined to give them the lie.   I will live and die a clean man.

DR. STOCKMANN.

And how will you manage t h a t?

MORTEN KIIL.

Y o u shall make me clean, Stockmann.

DR. STOCKMANN.

I!

MORTEN KIIL.

Do you know what money I've used to buy these shares with?   No, you can't know; but now I'll tell you.   It's the money Katrina and Petra and the boys are to have after my death.   For, you see, I've laid by something after all.

DR. STOCKMANN.

[*Flaring up.*] And you've taken Katrina's money and
done t h i s with it!

MORTEN KIIL.

Yes; the whole of it is invested in the Baths now. And
now I want to see if you're really so stark, staring mad,
after all, Stockmann. If you go on making out that these
beasts and other abominations dribble down from my
tannery, it'll be just as if you were to flay broad stripes
of Katrina's skin—and Petra's too, and the boys! No
decent father would ever do that—unless he were a madman.

DR. STOCKMANN.

[*Walking up and down.*] Yes, but I a m a madman;
I a m a madman!

MORTEN KIIL.

You surely can't be so raving, ramping mad where
your wife and children are concerned.

DR. STOCKMANN.

[*Stopping in front of him.*] Why couldn't you have
spoken to me before you went and bought all that rubbish?

MORTEN KIIL.

What's done can't be undone.

DR. STOCKMANN.

[*Walking restlessly about.*] If only I weren't so certain
about the affair——! But I am absolutely convinced
that I'm right.

MORTEN KIIL.

[*Weighing the pocket-book in his hand.*] If you stick to this lunacy, these aren't worth much.

[*Puts the book into his pocket.*

DR. STOCKMANN.

But, deuce take it! surely science ought to be able to hit upon some antidote, some sort of prophylactic——

MORTEN KIIL.

Do you mean something to kill the beasts?

DR. STOCKMANN.

Yes, or at least to make them harmless.

MORTEN KIIL.

Couldn't you try ratsbane?

DR. STOCKMANN.

Oh, nonsense, nonsense!—But since every one declares it's nothing but fancy, why fancy let it be! Let them have it their own way! Haven't the ignorant, narrow-hearted curs reviled me as an enemy of the people?— and weren't they on the point of tearing the clothes off my back?

MORTEN KIIL.

And they've smashed all your windows for you too!

DR. STOCKMANN.

Yes, and then there's one's duty to one's family! I must talk that over with Katrina; such things are more in her line.

MORTEN KIIL.

That's right! You just follow the advice of a sensible woman.

DR. STOCKMANN.

[*Turning upon him angrily.*] How could you act so preposterously! Risking Katrina's money, and putting me to this horrible torture! When I look at you, I seem to see the devil himself——!

MORTEN KIIL.

Then I'd better be off. But I must hear from you, yes or no, by two o'clock. If it's n o, all the shares go to the Hospital—and that this very day.

DR. STOCKMANN.

And what will Katrina get?

MORTEN KIIL.

Not a rap.
[*The door leading to the hall opens.* HOVSTAD *and* ASLAKSEN *are seen outside it.*

MORTEN KIIL.

Hullo! look at these two.

DR. STOCKMANN.

[*Staring at them.*] What! Do y o u actually venture to come here?

HOVSTAD.

Why, to be sure we do.

ASLAKSEN.

You see, we've something to discuss with you.

MORTEN KIIL.

[*Whispers.*]   Yes or no—by two o'clock.

ASLAKSEN.

[*With a glance at* HOVSTAD.]   Aha!

[MORTEN KIIL *goes out.*

DR. STOCKMANN.

Well, what do you want with me? Be brief.

HOVSTAD.

I can quite understand that you resent our attitude at the meeting yesterday——

DR. STOCKMANN.

Your attitude, you say? Yes, it was a pretty attitude! I call it the attitude of cowards—of old women—— Shame upon you!

HOVSTAD.

Call it what you will; but we c o u l d not act otherwise.

DR. STOCKMANN.

You d a r e d not, I suppose? Isn't that so?

HOVSTAD.

Yes, if you like to put it so.

ASLAKSEN.

But why didn't you just say a word to us beforehand? The merest hint to Mr. Hovstad or to me——

DR. STOCKMANN.

A hint? What about?

ASLAKSEN.

About what was really behind it all.

DR. STOCKMANN.

I don't in the least understand you?

ASLAKSEN.

[*Nods confidentially.*] Oh yes, you do, Dr. Stockmann.

HOVSTAD.

It's no good making a mystery of it any longer.

DR. STOCKMANN.

[*Looking from one to the other.*] Why, what in the devil's name——!

ASLAKSEN.

May I ask—isn't your father-in-law going about the town buying up all the Bath stock?

DR. STOCKMANN.

Yes, he has been buying Bath stock to-day but——

ASLAKSEN.

It would have been more prudent to let somebody else do that—some one not so closely connected with you.

HOVSTAD.

And then you ought not to have appeared in the matter under your own name. No one need have known that the attack on the Baths came from you. You should have taken me into your counsels, Dr. Stockmann.

DR. STOCKMANN.

[*Stares straight in front of him; a light seems to break in upon him, and he says as though thunder-struck.*] Is this possible? Can such things be?

ASLAKSEN.

[*Smiling.*] It's plain enough that they can. But they ought to be managed delicately, you understand.

HOVSTAD.

And there ought to be more people in it; for the responsibility always falls more lightly when there are several to share it.

DR. STOCKMANN.

[*Calmly.*] In one word, gentlemen—what is it you want?

ASLAKSEN.

Mr. Hovstad can best——

HOVSTAD.

No, you explain, Aslaksen.

ASLAKSEN.

Well, it's this: now that we know how the matter really stands, we believe we can venture to place the *People's Messenger* at your disposal.

DR. STOCKMANN.

You can venture to n o w, eh? But how about public opinion? Aren't you afraid of bringing down a storm upon us?

HOVSTAD.

We must manage to ride out the storm.

ASLAKSEN.

And you must be ready to put about quickly, Doctor. As soon as your attack has done its work——

DR. STOCKMANN.

As soon as my father-in-law and I have bought up the shares at a discount, you mean?

HOVSTAD.

I presume it is mainly on scientific grounds that you want to take the management of the Baths into your own hands.

DR. STOCKMANN.

Of course; it was on scientific grounds that I got the old Badger to stand in with me. And then we'll tinker up the water-works a little, and potter about a bit down at the beach, without its costing the town sixpence.   That ought to do the business?   Eh?

HOVSTAD.

I think so—if you have the *Messenger* to back you up.

ASLAKSEN.

In a free community the press is a power, Doctor.

DR. STOCKMANN.

Yes, indeed; and so is public opinion.   And you, Mr. Aslaksen—I suppose you will answer for the House-owners' Association?

ASLAKSEN.

Both for the House-owners' Association and the Temperance Society.   You may make your mind easy.

DR. STOCKMANN.

But, gentlemen—really I'm quite ashamed to mention such a thing—but—what return——?

HOVSTAD.

Of course, we should prefer to give you our support for nothing.   But the *Messenger* is not very firmly established; it's not getting on as it ought to; and I should be very sorry to have to stop the paper just now, when there's so much to be done in general politics.

DR. STOCKMANN.

Naturally; that would be very hard for a friend of the people like you.   [*Flaring up.*]   But I—I am an enemy

of the people! [*Striding about the room.*] Where's my
stick? Where the devil is my stick?

HOVSTAD.

What do you mean?

ASLAKSEN.

Surely you wouldn't——

DR. STOCKMANN.

[*Standing still.*] And suppose I don't give you a single farthing out of all my shares? You must remember
we rich folk don't like parting with our money.

HOVSTAD.

And you must remember that this business of the shares
can be represented in two ways.

DR. STOCKMANN.

Yes, you are the man for that; if I don't come to the
rescue of the *Messenger*, you'll manage to put a vile com-
plexion on the affair; you'll hunt me down, I suppose—
bait me—try to throttle me as a dog throttles a hare!

HOVSTAD.

That's a law of nature—every animal fights for its own
subsistence.

ASLAKSEN.

And must take its food where it can find it, you know.

DR. STOCKMANN.

Then see if you can't find some out in the gutter;
[*Striding about the room*] for now, by heaven! we shall
see which is the strongest animal of us three.   [*Finds his
umbrella and brandishes it.*]   Now, look here——!

HOVSTAD.

You surely don't mean to assault us!

ASLAKSEN.

I say, be careful with that umbrella!

DR. STOCKMANN.

Out at the window with you, Mr. Hovstad!

HOVSTAD.

[*By the hall door.*]   Are you utterly crazy?

DR. STOCKMANN.

Out at the window, Mr. Aslaksen!   Jump I tell you!
Be quick about it!

ASLAKSEN.

[*Running round the writing-table.*]   Moderation, Doctor; I'm not at all strong; I can't stand much——
[*Screams.*]   Help! help!

MRS. STOCKMANN, PETRA, *and* HORSTER *enter from
sitting-room.*

MRS. STOCKMANN.

Good heavens, Thomas! what c a n be the matter?

DR. STOCKMANN.

[*Brandishing the umbrella.*] Jump! I tell you! Out into the gutter!

HOVSTAD.

An unprovoked assault! I call you to witness, Captain Horster. [*Rushes off through the hall.*

ASLAKSEN.

[*Bewildered.*] If one only knew the local situation——!¹ [*He slinks out by the sitting-room door.*

MRS. STOCKMANN.

[*Holding back the* DOCTOR.] Now, do restrain yourself, Thomas!

DR. STOCKMANN.

[*Throwing down the umbrella.*] I'll be hanged if they haven't got off after all.

MRS. STOCKMANN.

Why, what can they have wanted with you?

DR. STOCKMANN.

I'll tell you afterwards; I have other things to think of now. [*Goes to the table and writes on a visiting-card.*] Look here, Katrina: what's written here?

---

¹ "De lokale forholde"—the local conditions, or the circumstances of the locality, a phrase constantly in Aslaksen's mouth in *The League of Youth*. In the present context it is about equivalent to "the lie of the land."

MRS. STOCKMANN.

Three big N o e s; what does that mean ?

DR. STOCKMANN.

That I'll tell you afterwards, too.   [*Handing the card.*]
There, Petra; let smudgy-face run to the Badger's with
this as fast as she can.   Be quick!
        .[PETRA *goes out through the hall with the card.*

DR. STOCKMANN.

Well, if I haven't had visits to-day from all the emis-
saries of the devil!   But now I'll sharpen my pen against
them till it becomes a goad; I'll dip it in gall and venom;
I'll hurl my inkstand straight at their skulls.

MRS. STOCKMANN.

You forget we are going away, Thomas.

PETRA *returns.*

DR. STOCKMANN.

Well?

PETRA.

She has gone.

DR. STOCKMANN.

Good.   Going away, do you say ?   No, I'll be damned
if we do; we stay where we are, Katrina!

PETRA.

Stay!

MRS. STOCKMANN.

Here in the town?

DR. STOCKMANN.

Yes, here; the field of battle is here; here the fight must be fought; here I will conquer! As soon as my trousers are mended, I shall go out into the town and look for a house; we must have a roof over our heads for the winter.

HORSTER.

That you can have in my house.

DR. STOCKMANN.

Can I?

HORSTER.

Yes, there's no difficulty about that. I have room enough, and I'm hardly ever at home myself.

MRS. STOCKMANN.

Oh, how kind of you, Captain Horster.

PETRA.

Thank you!

DR. STOCKMANN.

[*Shaking his hand.*] Thanks, thanks! So that is off my mind. And this very day I shall set to work in earnest. Oh, there's no end of work to be done here, Katrina! It's a good thing I shall have all my time at my disposal now; for you must know I've had notice from the Baths——

MRS. STOCKMANN.

[*Sighing.*]   Oh yes, I was expecting that.

DR. STOCKMANN.

——And now they want to take away my practice as well.   But let them!   The poor I shall keep anyhow—those that can't pay; and, good Lord! it's they that need me most.   But by heaven! I'll make them listen to me; I'll preach to them in season and out of season, as the saying goes.

MRS. STOCKMANN.

My dear Thomas, I should have thought you had learnt what good preaching does.

DR. STOCKMANN.

You really are absurd, Katrina.   Am I to let myself be beaten off the field by public opinion, and the compact majority, and all that sort of devilry?   No, thank you!   Besides, my point is so simple, so clear and straightforward.   I only want to drive it into the heads of these curs that the Liberals are the craftiest foes free men have to face; that party-programmes wring the necks of all young and living truths; that considerations of expediency turn justice and morality upside down, until life here becomes simply unlivable.   Come, Captain Horster, don't you think I shall be able to make the people understand that?

HORSTER.

Maybe; I don't know much about these things myself.

DR. STOCKMANN.

Well, you see—this is the way of it! It's the party-leaders that must be exterminated. For a party-leader is just like a wolf, you see—like a ravening wolf; he must devour a certain number of smaller animals a year, if he's to exist at all. Just look at Hovstad and Aslaksen! How many small animals they polish off—or at least mangle and maim, so that they're fit for nothing else but to be house-owners and subscribers to the *People's Messenger!* [*Sits on the edge of the table.*] Just come here, Katrina—see how bravely the sun shines to-day! And how the blessëd fresh spring air blows in upon me!

MRS. STOCKMANN.

Yes, if only we could live on sunshine and spring air, Thomas.

DR. STOCKMANN.

Well, you'll have to pinch and save to eke them out—and then we shall get on all right. That's what troubles me least. No, what d o e s trouble me is that I don't see any man free enough and high-minded enough to dare to take up my work after me.

PETRA.

Oh, don't think about that, father; you have time enough before you.—Why, see, there are the boys already.

EILIF *and* MORTEN *enter from the sitting-room.*

MRS. STOCKMANN.

Have you a holiday to-day?

MORTEN.

No; but we had a fight with the other fellows in play-time——

EILIF.

That's not true; it was the other fellows that fought us.

MORTEN.

Yes, and then Mr. Rörlund said we had better stop at home for a few days.

DR. STOCKMANN.

[*Snapping his fingers and springing down from the table.*] Now I have it! Now I have it, on my soul! You shall never set foot in school again!

THE BOYS.

Never go to school!

MRS. STOCKMANN.

Why, Thomas——

DR. STOCKMANN.

Never, I say! I shall teach you myself—that's to say, I won't teach you any mortal thing——

MORTEN.

Hurrah!

DR. STOCKMANN.

——but I shall help you to grow into free, high-minded men.—Look here, you'll have to help me, Petra.

PETRA.

Yes, father, you may be sure I will.

DR. STOCKMANN.

And we'll have our school in the room where they reviled me as an enemy of the people. But we must have more pupils. I must have at least a dozen boys to begin with.

MRS. STOCKMANN.

You'll never get them in this town.

DR. STOCKMANN.

We shall see. [*To the boys.*] Don't you know any street urchins—any regular ragamuffins——?

MORTEN.

Yes, father, I know lots!

DR. STOCKMANN.

That's all right; bring me a few of them. I shall experiment with the street-curs for once in a way; there are sometimes excellent heads amongst them.

MORTEN.

But what are we to do when we've grown into free and high-minded men?

DR. STOCKMANN.

Drive all the wolves out to the far west, boys!
[EILIF *looks rather doubtful;* MORTEN *jumps about shouting "Hurrah!"*

MRS. STOCKMANN.

If only the wolves don't drive you out, Thomas.

DR. STOCKMANN.

Are you quite mad, Katrina! D r i v e me o u t!
Now that I am the strongest man in the town?

MRS. STOCKMANN.

The strongest—now?

DR. STOCKMANN.

Yes, I venture to say this: that now I am one of the
strongest men in the whole world.

MORTEN.

I say, what fun!

DR. STOCKMANN.

[*In a subdued voice.*]   Hush; you mustn't speak about
it yet: but I have made a great discovery.

MRS. STOCKMANN.

What, another?

DR. STOCKMANN.

Yes, of course! [*Gathers them about him, and speaks
confidentially.*]   This is what I have discovered, you see:
the strongest man in the world is he who stands most
alone.

MRS. STOCKMANN.

[*Shakes her head, smiling.*]   Ah, Thomas dear——!

PETRA.

[*Grasping his hands cheerily.*]   Father!

THE END.

THE WILD DUCK

THE WILD DUCK

INTRODUCTION *

THE first mention of *The Wild Duck* (as yet unnamed) occurs in a letter from Ibsen to George Brandes, dated Rome, June 12, 1883, some six months after the appearance of *An Enemy of the People.* "I am revolving in my mind just now," he says, "the plan of a new dramatic work in four acts. From time to time a variety of whimsies gathers in one's mind, and one wants to find an outlet for them. But as the play will neither deal with the Supreme Court nor with the Absolute Veto, nor even with the Pure Flag, it can hardly count upon attracting much attention in Norway. Let us hope, however, that it may find a hearing elsewhere." The allusion in this passage is to the great constitutional struggle of 1880–84, of which some account will have to be given in the Introduction to *Rosmersholm.* The "Pure Flag" agitation aimed at, and obtained, the exclusion from the Norwegian flag of the mark of union with Sweden, and was thus a preliminary step towards the severance of the two kingdoms. The word which I have translated "whimsies" is in the original *galskaber,* which might be literally rendered "mad fancies" or "crazy notions." This word, or *galskab* in the singular, was Ibsen's favourite term for his conceptions as they grew up in his mind. I well remember

* Copyright, 1907, by Charles Scribner's Sons.

221

his saying to me, while he was engaged on *The Lady from the Sea*, "I hope to have some tomfoolery [*galskab*] ready for next year." Sometimes he would vary the expression and say *djævelskab*, or "devilry."

Of this particular "tomfoolery" we hear no more for a full year. Then, at the end of June, 1884, he writes in almost identical terms to Brandes and to Theodor Caspari, announcing its completion in the rough. His letter to Caspari is dated Rome, June 27. "All last winter," he says, "I have been pondering over some new whimsies, and have wrestled with them till at last they took dramatic form in a five-act play which I have just completed. That is to say, I have completed the rough draft of it. Now comes the more delicate elaboration, the more energetic individualisation of the characters and their methods of expression. In order to find the requisite quiet and solitude for this work, I am going in a few days to Gossensass, in the Tyrol." This little glimpse into his workshop is particularly interesting.

It becomes all the more interesting when, on turning to the *Literary Remains*, we find that the rough draft, which Ibsen took with him to Gossensass, has been preserved, so that we can see, on comparing the two forms, what he meant by "elaboration and individualisation."

The draft of the first act contains 208 speeches, the completed act 302; which practically means that in the process of elaboration the act became half as long again. It is scarcely too much to say that everything that is most characteristic is added in the revision. The idea of making Old Ekdal an ex-officer was an afterthought. In the

draft we are told that he was a lawyer, and we gather that
he had made himself useful to Werle in some question-
able transactions, and was afterwards deserted by him.
On the other hand, a small touch of rebellion on Old Ekdal's part against the familiarity with which he is treated
by Werle's butler has disappeared from the final form.
I venture to think that the chatter of the Chamberlains
has not been improved in the revision. Each of them,
by the way, figures under his name in the draft, and not
under a mere description. Gregers Werle was originally
supposed to have been living in Paris, not playing the
hermit at "the works." He was apparently conceived
as more of a man of the world than he ultimately became.
When one of the Chamberlains complains of his digestion, Gregers remarks, "There are remedies for everything, Mr. Flor—else why do you suppose that an all-wise
Providence has created mineral waters?"—a speech which
another Chamberlain reproves as "Parisian," and which,
indeed, would scarcely harmonise with the later conception of his character. The Werle family was originally
named "Walle"—the change to Werle suddenly occurs
in the middle of the act, at the point where Old Ekdal
passes through the room. There is no allusion to the fact
of there having been thirteen at table; but the idea had
evidently occurred to Ibsen before he drafted the second
act, in which he makes Hialmar say, "There were twelve
or fourteen of us." Of the scene between Hialmar and
Gregers, so indispensable to the ultimate development,
there is only the slightest trace. In the scene between
Gregers and Werle, Gregers evidently knows that Hialmar is married to his father's ex-mistress, but it is not

clear how he has learnt the fact. Old Werle makes no allusion to "people who dive to the bottom the moment they get a couple of slugs in their body," whence it would almost seem that the symbol of the wild duck, which was to give the play its title, had not yet entered the poet's mind.

The draft of the second act is very fragmentary, but we can see that all the leading ideas of the play—except one—are already present to Ibsen's mind. The three remaining acts are pretty fully drafted; nor did the poet seriously depart from the main lines here laid down. What he did was to fill in and enrich the characterisation. Hedvig in particular gains immensely in the revision. In the draft she is comparatively commonplace; much of the delicacy and beauty of the character, which make her fate so heartrending, came to the poet as an afterthought. And it is curious to note how one single invention, apparently trifling in itself, may almost be said to have transformed the character and the play—the invention, I mean, of Werle's weak eyes and Hedvig's threatened blindness. Nowhere in the draft is there any hint of this idea. The most admirably effective strand in the finished fabric was not at first on the poet's loom, but was woven in as an afterthought. It served a multiplicity of purposes: it helped out the plot, it added to the pathos of Hedvig's figure, and it illustrated Hialmar's selfishness in allowing her to strain her eyes over the retouching which he himself ought to have done. One can imagine the artist's joy in achieving so perfect an example of constructive economy. An idea which presents itself in rudimentary form in the draft is that of Hialmar Ekdal's "invention"—here called his "problem." The later development of this wonderful "invention" forms a very good specimen of Ibsen's method. The draft contains no hint of Hialmar's delightful exposition of the part played by the pistol in the tragedy of the House of Ekdal. Everywhere, on a close comparison of the texts, we see an intensive imagination lighting up, as it were, what was at first somewhat cold and colourless. In this case, as in many others, Ibsen's final working-over may be compared to a switching-on of the electricity.

From Gossensass he wrote to Hegel on September 2: "Herewith I send you the manuscript of my new play, *The Wild Duck*, which has occupied me daily for the past four months, and from which I cannot part without a sense of regret. The characters in this play, despite their many frailties, have, in the course of our long daily association, endeared themselves to me. However, I hope they will also find good and kind friends among the great reading public, and not least among the player-folk, to whom they all, without exception, offer problems worth the solving. But the study and presentation of these personages will not be easy. . . . This new play in some ways occupies a place apart among my dramatic productions; its method of development [literally, of advance] is in many respects divergent from that of its predecessors. But for the present I shall say no more on this subject. The critics will no doubt discover the points in question; at all events, they will find a good deal to wrangle about, a good deal to interpret. Moreover, I think *The Wild Duck* may perhaps lure some of our younger dramatists into new paths, and this I hold to be desirable."

The play was published on November 11, 1884, and was acted at all the leading theatres of Scandinavia in January or February, 1885. Ibsen's estimate of its acting value was fully justified. It everywhere proved itself immensely effective on the stage, and Hialmar, Gina, and Hedvig have made, or greatly enhanced, the reputation of many an actor and actress. Hialmar was one of the chief successes of Emil Poulsen, the leading Danish actor of his day, who placed the second act of *The Wild Duck* in the programme of his farewell performance. It took more than three years for the play to reach the German stage. It was first acted in Berlin in March, 1888; but thereafter it rapidly spread throughout Germany and Austria, and everywhere took firm hold. It was on several occasions, and in various cities, selected for performance in Ibsen's presence, as representing the best that the local theatre could do. In Paris it was produced at the Théâtre-Libre in 1891, and was pronounced by Francisque Sarcey to be "obscure, incoherent, insupportable," but nevertheless to leave "a profound impression." In London it was first produced by the Independent Theatre Society on May 4, 1894, Mr. W. L. Abingdon playing Hialmar, and Miss Winifred Fraser giving a delightful performance of Hedvig. The late Clement Scott's pronouncement on it was that "to make a fuss about so feeble a production was to insult dramatic literature and to outrage common sense." It was repeated at the Globe Theatre in May, 1897, with Mr. Laurence Irving as Hialmar and Miss Fraser again as Hedvig. In October, 1905, it was revived at the Court Theatre, with Mr. Granville Barker as Hialmar and Miss Dorothy Minto as Hedvig.

Of American performances I find no record. It has been acted in Italy and in Greece, I know not with what success. The fact that it has no part for a "leading lady" has rendered it less of an international stock-piece than *A Doll's House*, *Hedda Gabler*, or even *Rosmersholm*.

There can be no doubt that *The Wild Duck* marks a reaction in the poet's mood, following upon the eager vivacity wherewith, in *An Enemy of the People*, he had flung his defiance at the "compact Liberal majority," which, as the reception of *Ghosts* had proved, could not endure to be told the truth. Having said his say and liberated his soul, he now began to ask himself whether human nature was, after all, capable of assimilating the strong meat of truth—whether illusion might not be, for the average man, the only thing that could make life livable. It would be too much to say that the play gives a generally affirmative answer to this question. On the contrary, its last lines express pretty clearly the poet's firm conviction that if life cannot reconcile itself with truth, then life may as well go to the wall. Nevertheless his very devotion to truth forces him to realise and admit that it is an antitoxin which, rashly injected at wrong times or in wrong doses, may produce disastrous results. It ought not to be indiscriminately administered by "quacksalvers."

Gregers Werle is unquestionably a piece of ironic self-portraiture. In his habit of "pestering people, in their poverty, with the claim of the ideal," the poet adumbrates his own conduct from *Brand* onwards, but especially in *Ghosts* and *An Enemy of the People*. Relling, again, is an embodiment of the mood which was dominant during the conception of the play—the mood of pitying contempt for that poor thing human nature, as embodied in Hialmar. An actor who, in playing the part of Relling, made up as Ibsen himself, has been blamed for having committed a fault, not only of taste, but of interpretation, since Gregers (it is maintained) is the true Ibsen. But the fact is that both characters represent the poet. They embody the struggle in his mind between idealism and cynical despondency. There can be no doubt, however, that in some measure he consciously identified himself with Gregers. In a letter to Mr. Gosse, written in 1872, he had employed in his own person the very phrase, *den ideale fordring*—"the claim of the ideal"—which is Gregers' watchword. The use of this sufficiently obvious phrase, however, does not mean much. Far stronger evidence of identification is afforded by John Paulsen[1] in some anecdotes he relates of Ibsen's habits of "self-help"—evidence which we may all the more safely accept, as Herr Paulsen seems to have been unconscious of its bearing upon the character of Gregers. "Ibsen," he says, "was always bent upon doing things himself, so as not to give trouble to servants. His ideal was 'the self-made man.'[2] Thus, if a button came off one of his garments he would retire to his own room, lock the door, and after many comical and unnecessary preliminaries proceed to sew on the button himself, with the same care with which he wrote the fair copy of a new play. Such an important task he could not possibly entrust to any one else, not even to his wife. One of his paradoxes was that 'a woman

[1] *Samliv med Ibsen*, p. 33.
[2] Herr Paulsen uses the English words; but it will appear from the sequel that Ibsen's ideal was not so much the self-made as the self-mended man.

never knew how to sew on a button so that it would hold.'
But if he himself sewed it on, it held to all eternity. Fru
Ibsen smiled roguishly and subtly when the creator of
Nora came out with such anti-feminist sentiments. Afterwards she told me in confidence, 'It is true that Ibsen
himself sews on his vagrant buttons; but the fact that
they hold so well is *my* doing, for, without his knowledge,
I always "finish them off," which he forgets to do. But
don't disturb his conviction: it makes him so happy.' "

"One winter day in Munich," Herr Paulsen continues,
"Ibsen asked me with a serious and even anxious coun-
tenance, 'Tell me one thing, Paulsen—do you black your
own boots every morning?' I was taken aback, and
doubtless looked quite guilty as I answered, 'No.' I had
a vaguely uncomfortable sense that I had failed in a duty
to myself and to society. 'But you really ought to do so.
It will make you feel a different man. One should never
let others do what one can do oneself. If you begin with
blacking your boots, you will get on to putting your room
in order, laying the fire, etc. In this way you will at last
find yourself an emancipated man, independent of Tom,
Dick, or Harry.' I promised to follow his advice, but
have unfortunately not kept my word." It is evident
that Ibsen purposely transferred to Gregers this characteristic of his own; and the sentiments with which
Gina regards it are probably not unlike those which
Fru Ibsen may from time to time have manifested. We
could scarcely demand clearer proof that in Gregers the
poet was laughing at himself.

To Hedvig, Ibsen gave the name of his only sister, and
in many respects she seems to have served as a model for

the character. She was the poet's favourite among all his relatives. "You are certainly the best of us," he wrote to her in 1869. Björnstjerne Björnson said, after making her acquaintance, that he now understood what a large element of heredity there was in Ibsen's bent towards mysticism. We may be sure that Hedvig's researches among the books left by the old sea-captain, and her dislike for the frontispiece of Harrison's *History of London*, are remembered traits from the home-life of the poet's childhood. It does not seem to be known who had the honour of "sitting for" the character of Hialmar. Probably he is a composite of many originals. Moreover, he is obviously a younger brother of Peer Gynt. Deprive Peer Gynt of his sense of humour, and clip the wings of his imagination, and you have Hialmar Ekdal.

I confess I do not know quite definitely what Ibsen had in mind when he spoke of *The Wild Duck* holding "a place apart" among his productions, and exemplifying a technique (for he is evidently thinking of its technical development) "divergent" from that of its predecessors. I should rather say that it marked the continuation and consummation of the technical method which he had been elaborating from *Pillars of Society* onward. It is the first example of what we may term his retrospective method, in its full complexity. *Pillars of Society* and *A Doll's House* may be called semi-retrospective; something like half of the essential action takes place before the eyes of the audience. *Ghosts* is almost wholly retrospective; as soon as the past has been fully unravelled the action is over, and only the catastrophe remains; but in this case the past to be unravelled is comparatively simple and easy

of disentanglement. *An Enemy of the People* is scarcely
retrospective at all; almost the whole of its action falls
within the frame of the picture.   In *The Wild Duck*, on
the other hand, the unravelling of the past is a task of
infinite subtlety and elaborate art.   The execution of this
task shows a marvellous and hitherto unexampled grasp
of mind.   Never before, certainly, had the poet displayed
such an amazing power of fascinating and absorbing us
by the gradual withdrawal of veil after veil from the past;
and as every event was also a trait of character, it followed that never before had his dialogue been so satu-
rated, as it were, with character-revelation.   The development of the drama reminds one of the practice (in itself
a very bad practice) of certain modern stage-managers,
who are fond of raising their curtain on a dark scene,
and then gradually lighting it up by a series of touches on
the electric switchboard.   First there comes a glimmer
from the right, then a flash from the left; then the background is suffused with light, so that we see objects standing out against it in profile, but cannot as yet discern their
details.   Then comes a ray from this batten, a gleam from
that; here a penetrating shaft of light, there a lambent
glow; until at last the footlights are turned on at full, and
every nook and cranny of the scene stands revealed in a
blaze of luminosity.   But Ibsen's switchboard is far more
subtly divided than that of even the most modern theatre.   At every touch upon it, some single, cunningly-
placed, ingeniously-dissembled burner kindles, almost
unnoticed save by the most watchful eye; so that the full
light spreads over the scene as imperceptibly as dawn
grows into day.

It seems to me, then, that *The Wild Duck* is a consummation rather than a new departure. Assuredly it marks the summit of the poet's achievement (in modern prose) up to that date. Its only possible rival is *Ghosts;* and who does not feel the greater richness, depth, suppleness, and variety of the later play? It gives us, in a word, a larger segment of life.

THE WILD DUCK

(1884)

CHARACTERS

WERLE, *a merchant, manufacturer, etc.*
GREGERS WERLE, *his son.*
OLD EKDAL.
HIALMAR EKDAL, *his son, a photographer.*
GINA EKDAL, *Hialmar's wife.*
HEDVIG, *their daughter, a girl of fourteen.*
MRS. SÖRBY, *Werle's housekeeper.*
RELLING, *a doctor.*
MOLVIK, *a student of theology.*
GRÅBERG, *Werle's bookkeeper.*
PETTERSEN, *Werle's servant.*
JENSEN, *a hired waiter.*
A FLABBY GENTLEMAN.
A THIN-HAIRED GENTLEMAN.
A SHORT-SIGHTED GENTLEMAN.
Six other gentlemen, guests at Werle's dinner-party.
Several hired waiters.

———

The first act passes in Werle's house, the remaining acts at Hialmar Ekdal's.

Pronunciation of Names: Gregers Werle=Grayghers Verlë; Hialmar Ekdal=Yalmar Aykdal; Gina=Gheena; Gråberg=Groberg; Jensen=Yensen.

THE WILD DUCK

PLAY IN FIVE ACTS

ACT FIRST

At WERLE'S *house. A richly and comfortably furnished study; bookcases and upholstered furniture; a writing-table, with papers and documents, in the centre of the room; lighted lamps with green shades, giving a subdued light. At the back, open folding-doors with curtains drawn back. Within is seen a large and handsome room, brilliantly lighted with lamps and branching candlesticks. In front, on the right (in the study), a small baize door leads into* WERLE'S *office. On the left, in front, a fireplace with a glowing coal fire, and farther back a double door leading into the dining-room.*

WERLE'S *servant,* PETTERSEN, *in livery, and* JENSEN, *the hired waiter, in black, are putting the study in order. In the large room, two or three other hired waiters are moving about, arranging things and lighting more candles. From the dining-room, the hum of conversation and laughter of many voices are heard; a glass is tapped with a knife; silence follows, and a toast is proposed; shouts of " Bravo ! " and then again a buzz of conversation.*

PETTERSEN.

[*Lights a lamp on the chimney-place and places a shade over it.*] Hark to them, Jensen! now the old man's on his legs holding a long palaver about Mrs. Sörby.

JENSEN.

[*Pushing forward an arm-chair.*] Is it true, what folks say, that they're—very good friends, eh?

PETTERSEN.

Lord knows.

JENSEN.

I've heard tell as he's been a lively customer in his day.

PETTERSEN.

May be.

JENSEN.

And he's giving this spread in honour of his son, they say.

PETTERSEN.

Yes. His son came home yesterday.

JENSEN.

This is the first time I ever heard as Mr. Werle h a d a son.

PETTERSEN.

Oh yes, he has a son, right enough. But he's a fixture, as you might say, up at the Höidal works. He's never once come to town all the years I've been in service here.

A WAITER.

[*In the doorway of the other room.*]   Pettersen, here's an old fellow wanting——

PETTERSEN.

[*Mutters.*]   The devil—who's this now?

OLD EKDAL *appears from the right, in the inner room. He is dressed in a threadbare overcoat with a high collar; he wears woollen mittens, and carries in his hand a stick and a fur cap.   Under his arm, a brown paper parcel.   Dirty red-brown wig and small grey moustache.*

PETTERSEN.

[*Goes towards him.*]   Good Lord—what do y o u want here?

EKDAL.

[*In the doorway.*]   Must get into the office, Pettersen.

PETTERSEN.

The office was closed an hour ago, and——

EKDAL.

So they told me at the front door.   But Gråberg's in there still.   Let me slip in this way, Pettersen; there's a good fellow.   [*Points towards the baize door.*]   It's not the first time I've come this way.

PETTERSEN.

Well, you may pass.   [*Opens the door.*]   But mind you go out again the proper way, for we've got company.

EKDAL.

I know, I know—h'm! Thanks, Pettersen, good old friend! Thanks! [*Mutters softly.*] Ass!
[*He goes into the office;* PETTERSEN *shuts the door after him.*

JENSEN.

Is h e one of the office people?

PETTERSEN.

No, he's only an outside hand that does odd jobs of copying. But he's been a tip-topper in his day, has old Ekdal.

JENSEN.

You can see he's been through a lot.

PETTERSEN.

Yes; he was an army officer, you know.

JENSEN.

You don't say so?

PETTERSEN.

No mistake about it. But then he went into the timber trade or something of the sort. They say he once played Mr. Werle a very nasty trick. They were partners in the Höidal works at the time. Oh, I know old Ekdal well, I do. Many a nip of bitters and bottle of ale we two have drunk at Madam Eriksen's.

JENSEN.

He don't look as if he'd much to stand treat with.

PETTERSEN.

Why, bless you, Jensen, it's m e that stands treat. I always think there's no harm in being a bit civil to folks that have seen better days.

JENSEN.

Did he go bankrupt then?

PETTERSEN.

Worse than that. He went to prison.

JENSEN.

To prison!

PETTERSEN.

Or perhaps it was the Penitentiary. [*Listens.*] Sh! They're leaving the table.

The dining-room door is thrown open from within, by a couple of waiters. MRS. SÖRBY *comes out conversing with two gentlemen. Gradually the whole company follows, amongst them* WERLE. *Last come* HIALMAR EKDAL *and* GREGERS WERLE.

MRS. SÖRBY.

[*In passing, to the servant.*] Tell them to serve the coffee in the music-room, Pettersen.

PETTERSEN.

Very well, Madam.
[*She goes with the two gentlemen into the inner room, and thence out to the right.* PETTERSEN *and* JENSEN *go out the same way.*

A Flabby Gentleman.

[*To a* Thin-haired Gentleman.] Whew! What a dinner!—It was no joke to do it justice!

The Thin-haired Gentleman.

Oh, with a little good-will one can get through a lot in three hours.

The Flabby Gentleman.

Yes, but afterwards, afterwards, my dear Chamberlain!

A Third Gentleman.

I hear the coffee and maraschino are to be served in the music-room.

The Flabby Gentleman.

Bravo! Then perhaps Mrs. Sörby will play us something.

The Thin-haired Gentleman.

[*In a low voice.*] I hope Mrs. Sörby mayn't play us a tune we don't like, one of these days!

The Flabby Gentleman.

Oh no, not she! Bertha will never turn against her old friends. [*They laugh and pass into the inner room.*

Werle.

[*In a low voice, dejectedly.*] I don't think anybody noticed it, Gregers.

GREGERS.

[*Looks at him.*]   Noticed what?

WERLE.

Did you not notice it either?

GREGERS.

What do you mean?

WERLE.

We were thirteen at table.

GREGERS.

Indeed?   Were there thirteen of us?

WERLE.

[*Glances towards* HIALMAR EKDAL.]   Our usual party
is twelve.   [*To the others.*]   This way, gentlemen!
    [WERLE *and the others, all except* HIALMAR *and*
        GREGERS, *go out by the back, to the right.*

HIALMAR.

[*Who has overheard the conversation.*]   You ought not
to have invited me, Gregers.

GREGERS.

What!   Not ask my best and only friend to a party
supposed to be in my honour——?

HIALMAR.

But I don't think your father likes it.   You see I am
quite outside his circle.

GREGERS.

So I hear.   But I wanted to see you and have a talk
with you, and I certainly shan't be staying long.—Ah, we
two old schoolfellows have drifted far apart from each
other.   It must be sixteen or seventeen years since we
met.

HIALMAR.

Is it so long?

GREGERS.

It is indeed.   Well, how goes it with you?   You look
well.   You have put on flesh, and grown almost stout.

HIALMAR.

Well, "stout" is scarcely the word; but I daresay I look
a little more of a man than I used to.

GREGERS.

Yes, you do; your outer man is in first-rate condition.

HIALMAR.

[*In a tone of gloom.*]   Ah, but the inner man!   That is
a very different matter, I can tell you!   Of course you
know of the terrible catastrophe that has befallen me and
mine since last we met.

GREGERS.

[*More softly.*]   How are things going with your father
now?

HIALMAR.

Don't let us talk of it, old fellow.   Of course my poor
unhappy father lives with me.   He hasn't another soul

in the world to care for him.   But you can understand
that this is a miserable subject for me.—Tell me, rather,
how you have been getting on up at the works.

GREGERS.

I have had a delightfully lonely time of it—plenty of
leisure to think and think about things.   Come over here;
we may as well make ourselves comfortable.

[*He seats himself in an arm-chair by the fire and draws*
HIALMAR *down into another alongside of it.*

HIALMAR.

[*Sentimentally.*]   After all, Gregers, I thank you for in-
viting me to your father's table; for I take it as a sign
that you have got over your feeling against me.

GREGERS.

[*Surprised.*]   How could you imagine I had any feeling against you?

HIALMAR.

You had at first, you know.

GREGERS.

How at first?

HIALMAR.

After the great misfortune.   It was natural enough
that you should.   Your father was within an ace of being
drawn into that—well, that terrible business.

GREGERS.

Why should that give me any feeling against you?
Who can have put that into your head?

HIALMAR.

I know it did, Gregers; your father told me so himself.

GREGERS.

[*Starts.*] My father! Oh indeed. H'm.—Was that why you never let me hear from you?—not a single word.

HIALMAR.

Yes.

GREGERS.

Not even when you made up your mind to become a photographer?

HIALMAR.

Your father said I had better not write to you at all, about anything.

GREGERS.

[*Looking straight before him.*] Well well, perhaps he was right.—But tell me now, Hialmar: are you pretty well satisfied with your present position?

HIALMAR.

[*With a little sigh.*] Oh yes, I am; I have really no cause to complain. At first, as you may guess, I felt it a little strange. It was such a totally new state of things for me. But of course my whole circumstances were totally changed. Father's utter, irretrievable ruin,—the shame and disgrace of it, Gregers——

GREGERS.

[*Affected.*] Yes, yes; I understand.

HIALMAR.

I couldn't think of remaining at college; there wasn't
a shilling to spare; on the contrary, there were debts—
mainly to your father I believe——

GREGERS.

H'm——

HIALMAR.

In short, I thought it best to break, once for all, with
my old surroundings and associations. It was your
father that specially urged me to it; and since he interested himself so much in me——

GREGERS.

My father did?

HIALMAR.

Yes, you surely knew that, didn't you?   Where do you
suppose I found the money to learn photography, and to
furnish a studio and make a start?   All that costs a pretty
penny, I can tell you.

GREGERS.

And my f a t h e r provided the money?

HIALMAR.

Yes, my dear fellow, didn't you know?   I understood
him to say he had written to you about it.

GREGERS.

Not a word about h i s part in the business.   He must
have forgotten it.   Our correspondence has always been
purely a business one.   So it was my father that——!

HIALMAR.

Yes, certainly. He didn't wish it to be generally known; but he it was. And of course it was he, too, that put me in a position to marry. Don't you—don't you know about that either?

GREGERS.

No, I haven't heard a word of it. [*Shakes him by the arm.*] But, my dear Hialmar, I can't tell you what pleasure all this gives me—pleasure, and self-reproach. I have perhaps done my father injustice after all—in some things. This proves that he has a heart. It shows a sort of compunction——

HIALMAR.

Compunction——?

GREGERS.

Yes, yes—whatever you like to call it. Oh, I can't tell you how glad I am to hear this of father.—So you are a married man, Hialmar! That is further than I shall ever get. Well, I hope you are happy in your married life?

HIALMAR.

Yes, thoroughly happy. She is as good and capable a wife as any man could wish for. And she is by no means without culture.

GREGERS.

[*Rather surprised.*] No, of course not.

HIALMAR.

You see, life is itself an education. Her daily intercourse with me—— And then we know one or two rather remarkable men, who come a good deal about us. I assure you, you would hardly know Gina again.

GREGERS.

Gina?

HIALMAR.

Yes; had you forgotten that her name was Gina?

GREGERS.

Whose name? I haven't the slightest idea——

HIALMAR.

Don't you remember that she used to be in service here?

GREGERS.

[*Looks at him.*] Is it Gina Hansen——?

HIALMAR.

Yes, of course it is Gina Hansen.

GREGERS.

——who kept house for us during the last year of my mother's illness?

HIALMAR.

Yes, exactly. But, my dear friend, I'm quite sure your father told you that I was married.

GREGERS.

[*Who has risen.*] Oh yes, he mentioned it; but not that—— [*Walking about the room.*] Stay—perhaps he did—now that I think of it. My father always writes such short letters. [*Half seats himself on the arm of the chair.*] Now, tell me, Hialmar—this is interesting—how did you come to know Gina—your wife?

HIALMAR.

The simplest thing in the world. You know Gina did not stay here long; everything was so much upset at that time, owing to your mother's illness and so forth, that Gina was not equal to it all; so she gave notice and left. That was the year before your mother died—or it may have been the same year.

GREGERS.

It was the same year. I was up at the works then. But afterwards——?

HIALMAR.

Well, Gina lived at home with her mother, Madam Hansen, an excellent hard-working woman, who kept a little eating-house. She had a room to let too; a very nice comfortable room.

GREGERS.

And I suppose you were lucky enough to secure it?

HIALMAR.

Yes; in fact, it was your father that recommended it to me. So it was there, you see, that I really came to know Gina.

GREGERS.

And then you got engaged?

HIALMAR.

Yes. It doesn't take young people long to fall in love——; h'm——

GREGERS.

[*Rises and moves about a little.*] Tell me: was it after your engagement—was it then that my father—I mean was it then that you began to take up photography?

HIALMAR.

Yes, precisely. I wanted to make a start, and to set up house as soon as possible; and your father and I agreed that this photography business was the readiest way. Gina thought so too. Oh, and there was another thing in its favour, by-the-bye: it happened, luckily, that Gina had learnt to retouch.

GREGERS.

That chimed in marvellously.

HIALMAR.

[*Pleased, rises.*] Yes, didn't it? Don't you think it was a marvellous piece of luck?

GREGERS.

Oh, unquestionably. My father seems to have been almost a kind of providence for you.

HIALMAR.

[*With emotion.*] He did not forsake his old friend's son in the hour of his need. For he has a heart, you see.

MRS. SÖRBY.

[*Enters, arm-in-arm with* WERLE.]   Nonsense, my dear
Mr. Werle; you mustn't stop there any longer staring at
all the lights.   It's very bad for you.

WERLE.

[*Lets go her arm and passes his hand over his eyes.*]   I
daresay you are right.
      [PETTERSEN *and* JENSEN *carry round refreshment
      trays.*]

MRS. SÖRBY.

[*To the Guests in the other room.*]   This way, if you
please, gentlemen.   Whoever wants a glass of punch
must be so good as to come in here.

THE FLABBY GENTLEMAN.

[*Comes up to* MRS. SÖRBY.]   Surely, it isn't possible
that you have suspended our cherished right to smoke?

MRS. SÖRBY.

Yes.   No smoking here, in Mr. Werle's sanctum,
Chamberlain.

THE THIN-HAIRED GENTLEMAN.

When did you enact these stringent amendments on
the cigar law, Mrs. Sörby?

MRS. SÖRBY.

After the last dinner, Chamberlain, when certain persons permitted themselves to overstep the mark.

The Thin-haired Gentleman.

And may one never overstep the mark a little bit, Madame Bertha?   Not the least little bit?

Mrs. Sörby.

Not in any respect whatsoever, Mr. Balle.
[*Most of the guests have assembled in the study; servants hand round glasses of punch.*

Werle.

[*To* Hialmar, *who is standing beside a table.*]   What are you studying so intently, Ekdal?

Hialmar.

Only an album, Mr. Werle.

The Thin-haired Gentleman.

[*Who is wandering about.*]   Ah, photographs!   They are quite in your line of course.

The Flabby Gentleman.

[*In an arm-chair.*]   Haven't you brought any of your own with you?

Hialmar.

No, I haven't.

The Flabby Gentleman.

You ought to have; it's very good for the digestion to sit and look at pictures.

THE THIN-HAIRED GENTLEMAN.

And it contributes to the entertainment, you know.

THE SHORT-SIGHTED GENTLEMAN.

And all contributions are thankfully received.

MRS. SÖRBY.

The Chamberlains think that when one is invited out to dinner, one ought to exert oneself a little in return, Mr. Ekdal.

THE FLABBY GENTLEMAN.

Where one dines so well, that duty becomes a pleasure.

THE THIN-HAIRED GENTLEMAN.

And when it's a case of the struggle for existence, you know——

MRS. SÖRBY.

I quite agree with you!
[*They continue the conversation, with laughter and joking.*

GREGERS.

[*Softly.*] You must join in, Hialmar.

HIALMAR.

[*Writhing.*] What am I to talk about?

THE FLABBY GENTLEMAN.

Don't you think, Mr. Werle, that Tokay may be considered one of the more wholesome sorts of wine?

WERLE.

[*By the fire.*] I can answer for the Tokay you had
to-day, at any rate; it's of one of the very finest seasons.
Of course you would notice that.

THE FLABBY GENTLEMAN.

Yes, it had a remarkably delicate flavour.

HIALMAR.

[*Shyly.*] Is there any difference between the seasons?

THE FLABBY GENTLEMAN.

[*Laughs.*] Come! That's good!

WERLE.

[*Smiles.*] It really doesn't pay to set fine wine before
you.

THE THIN-HAIRED GENTLEMAN.

Tokay is like photographs, Mr. Ekdal: they both need
sunshine. Am I not right?

HIALMAR.

Yes, light is important no doubt.

MRS. SÖRBY.

And it's exactly the same with Chamberlains—they,
too, depend very much on sunshine,[1] as the saying is.

THE THIN-HAIRED GENTLEMAN.

Oh fie! That's a very threadbare sarcasm!

[1] The "sunshine" of Court favour.

THE SHORT-SIGHTED GENTLEMAN.

Mrs. Sörby is coming out——

THE FLABBY GENTLEMAN.

——and at our expense, too. [*Holds up his finger reprovingly.*] Oh, Madame Bertha, Madame Bertha!

MRS. SÖRBY.

Yes, and there's not the least doubt that the seasons differ greatly. The old vintages are the finest.

THE SHORT-SIGHTED GENTLEMAN.

Do you reckon me among the old vintages?

MRS. SÖRBY.

Oh, far from it.

THE THIN-HAIRED GENTLEMAN.

There now! But m e, dear Mrs. Sörby——?

THE FLABBY GENTLEMAN.

Yes, and me? What vintage should you say that we belong to?

MRS. SÖRBY.

Why, to the sweet vintages, gentlemen.
　[*She sips a glass of punch. The gentlemen laugh and
　　flirt with her.*

WERLE.

Mrs. Sörby can always find a loop-hole—when she wants to. Fill your glasses, gentlemen! Pettersen, will

you see to it——! Gregers, suppose we have a glass together. [GREGERS *does not move.*] Won't you join us,
Ekdal? I found no opportunity of drinking with you at
table.

　　[GRÅBERG, *the Bookkeeper, looks in at the baize door.*

GRÅBERG.

Excuse me, sir, but I can't get out.

WERLE.

Have you been locked in again?

GRÅBERG.

Yes, and Flakstad has carried off the keys.

WERLE.

Well, you can pass out this way.

GRÅBERG.

But there's some one else——

WERLE.

All right; come through, both of you. Don't be afraid.

　　[GRÅBERG *and* OLD EKDAL *come out of the office.*

WERLE.

[*Involuntarily.*] Ugh!
　　[*The laughter and talk among the Guests cease.*
　　HIALMAR *starts at the sight of his father, puts down*
　　his glass, and turns towards the fireplace.

EKDAL.

[*Does not look up, but makes little bows to both sides as he passes, murmuring.*] Beg pardon, come the wrong way. Door locked—door locked. Beg pardon.

  [*He and* GRÅBERG *go out by the back, to the right.*

WERLE.

[*Between his teeth.*] That idiot Gråberg!

GREGERS.

[*Open-mouthed and staring, to* HIALMAR.] Why surely that wasn't——!

THE FLABBY GENTLEMAN.

What's the matter? Who was it?

GREGERS.

Oh, nobody, only the bookkeeper and some one with him.

THE SHORT-SIGHTED GENTLEMAN.

[*To* HIALMAR.] Did y o u know that man?

HIALMAR.

I don't know—I didn't notice——

THE FLABBY GENTLEMAN.

What the deuce has come over every one?

  [*He joins another group who are talking softly.*

MRS. SÖRBY.

[*Whispers to the Servant.*]   Give him something to take with him;—something good, mind!

PETTERSEN.

[*Nods.*]   I'll see to it.   [*Goes out.*

GREGERS.

[*Softly and with emotion, to* HIALMAR.]   So that was really he!

HIALMAR.

Yes.

GREGERS.

And you could stand there and deny that you knew him!

HIALMAR.

[*Whispers vehemently.*]   But how c o u l d I——!

GREGERS.

——acknowledge your own father?

HIALMAR.

[*With pain.*]   Oh, if you were in my place——
    [*The conversation amongst the Guests, which has been carried on in a low tone, now swells into constrained joviality.*]

THE THIN-HAIRED GENTLEMAN.

[*Approaching* HIALMAR *and* GREGERS *in a friendly manner.*]   Aha!   Reviving old college memories, eh?

Don't you smoke, Mr. Ekdal? May I give you a light?
Oh, by-the-bye, we mustn't——

HIALMAR.

No, thank you, I won't——

THE FLABBY GENTLEMAN.

Haven't you a nice little poem you could recite to us,
Mr. Ekdal? You used to recite so charmingly.

HIALMAR.

I am sorry I can't remember anything.

THE FLABBY GENTLEMAN.

Oh, that's a pity. Well, what shall we do, Balle?
[*Both Gentlemen move away and pass into the other
room.*

HIALMAR.

[*Gloomily.*] Gregers—I am going! When a man has
felt the crushing hand of Fate, you see—— Say good-
bye to your father for me.

GREGERS.

Yes, yes. Are you going straight home?

HIALMAR.

Yes. Why?

GREGERS.

Oh, because I may perhaps look in on you later.

HIALMAR.

No, you mustn't do that. You must not come to my home. Mine is a melancholy abode, Gregers; especially after a splendid banquet like this. We can always arrange to meet somewhere in the town.

MRS. SÖRBY.

[*Who has quietly approached.*] Are you going, Ekdal?

HIALMAR.

Yes.

MRS. SÖRBY.

Remember me to Gina.

HIALMAR.

Thanks.

MRS. SÖRBY.

And say I am coming up to see her one of these days.

HIALMAR.

Yes, thank you. [*To* GREGERS.] Stay here; I will slip out unobserved.

[*He saunters away, then into the other room, and so out to the right.*

MRS. SÖRBY.

[*Softly to the Servant, who has come back.*] Well, did you give the old man something?

PETTERSEN.

Yes; I sent him off with a bottle of cognac.

MRS. SÖRBY.

Oh, you might have thought of something better than that.

PETTERSEN.

Oh no, Mrs. Sörby; cognac is what he likes best in the world.

THE FLABBY GENTLEMAN.

[*In the doorway with a sheet of music in his hand.*] Shall we play a duet, Mrs. Sörby?

MRS. SÖRBY.

Yes, suppose we do.

THE GUESTS.

Bravo, bravo!
[*She goes with all the Guests through the back room, out to the right.* GREGERS *remains standing by the fire.* WERLE *is looking for something on the writing-table, and appears to wish that* GREGERS *would go; as* GREGERS *does not move,* WERLE *goes towards the door.*

GREGERS.

Father, won't you stay a moment?

WERLE.

[*Stops.*]   What is it?

GREGERS.

I must have a word with you.

WERLE.

Can it not wait till we are alone?

GREGERS.

No, it cannot; for perhaps we shall never be alone together.

WERLE.

[*Drawing nearer.*]　What do you mean by that?
　[*During what follows, the pianoforte is faintly heard
　　from the distant music-room.*

GREGERS.

How has that family been allowed to go so miserably
to the wall?

WERLE.

You mean the Ekdals, I suppose.

GREGERS.

Yes, I mean the Ekdals.　Lieutenant Ekdal was once
so closely associated with you.

WERLE.

Much too closely; I have felt that to my cost for many
a year.　It is thanks to him that I—yes *I*—have had a
kind of slur cast upon my reputation.

GREGERS.

[*Softly.*]　Are you sure that h e alone was to blame?

WERLE.

Who else do you suppose——?

GREGERS.

You and he acted together in that affair of the forests——

WERLE.

But was it not Ekdal that drew the map of the tracts we had bought—that fraudulent map! It was he who felled all that timber illegally on Government ground. In fact, the whole management was in his hands.   I was quite in the dark as to what Lieutenant Ekdal was doing.

GREGERS.

Lieutenant Ekdal himself seems to have been very much in the dark as to what he was doing.

WERLE.

That may be.   But the fact remains that he was found guilty and I acquitted.

GREGERS.

Yes, I know that nothing was proved against you.

WERLE.

Acquittal is acquittal.   Why do you rake up these old miseries that turned my hair grey before its time?   Is that the sort of thing you have been brooding over up there, all these years?   I can assure you, Gregers, here in the town the whole story has been forgotten long ago —so far as *I* am concerned.

GREGERS.

But that unhappy Ekdal family.

WERLE.

What would you have had me do for the people?
When Ekdal came out of prison he was a broken-down
being, past all help.   There are people in the world who
dive to the bottom the moment they get a couple of slugs
in their body, and never come to the surface again.   You
may take my word for it, Gregers, I have done all I
could without positively laying myself open to all sorts
of suspicion and gossip——

GREGERS.

Suspicion——?   Oh, I see.

WERLE.

I have given Ekdal copying to do for the office, and I
pay him far, far more for it than his work is worth——

GREGERS.

[*Without looking at him.*]   H'm; t h a t I don't doubt

WERLE.

You laugh?   Do you think I am not telling you the
truth?   Well, I certainly can't refer you to my books,
for I never enter payments of that sort.

GREGERS.

[*Smiles coldly.*]   No, there are certain payments it is
best to keep no account of.

WERLE.

[*Taken aback.*]   What do you mean by t h a t ?

GREGERS.

[*Mustering up courage.*]   Have you entered what it cost you to have Hialmar Ekdal taught photography?

WERLE.

I?   How "entered" it?

GREGERS.

I have learnt that it was you who paid for his training. And I have learnt, too, that it was you who enabled him to set up house so comfortably.

WERLE.

Well, and yet you talk as though I had done nothing for the Ekdals!   I can assure you these people have cost me enough in all conscience.

GREGERS

Have you entered any of these expenses in your books?

WERLE.

Why do you ask?

GREGERS.

Oh, I have my reasons.   Now tell me: when you interested yourself so warmly in your old friend's son—it was just before his marriage, was it not?

WERLE.

Why, deuce take it—after all these years, how can
I——?

GREGERS.

You wrote me a letter about that time—a business
letter, of course; and in a postscript you mentioned—
quite briefly—that Hialmar Ekdal had married a Miss
Hansen.

WERLE.

Yes, that was quite right.   That was her name.

GREGERS.

But you did not mention that this Miss Hansen was
Gina Hansen—our former housekeeper.

WERLE.

[*With a forced laugh of derision.*]   No; to tell the truth,
it didn't occur to me that you were so particularly interested in our former housekeeper.

GREGERS.

No more I was.   But [*lowers his voice*] there were
others in this house who w e r e particularly interested
in her.

WERLE.

What do you mean by that?   [*Flaring up.*]   You are
not alluding to me, I hope?

GREGERS.

[*Softly but firmly.*]   Yes, I am alluding to you.

WERLE.

And you dare——! You presume to——! How can that ungrateful hound—that photographer fellow—how dare he go making such insinuations!

GREGERS.

Hialmar has never breathed a word about this. I don't believe he has the faintest suspicion of such a thing.

WERLE.

Then where have you got it from? Who can have put such notions in your head?

GREGERS.

My poor unhappy mother told me; and that the very last time I saw her.

WERLE.

Your mother! I might have known as much! You and she—you always held together. It was she who turned you against me, from the first.

GREGERS.

No, it was all that she had to suffer and submit to, until she broke down and came to such a pitiful end.

WERLE.

Oh, she had nothing to suffer or submit to; not more than most people, at all events. But there's no getting on with morbid, overstrained creatures—that I have learnt to my cost.—And you could go on nursing such a suspicion—burrowing into all sorts of old rumours and slanders against your own father! I must say, Gregers, I really think that at your age you might find something more useful to do.

GREGERS.

Yes, it is high time.

WERLE.

Then perhaps your mind would be easier than it seems to be now. What can be your object in remaining up at the works, year out and year in, drudging away like a common clerk, and not drawing a farthing more than the ordinary monthly wage? It is downright folly.

GREGERS.

Ah, if I were only sure of t h a t.

WERLE.

I understand you well enough. You want to be independent; you won't be beholden to me for anything. Well, now there happens to be an opportunity for you to become independent, your own master in everything.

GREGERS.

Indeed? In what way——?

WERLE.

When I wrote you insisting on your coming to town at once—h'm——

GREGERS.

Yes, what is it you really want of me? I have been waiting all day to know.

WERLE.

I want to propose that you should enter the firm, as partner.

GREGERS.

I? Join your firm? As partner?

WERLE.

Yes. It would not involve our being constantly together. You could take over the business here in town, and I should move up to the works.

GREGERS.

Y o u would?

WERLE.

The fact is, I am not so fit for work as I once was. I am obliged to spare my eyes, Gregers; they have begun to trouble me.

GREGERS.

They have always been weak.

WERLE.

Not as they are now. And besides, circumstances might possibly make it desirable for me to live up there— for a time, at any rate.

GREGERS.

That is certainly quite a new idea to me.

WERLE.

Listen, Gregers: there are many things that stand between us; but we are father and son after all. We ought

surely to be able to come to some sort of understanding
with each other.

GREGERS.

Outwardly, you mean, of course?

WERLE.

Well, even that would be something.   Think it over,
Gregers.   Don't you think it ought to be possible?   Eh?

GREGERS.

[*Looking at him coldly.*]   There is something behind
all this.

WERLE.

How so?

GREGERS.

You want to make use of me in some way.

WERLE.

In such a close relationship as ours, the one can always be useful to the other.

GREGERS.

Yes, so people say.

WERLE.

I want very much to have you at home with me for a
time.   I am a lonely man, Gregers; I have always felt
lonely, all my life through; but most of all now that I am
getting up in years.   I feel the need of some one about
me——

GREGERS.

You have Mrs. Sörby.

WERLE.

Yes, I have her; and she has become, I may say, almost indispensable to me. She is lively and even-tempered; she brightens up the house; and that is a very great thing for me.

GREGERS.

Well then, you have everything just as you wish it.

WERLE.

Yes, but I am afraid it can't last. A woman so situated may easily find herself in a false position, in the eyes of the world. For that matter it does a man no good, either.

GREGERS.

Oh, when a man gives such dinners as you give, he can risk a great deal.

WERLE.

Yes, but how about the woman, Gregers? I fear she won't accept the situation much longer; and even if she did—even if, out of attachment to me, she were to take her chance of gossip and scandal and all that——? Do you think, Gregers—you with your strong sense of justice——

GREGERS.

[Interrupts him.] Tell me in one word: are you thinking of marrying her?

WERLE.

Suppose I were thinking of it ?   What then ?

GREGERS.

That's what I say: what then ?

WERLE.

Should you be inflexibly opposed to it ?

GREGERS.

Not at all.   Not by any means.

WERLE.

I was not sure whether your devotion to your mother's memory——

GREGERS.

I am not overstrained.

WERLE.

Well, whatever you may or may not be, at all events you have lifted a great weight from my mind.   I am extremely pleased that I can reckon on your concurrence in this matter.

GREGERS.

[*Looking intently at him.*]   Now I see the use you want to put me to.

WERLE.

Use to put you to ?   What an expression !

GREGERS.

Oh, don't let us be nice in our choice of words—not when we are alone together, at any rate. [*With a short laugh.*] Well well! So this is what made it absolutely essential that I should come to town in person. For the sake of Mrs. Sörby, we are to get up a pretence at family life in the house—a tableau of filial affection! That will be something new indeed.

WERLE.

How dare you speak in that tone!

GREGERS.

Was there ever any family life here? Never since I can remember. But now, forsooth, your plans demand something of the sort. No doubt it will have an excellent effect when it is reported that the son has hastened home, on the wings of filial piety, to the grey-haired father's wedding-feast. What will then remain of all the rumours as to the wrongs the poor dead mother had to submit to? Not a vestige. Her son annihilates them at one stroke.

WERLE.

Gregers—I believe there is no one in the world you detest as you do me.

GREGERS.

[*Softly.*] I have seen you at too close quarters.

WERLE.

You have seen me with your mother's eyes. [*Lowers his voice a little.*] But you should remember that her eyes were—clouded now and then.

GREGERS.

[*Quivering.*] I see what you are hinting at.   But who was to blame for mother's unfortunate weakness?   Why you, and all those ——! The last of them was this woman that you palmed off upon Hialmar Ekdal, when you were—— Ugh!

WERLE.

[*Shrugs his shoulders.*] Word for word as if it were your mother speaking!

GREGERS.

[*Without heeding.*] And there he is now, with his great, confiding, childlike mind, compassed about with all this treachery—living under the same roof with such a creature, and never dreaming that what he calls his home is built upon a lie! [*Comes a step nearer.*] When I look back upon your past, I seem to see a battle-field with shattered lives on every hand.

WERLE.

I begin to think the chasm that divides us is too wide.

GREGERS.

[*Bowing, with self-command.*] So I have observed; and therefore I take my hat and go.

WERLE.

You are going!   Out of the house?

GREGERS.

Yes.   For at last I see my mission in life.

WERLE.

What mission?

GREGERS.

You would only laugh if I told you.

WERLE.

A lonely man doesn't laugh so easily, Gregers.

GREGERS.

[*Pointing towards the background.*]   Look, father,—
the Chamberlains are playing blind-man's-buff with Mrs.
Sörby.—Good-night and good-bye.
   [*He goes out by the back to the right.   Sounds of
       laughter and merriment from the Company, who
       are now visible in the outer room.*

WERLE.

[*Muttering contemptuously after* GREGERS.]   Ha——!
Poor wretch—and he says he is not overstrained!

ACT SECOND

HIALMAR EKDAL'S *studio, a good-sized room, evidently in the top storey of the building. On the right, a sloping roof of large panes of glass, half-covered by a blue curtain. In the right-hand corner, at the back, the entrance door; farther forward, on the same side, a door leading to the sitting-room. Two doors on the opposite side, and between them an iron stove. At the back, a wide double sliding-door. The studio is plainly but comfortably fitted up and furnished. Between the doors on the right, standing out a little from the wall, a sofa with a table and some chairs; on the table a lighted lamp with a shade; beside the stove an old arm-chair. Photographic instruments and apparatus of different kinds lying about the room. Against the back wall, to the left of the double door, stands a bookcase containing a few books, boxes, and bottles of chemicals, instruments, tools, and other objects. Photographs and small articles, such as camel's-hair brushes, paper, and so forth, lie on the table.* GINA EKDAL *sits on a chair by the table, sewing.* HEDVIG *is sitting on the sofa, with her hands shading her eyes and her thumbs in her ears, reading a book.*

GINA.

[*Glances once or twice at* HEDVIG, *as if with secret anxiety; then says:*]   Hedvig!

HEDVIG.

[*Does not hear.*]

GINA.

[*Repeats more loudly.*]   Hedvig!

HEDVIG.

[*Takes away her hands and looks up.*]   Yes, mother?

GINA.

Hedvig dear, you mustn't sit reading any longer now.

HEDVIG.

Oh mother, mayn't I read a little more?   Just a little bit?

GINA.

No no, you must put away your book now.   Father doesn't like it; he never reads hisself in the evening.

HEDVIG.

[*Shuts the book.*]   No, father doesn't care much about reading.

GINA.

[*Puts aside her sewing and takes up a lead pencil and a little account-book from the table.*]   Can you remember how much we paid for the butter to-day?

HEDVIG.

It was one crown sixty-five.

GINA.

That's right.   [*Puts it down.*]   It's terrible what a lot of butter we get through in this house.   Then there was

the smoked sausage, and the cheese—let me see—[*Writes*]
—and the ham—[*Adds up.*]   Yes, that makes just——

HEDVIG.

And then the beer.

GINA.

Yes, to be sure. [*Writes.*]   How it do mount up!
But we can't manage with no less.

HEDVIG.

And then you and I didn't need anything hot for dinner, as father was out.

GINA.

No; that was so much to the good.   And then I took
eight crowns fifty for the photographs.

HEDVIG.

Really!   So much as that?

GINA.

Exactly eight crowns fifty.
[*Silence.   GINA takes up her sewing again, HEDVIG
takes paper and pencil and begins to draw, shading
her eyes with her left hand.*

HEDVIG.

Isn't it jolly to think that father is at Mr. Werle's big
dinner-party?

GINA.

You know he's not really Mr. Werle's guest. It was the son invited him. [*After a pause.*] We have nothing to do with that Mr. Werle.

HEDVIG.

I'm longing for father to come home. He promised to ask Mrs. Sörby for something nice for me.

GINA.

Yes, there's plenty of good things going in t h a t house, I can tell you.

HEDVIG.

[*Goes on drawing.*] And I believe I'm a little hungry too.

[OLD EKDAL, *with the paper parcel under his arm and another parcel in his coat pocket, comes in by the entrance door.*

GINA.

How late you are to-day, grandfather!

EKDAL.

They had locked the office door. Had to wait in Grå-berg's room. And then they let me through—h'm.

HEDVIG.

Did you get some more copying to do, grandfather?

EKDAL.

This whole packet. Just look.

GINA.

That's capital.

HEDVIG.

And you have another parcel in your pocket.

EKDAL.

Eh? Oh never mind, that's nothing. [*Puts his stick away in a corner.*] This work will keep me going a long time, Gina. [*Opens one of the sliding-doors in the back wall a little.*] Hush! [*Peeps into the room for a moment, then pushes the door carefully to again.*] Hee-hee! They're fast asleep, all the lot of them. And she's gone into the basket herself. Hee-hee!

HEDVIG.

Are you sure she isn't cold in that basket, grandfather?

EKDAL.

Not a bit of it! Cold? With all that straw? [*Goes towards the farther door on the left.*] There are matches in here, I suppose.

GINA.

The matches is on the drawers.

[EKDAL *goes into his room.*

HEDVIG.

It's nice that grandfather has got all that copying.

GINA.

Yes, poor old father; it means a bit of pocket-money for him.

HEDVIG.

And he won't be able to sit the whole forenoon down at that horrid Madam Eriksen's.

GINA.

No more he won't.   [*Short silence.*

HEDVIG.

Do you suppose they are still at the dinner-table?

GINA.

Goodness knows; as like as not.

HEDVIG.

Think of all the delicious things father is having to eat! I'm certain he'll be in splendid spirits when he comes.   Don't you think so, mother?

GINA.

Yes; and if only we could tell him that we'd got the room let——

HEDVIG.

But we don't need that this evening.

GINA.

Oh, we'd be none the worse of it, I can tell you.   It's no use to us as it is.

HEDVIG.

I mean we don't need it this evening, for father will be in a good humour at any rate.   It is best to keep the letting of the room for another time.

GINA.

[*Looks across at her.*] You like having some good news to tell father when he comes home in the evening?

HEDVIG.

Yes; for then things are pleasanter somehow.

GINA.

[*Thinking to herself.*] Yes, yes, there's something in that.

[OLD EKDAL *comes in again and is going out by the foremost door to the left.*

GINA.

[*Half turning in her chair.*] Do you want something out of the kitchen, grandfather?

EKDAL.

Yes, yes, I do. Don't you trouble. [*Goes out.*

GINA.

He's not poking away at the fire, is he? [*Waits a moment.*] Hedvig, go and see what he's about.

[EKDAL *comes in again with a small jug of steaming hot water.*

HEDVIG.

Have you been getting some hot water, grandfather?

EKDAL.

Yes, hot water. Want it for something. Want to write, and the ink has got as thick as porridge—h'm.

GINA.

But you'd best have your supper, first, grandfather. It's laid in there.

EKDAL.

Can't be bothered with supper, Gina. Very busy, I tell you. No one's to come to my room. No one—h'm.
[*He goes into his room;* GINA *and* HEDVIG *look at each other.*

GINA.

[*Softly.*] Can you imagine where he's got money from?

HEDVIG.

From Gråberg, perhaps.

GINA.

Not a bit of it. Gråberg always sends the money to me.

HEDVIG.

Then he must have got a bottle on credit somewhere.

GINA.

Poor grandfather, who'd give him credit?

HIALMAR EKDAL, *in an overcoat and grey felt hat, comes in from the right.*

GINA.

[*Throws down her sewing and rises.*] Why, Ekdal. Is that you already?

HEDVIG.

[*At the same time jumping up.*] Fancy your coming so soon, father!

HIALMAR.

[*Taking off his hat.*] Yes, most of the people were coming away.

HEDVIG.

So early?

HIALMAR.

Yes, it was a dinner-party, you know.

[*Is taking off his overcoat.*

GINA.

Let me help you.

HEDVIG.

Me too.

[*They draw off his coat; GINA hangs it up on the back wall.*

HEDVIG.

Were there many people there, father?

HIALMAR.

Oh no, not many. We were about twelve or fourteen at table.

GINA.

And you had some talk with them all?

HIALMAR.

Oh yes, a little; but Gregers took me up most of the time.

GINA.

Is Gregers as ugly as ever?

HIALMAR.

Well, he's not very much to look at.   Hasn't the old
man come home?

HEDVIG.

Yes, grandfather is in his room, writing.

HIALMAR.

Did he say anything?

GINA.

No, what should he say?

HIALMAR.

Didn't he say anything about——?   I heard something about his having been with Gråberg.   I'll go in
and see him for a moment.

GINA.

No, no, better not.

HIALMAR.

Why not?   Did he say he didn't want me to go in?

GINA.

I don't think he wants to see n o b o d y this evening——

HEDVIG.

[*Making signs.*]   H'm—h'm!

GINA.

[*Not noticing.*] ——he has been in to fetch hot water——

HIALMAR.

Aha!   Then he's——

GINA.

Yes, I suppose so.

HIALMAR.

Oh God! my poor old white-haired father!—Well, well; there let him sit and get all the enjoyment he can.
[OLD EKDAL, *in an indoor coat and with a lighted pipe, comes from his room.*

EKDAL.

Got home?   Thought it was you I heard talking.

HIALMAR.

Yes, I have just come.

EKDAL.

You didn't see me, did you?

HIALMAR.

No; but they told me you had passed through—so I thought I would follow you.

EKDAL.

H'm, good of you, Hialmar.—Who were they, all those fellows?

HIALMAR.

Oh, all sorts of people. There was Chamberlain Flor, and Chamberlain Balle, and Chamberlain Kaspersen, and Chamberlain—this, that, and the other—I don't know who all——

EKDAL.

[*Nodding.*] Hear that, Gina! Chamberlains every one of them!

GINA.

Yes, I hear as they're terrible genteel in that house nowadays.

HEDVIG.

Did the Chamberlains sing, father? Or did they read aloud?

HIALMAR.

No, they only talked nonsense. They wanted m e to recite something for them; but I knew better than that.

EKDAL.

You weren't to be persuaded, eh?

GINA.

Oh, you might have done it.

HIALMAR.

No; one mustn't be at everybody's beck and call. [*Walks about the room.*] That's not m y way, at any rate.

EKDAL.

No no; Hialmar's not to be had for the asking, he isn't.

HIALMAR.

I don't see why *I* should bother myself to entertain people on the rare occasions when I go into society. Let the others exert themselves. These fellows go from one great dinner-table to the next and gorge and guzzle day out and day in. It's for them to bestir themselves and do something in return for all the good feeding they get.

GINA.

But you didn't say that?

HIALMAR.

[*Humming.*]   Ho-ho-ho——; faith, I gave them a bit of my mind.

EKDAL.

Not the Chamberlains?

HIALMAR.

Oh, why not? [*Lightly.*]   After that, we had a little discussion about Tokay.

EKDAL.

Tokay!   There's a fine wine for you!

HIALMAR.

[*Comes to a standstill.*]   It m a y be a fine wine.   But of course you know the vintages differ; it all depends on how much sunshine the grapes have had.

GINA.

Why, you know everything, Ekdal.

EKDAL.

And did they dispute that?

HIALMAR.

They tried to; but they were requested to observe that
it was just the same with Chamberlains—that with them,
too, different batches were of different qualities.

GINA.

What things you do think of!

EKDAL.

Hee-hee! So they got that in their pipes too?

HIALMAR.

Right in their teeth.

EKDAL.

Do you hear that, Gina? He said it right in the very
teeth of all the Chamberlains.

GINA.

Fancy——! Right in their teeth!

HIALMAR.

Yes, but I don't want it talked about. One doesn't
speak of such things. The whole affair passed off quite
amicably of course. They were nice, genial fellows; I
didn't want to wound them—not I!

EKDAL.

Right in their teeth, though——!

HEDVIG.

[*Caressingly.*] How nice it is to see you in a dress-coat! It suits you so well, father.

HIALMAR.

Yes, don't you think so? And this one really sits to perfection. It fits almost as if it had been made for me; —a little tight in the arm-holes perhaps;—help me, Hedvig. [*Takes off the coat.*] I think I'll put on my jacket. Where is my jacket, Gina?

GINA.

Here it is.   [*Brings the jacket and helps him.*

HIALMAR.

That's it! Don't forget to send the coat back to Molvik first thing to-morrow morning.

GINA.

[*Laying it away.*] I'll be sure and see to it.

HIALMAR.

[*Stretching himself.*] After all, there's a more homely feeling about this. A free-and-easy indoor costume suits my whole personality better. Don't you think so, Hedvig?

HEDVIG.

Yes, father.

HIALMAR.

When I loosen my necktie into a pair of flowing ends
—like this—eh?

HEDVIG.

Yes, that goes so well with your moustache and the
sweep of your curls.

HIALMAR.

I should not call them curls exactly; I should rather
say locks.

HEDVIG.

Yes, they are too big for curls.

HIALMAR.

Locks describes them better.

HEDVIG.

[*After a pause, twitching his jacket.*]   Father.

HIALMAR.

Well, what is it?

HEDVIG.

Oh, you know very well.

HIALMAR.

No, really I don't——

HEDVIG.

[*Half laughing, half whimpering.*]   Oh yes, father;
now don't tease me any longer!

HIALMAR.

Why, what d o you mean?

HEDVIG.

[*Shaking him.*]   Oh what nonsense; come, where are they, father?   All the good things you promised me, you know?

HIALMAR.

Oh—if I haven't forgotten all about them!

HEDVIG.

Now you're only teasing me, father!   Oh, it's too bad of you!   Where have you put them?

HIALMAR.

No, I positively forgot to get anything.   But wait a little!   I have something else for you, Hedvig.
      [*Goes and searches in the pockets of the coat.*

HEDVIG.

[*Skipping and clapping her hands.*]   Oh mother, mother!

GINA.

There, you see; if you only give him time——

HIALMAR.

[*With a paper.*]   Look, here it is.

HEDVIG.

That?   Why, that's only a paper.

HIALMAR.

That is the bill of fare, my dear; the whole bill of fare.
Here you see: " Menu "—that means bill of fare

HEDVIG.

Haven't you anything else?

HIALMAR.

I forgot the other things, I tell you.   But you may
take my word for it, these dainties are very unsatisfying.
Sit down at the table and read the bill of fare, and then
I'll describe to you how the dishes taste.   Here you are,
Hedvig.

HEDVIG.

[*Gulping down her tears.*]   Thank you.
   [*She seats herself, but does not read;* GINA *makes signs
   to her;* HIALMAR *notices it.*

HIALMAR.

[*Pacing up and down the room.*]   It's monstrous what
absurd things the father of a family is expected to think
of; and if he forgets the smallest trifle, he is treated to
sour faces at once.   Well, well, one gets used to that too.
[*Stops near the stove, by the old man's chair.*]   Have you
peeped in there this evening, father?

EKDAL.

Yes, to be sure I have.   She's gone into the basket.

HIALMAR.

Ah, she h a s gone into the basket.   Then she's beginning to get used to it.

EKDAL.

Yes; just as I prophesied. But you know there are still a few little things——

HIALMAR.

A few improvements, yes.

EKDAL.

They've g o t to be made, you know.

HIALMAR.

Yes, let us have a talk about the improvements, father. Come, let us sit on the sofa.

EKDAL.

All right.   H'm—-think I'll just fill my pipe first.   Must clean it out, too.   H'm.   [*He goes into his room.*

GINA.

[*Smiling to* HIALMAR.]   His pipe!

HIALMAR.

Oh yes, yes, Gina; let him alone—the poor ship-wrecked old man.—Yes, these improvements—we had better get them out of hand to-morrow.

GINA.

You'll hardly have time to-morrow, Ekdal.

HEDVIG.

[*Interposing.*]   Oh yes he will, mother!

GINA.

——for remember them prints that has to be retouched; they've sent for them time after time.

HIALMAR.

There now! those prints again! I shall get them finished all right! Have any new orders come in?

GINA.

No, worse luck; to-morrow I have nothing but those two sittings, you know.

HIALMAR.

Nothing else? Oh no, if people won't set about things with a will——

GINA.

But what more can I do? Don't I advertise in the papers as much as we can afford?

HIALMAR.

Yes, the papers, the papers; you see how much good t h e y do. And I suppose no one has been to look at the room either?

GINA.

No, not yet.

HIALMAR.

That was only to be expected. If people won't keep their eyes open——. Nothing can be done without a real effort, Gina!

HEDVIG.

[*Going towards him.*] Shall I fetch you the flute, father?

HIALMAR.

No; no flute for me; *I* want no pleasures in this world. [*Pacing about.*] Yes, indeed I will work to-morrow; you shall see if I don't. You may be sure I shall work as long as my strength holds out.

GINA.

But my dear good Ekdal, I didn't mean it in t h a t way.

HEDVIG.

Father, mayn't I bring in a bottle of beer?

HIALMAR.

No, certainly not. I require nothing, nothing—— [*Comes to a standstill.*] Beer? Was it beer you were talking about?

HEDVIG.

[*Cheerfully.*] Yes, father; beautiful fresh beer.

HIALMAR.

Well—since you insist upon it, you may bring in a bottle.

GINA.

Yes, do; and we'll be nice and cosy.
                    [HEDVIG *runs towards the kitchen door.*

HIALMAR.

[*By the stove, stops her, looks at her, puts his arm round her neck and presses her to him.*] Hedvig, Hedvig!

HEDVIG.

[*With tears of joy.*] My dear, kind father!

HIALMAR.

No, don't call me that. Here have I been feasting at the rich man's table,—battening at the groaning board——! And I couldn't even——!

GINA.

[*Sitting at the table.*] Oh nonsense, nonsense, Ekdal.

HIALMAR.

It's not nonsense! And yet you mustn't be too hard upon me. You know that I love you for all that.

HEDVIG.

[*Throwing her arms round him.*] And we love you, oh so dearly, father!

HIALMAR.

And if I am unreasonable once in a while,—why then —you must remember that I am a man beset by a host of cares. There, there! [*Dries his eyes.*] No beer at such a moment as this. Give me the flute.

[HEDVIG *runs to the bookcase and fetches it.*

HIALMAR.

Thanks! That's right. With my flute in my hand and you two at my side—ah——!

[HEDVIG *seats herself at the table near* GINA; HIAL-
MAR *paces backwards and forwards, pipes up vig-
orously, and plays a Bohemian peasant dance, but
in a slow plaintive tempo, and with sentimental expression.*

HIALMAR.

[*Breaking off the melody, holds out his left hand to* GINA,
and says with emotion:]   Our roof may be poor and humble, Gina; but it is home.   And· with all my heart I say:
here dwells my happiness.

[*He begins to play again; almost immediately after, a
knocking is heard at the entrance door.*

GINA.

[*Rising.*]   Hush, Ekdal,—I think there's some one at the door.

HIALMAR.

[*Laying the flute on the bookcase.*]   There!   Again!

[GINA *goes and opens the door.*

GREGERS WERLE.

[*In the passage.*]   Excuse me——

GINA.

[*Starting back slightly.*]   Oh!

GREGERS.

——does not Mr. Ekdal, the photographer, live here?

GINA.

Yes, he does.

HIALMAR.

[*Going towards the door.*] Gregers! You here after all? Well, come in then.

GREGERS.

[*Coming in.*] I told you I would come and look you up.

HIALMAR.

But this evening——? Have you left the party?

GREGERS.

I have left both the party and my father's house.— Good evening, Mrs. Ekdal. I don't know whether you recognise me?

GINA.

Oh yes; it's not difficult to know young Mr. Werle again.

GREGERS.

No, I am like my mother; and no doubt you remember her.

HIALMAR.

Left your father's house, did you say?

GREGERS.

Yes, I have gone to a hotel.

HIALMAR.

Indeed. Well, since you're here, take off your coat and sit down.

GREGERS.

Thanks.

[*He takes off his overcoat. He is now dressed in a plain grey suit of a countrified cut.*

HIALMAR.

Here, on the sofa. Make yourself comfortable.

[GREGERS *seats himself on the sofa;* HIALMAR *takes a chair at the table.*

GREGERS.

[*Looking around him.*] So these are your quarters, Hialmar—this is your home.

HIALMAR.

This is the studio, as you see——

GINA.

But it's the largest of our rooms, so we generally sit here.

HIALMAR.

We used to live in a better place; but this flat has one great advantage: there are such capital outer rooms——

GINA.

And we have a room on the other side of the passage that we can let.

GREGERS.

[*To* HIALMAR.] Ah—so you have lodgers too?

HIALMAR.

No, not yet. They're not so easy to find, you see; you have to keep your eyes open. [*To* HEDVIG.] What about that beer, eh?

[HEDVIG *nods and goes out into the kitchen.*

GREGERS.

So that is your daughter?

HIALMAR.

Yes, that is Hedvig.

GREGERS.

And she is your only child?

HIALMAR.

Yes, the only one. She is the joy of our lives, and— [*lowering his voice*]—at the same time our deepest sorrow, Gregers.

GREGERS.

What do you mean?

HIALMAR.

She is in serious danger of losing her eyesight.

GREGERS.

Becoming blind?

HIALMAR.

Yes. Only the first symptoms have appeared as yet, and she may not feel it much for some time. But the doctor has warned us. It is coming, inexorably.

GREGERS.

What a terrible misfortune! How do you account for it?

HIALMAR.

[*Sighs.*]   Hereditary, no doubt.

GREGERS.

[*Starting.*]   Hereditary?

GINA.

Ekdal's mother had weak eyes.

HIALMAR.

Yes, so my father says; I can't remember her.

GREGERS.

Poor child!   And how does she take it?

HIALMAR.

Oh, you can imagine we haven't the heart to tell her of it. She dreams of no danger. Gay and careless and chirping like a little bird, she flutters onward into a life of endless night. [*Overcome.*]   Oh, it is cruelly hard on me, Gregers.

> [HEDVIG *brings a tray with beer and glasses, which she sets upon the table.*

HIALMAR.

[*Stroking her hair.*]   Thanks, thanks, Hedvig.
[HEDVIG *puts her arm round his neck and whispers
in his ear.*

HIALMAR.

No, no bread and butter just now.   [*Looks up.*]   But
perhaps you would like some, Gregers.

GREGERS.

[*With a gesture of refusal.*]   No, no thank you.

HIALMAR.

[*Still melancholy.*]   Well, you can bring in a little all
the same.   If you have a crust, that is all I want.   And
plenty of butter on it, mind.
[HEDVIG *nods gaily and goes out into the kitchen
again.*

GREGERS.

[*Who has been following her with his eyes.*]   She seems
quite strong and healthy otherwise.

GINA.

Yes.   In other ways there's nothing amiss with her,
thank goodness.

GREGERS.

She promises to be very like you, Mrs. Ekdal.   How
old is she now?

GINA.

Hedvig is close on fourteen; her birthday is the day
after to-morrow.

GREGERS.

She is pretty tall for her age, then.

GINA.

Yes, she's shot up wonderful this last year.

GREGERS.

It makes one realise one's own age to see these young people growing up.—How long is it now since you were married?

GINA.

We've been married—let me see—just on fifteen years.

GREGERS.

Is it so long as that?

GINA.

[*Becomes attentive; looks at him.*]   Yes, it is indeed.

HIALMAR.

Yes, so it is.   Fifteen years all but a few months. [*Changing his tone.*]   They must have been long years for you, up at the works, Gregers.

GREGERS.

They seemed long while I was living them; now they are over, I hardly know how the time has gone.
   [OLD EKDAL *comes from his room without his pipe, but with his old-fashioned uniform cap on his head; his gait is somewhat unsteady.*

Ekdal.

Come now, Hialmar, let's sit down and have a good talk about this—h'm—what was it again?

Hialmar.

[*Going towards him.*] Father, we have a visitor here—Gregers Werle.—I don't know if you remember him.

Ekdal.

[*Looking at* Gregers, *who has risen.*]   Werle?   Is that the son?   What does he want with me?

Hialmar.

Nothing; it's me he has come to see.

Ekdal.

Oh!   Then there's nothing wrong?

Hialmar.

No, no, of course not.

Ekdal.

[*With a large gesture.*]   Not that I'm afraid, you know; but——

Gregers.

[*Goes over to him.*]   I bring you a greeting from your old hunting-grounds, Lieutenant Ekdal.

Ekdal.

Hunting-grounds?

GREGERS.

Yes, up in Höidal, about the works, you know.

EKDAL.

Oh, up there.　Yes, I knew all those places well in the old days.

GREGERS.

You were a great sportsman then.

EKDAL.

So I was, I don't deny it.　You're looking at my uniform cap.　I don't ask anybody's leave to wear it in the house.　So long as I don't go out in the streets with it——
　　[HEDVIG *brings a plate of bread and butter, which she puts upon the table.*

HIALMAR.

Sit down, father, and have a glass of beer.　Help yourself, Gregers.
　　[EKDAL *mutters and stumbles over to the sofa.* GRE-GERS *seats himself on the chair nearest to him,* HIALMAR *on the other side of* GREGERS.　GINA *sits a little way from the table, sewing;* HEDVIG *stands beside her father.*

GREGERS.

Can you remember, Lieutenant Ekdal, how Hialmar and I used to come up and visit you in the summer and at Christmas?

EKDAL.

Did you? No, no, no; I don't remember it. But sure enough I've been a tidy bit of a sportsman in my day. I've shot bears too. I've shot nine of 'em, no less.

GREGERS.

[*Looking sympathetically at him.*] And now you never get any shooting?

EKDAL.

Can't just say that, sir. Get a shot now and then perhaps. Of course not in the old way. For the woods you see—the woods, the woods——! [*Drinks.*] Are the woods fine up there now?

GREGERS.

Not so fine as in your time. They have been thinned a good deal.

EKDAL.

Thinned? [*More softly, and as if afraid.*] It's dangerous work that. Bad things come of it. The woods revenge themselves.

HIALMAR.

[*Filling up his glass.*] Come—a little more, father.

GREGERS.

How can a man like you—such a man for the open air —live in the midst of a stuffy town, boxed within four walls?

EKDAL.

[*Laughs quietly and glances at* HIALMAR.]   Oh, it's not so bad here.   Not at all so bad.

GREGERS.

But don't you miss all the things that used to be a part of your very being—the cool sweeping breezes, the free life in the woods and on the uplands, among beasts and birds——?

EKDAL.

[*Smiling.*]   Hialmar, shall we let him see it?

HIALMAR.

[*Hastily and a little embarrassed.*]   Oh no no, father; not this evening.

GREGERS.

What does he want to show me?

HIALMAR.

Oh, it's only something—you can see it another time.

GREGERS.

[*Continues, to the old man.*]   You see I have been think-ing, Lieutenant Ekdal, that you should come up with me to the works; I am sure to be going back soon.   No doubt you could get some copying there too.   And here, you have nothing on earth to interest you—nothing to liven you up.

EKDAL.

[*Stares in astonishment at him.*] Have *I* nothing on earth to——!

GREGERS.

Of course you have Hialmar; but then he has his own family. And a man like you, who has always had such a passion for what is free and wild——

EKDAL.

[*Thumps the table.*] Hialmar, he s h a l l see it!

HIALMAR.

Oh, do you think it's worth while, father? It's all dark.

EKDAL.

Nonsense; it's moonlight. [*Rises.*] He s h a l l see it, I tell you. Let me pass! Come and help me, Hialmar.

HEDVIG.

Oh yes, do, father!

HIALMAR.

[*Rising.*] Very well then.

GREGERS.

[*To* GINA.] What is it?

GINA.

Oh, nothing so very wonderful, after all.
    [EKDAL *and* HIALMAR *have gone to the back wall and are each pushing back a side of the sliding door;*

HEDVIG *helps the old man;* GREGERS *remains standing by the sofa;* GINA *sits still and sews. Through the open doorway a large, deep irregular garret is seen with odd nooks and corners; a couple of stove-pipes running through it, from rooms below. There are skylights through which clear moonbeams shine in on some parts of the great room; others lie in deep shadow.*]

EKDAL.

[*To* GREGERS.]   You may come close up if you like.

GREGERS.

[*Going over to them.*]   Why, what is it?

EKDAL.

Look for yourself.   H'm.

HIALMAR.

[*Somewhat embarrassed.*]   This belongs to father, you understand.

GREGERS.

[*At the door, looks into the garret.*]   Why, you keep poultry, Lieutcnant Ekdal.

EKDAL.

Should think we d i d keep poultry.   They've gone to roost now.   But you should just see our fowls by daylight, sir!

HEDVIG.

And there's a——

EKDAL.

Sh—sh! don't say anything about it yet.

GREGERS.

And you have pigeons too, I see.

EKDAL.

Oh yes, haven't we just got pigeons! They have their nest-boxes up there under the roof-tree; for pigeons like to roost high, you see.

HIALMAR.

They aren't all common pigeons.

EKDAL.

Common! Should think not indeed! We have tumblers, and a pair of pouters, too. But come here! Can you see that hutch down there by the wall?

GREGERS.

Yes; what do you use it for?

EKDAL.

That's where the rabbits sleep, sir.

GREGERS.

Dear me; so you have rabbits too?

EKDAL.

Yes, you may take my word for it, we have rabbits! He wants to know if we have rabbits, Hialmar! H'm!

But now comes t h e thing, let me tell you! Here we have it! Move away, Hedvig. Stand here; that's right, —and now look down there.—Don't you see a basket with straw in it?

GREGERS.

Yes.   And I can see a fowl lying in the basket.

EKDAL.

H'm—"a fowl"——

GREGERS.

Isn't it a duck?

EKDAL.

[*Hurt.*] Why, of course it's a duck.

HIALMAR.

But what k i n d of duck, do you think?

HEDVIG.

It's not just a common duck——

EKDAL.

Sh!

GREGERS.

And it's not a Muscovy duck either.

EKDAL.

No, Mr.—Werle; it's not a Muscovy duck; for it's a wild duck!

GREGERS.

Is it really?   A wild duck?

EKDAL.

Yes, that's what it is.   That "fowl" as you call it—
is the wild duck.   It's our wild duck, sir.

HEDVIG.

My wild duck.   It belongs to me.

GREGERS.

And can it live up here in the garret?   Does it thrive?

EKDAL.

Of course it has a trough of water to splash about in,
you know.

HIALMAR.

Fresh water every other day.

GINA.

[*Turning towards* HIALMAR.]   But my dear Ekdal, it's
getting icy cold here.

EKDAL.

H'm, we had better shut up then.   It's as well not to
disturb their night's rest, too.   Close up, Hedvig.
      [HIALMAR *and* HEDVIG *push the garret doors together.*

EKDAL.

Another time you shall see her properly.   [*Seats himself in the arm-chair by the stove.*]   Oh, they're curious
things, these wild ducks, I can tell you.

GREGERS.

How did you manage to catch it, Lieutenant Ekdal?

EKDAL.

I didn't catch it. There's a certain man in this town whom we have to thank for it.

GREGERS.

[*Starts slightly.*] That man was not my father, was he?

EKDAL.

You've hit it. Your father and no one else. H'm.

HIALMAR.

Strange that you should guess that, Gregers.

GREGERS.

You were telling me that you owed so many things to my father; and so I thought perhaps——

GINA.

But we didn't get the duck from Mr. Werle himself——

EKDAL.

It's Håkon Werle we have to thank for her, all the same, Gina. [*To* GREGERS.] He was shooting from a boat, you see, and he brought her down. But your father's sight is not very good now. H'm; she was only wounded.

GREGERS.

Ah! She got a couple of slugs in her body, I suppose.

HIALMAR.

Yes, two or three.

HEDVIG.

She was hit under the wing, so that she couldn't fly.

GREGERS.

And I suppose she dived to the bottom, eh?

EKDAL.

[*Sleepily, in a thick voice.*] Of course. Always do that, wild ducks do. They shoot to the bottom as deep as they can get, sir—and bite themselves fast in the tangle and sea-weed—and all the devil's own mess that grows down there. And they never come up again.

GREGERS.

But y o u r wild duck came up again, Lieutenant Ekdal.

EKDAL.

He had such an amazingly clever dog, your father had. And that dog—he dived in after the duck and fetched her up again.

GREGERS.

[*Who has turned to* HIALMAR.] And then she was sent to you here?

Bust of Henrik Ibsen, about 1865

HIALMAR.

Not at once; at first your father took her home.   But she wouldn't thrive there; so Pettersen was told to put an end to her——

EKDAL.

[*Half asleep.*]   H'm—yes—Pettersen—that ass——

HIALMAR.

[*Speaking more softly.*]   That was how we got her, you see; for father knows Pettersen a little; and when he heard about the wild duck he got him to hand her over to us.

GREGERS.

And now she thrives as well as possible in the garret there?

HIALMAR.

Yes, wonderfully well.   She has got fat.   You see, she has lived in there so long now that she has forgotten her natural wild life; and it all depends on t h a t.

GREGERS.

You are right there, Hialmar.   Be sure you never let her get a glimpse of the sky and the sea——.   But I mustn't stay any longer; I think your father is asleep.

HIALMAR.

Oh, as for that——

GREGERS.

But, by-the-bye—you said you had a room to let—a spare room?

HIALMAR.

Yes; what then? Do you know of anybody——?

GREGERS.

Can *I* have that room?

HIALMAR.

You?

GINA.

Oh no, Mr. Werle, y o u——

GREGERS.

May I have the room? If so, I'll take possession first thing to-morrow morning.

HIALMAR.

Yes, with the greatest pleasure——

GINA.

But, Mr. Werle, I'm sure it's not at all the sort of room for y o u.

HIALMAR.

Why, Gina! how can you say that?

GINA.

Why, because the room's neither large enough nor light enough, and——

GREGERS.

That really doesn't matter, Mrs. Ekdal.

HIALMAR.

I call it quite a nice room, and not at all badly furnished either.

GINA.

But remember the pair of them underneath.

GREGERS.

What pair?

GINA.

Well, there's one as has been a tutor——

HIALMAR.

That's Molvik—Mr. Molvik, B.A.

GINA.

And then there's a doctor, by the name of Relling.

GREGERS.

Relling? I know him a little; he practised for a time up in Höidal.

GINA.

They're a regular rackety pair, they are. As often as not, they're out on the loose in the evenings; and then they come home at all hours, and they're not always just——

GREGERS.

One soon gets used to that sort of thing. I daresay I shall be like the wild duck——

GINA.

H'm; I think you ought to sleep upon it first, anyway.

GREGERS.

You seem very unwilling to have me in the house, Mrs. Ekdal.

GINA.

Oh no! What makes you think t h a t?

HIALMAR.

Well, you really behave strangely about it, Gina. [*To* GREGERS.] Then I suppose you intend to remain in the town for the present?

GREGERS.

[*Putting on his overcoat.*] Yes, now I intend to remain here.

HIALMAR.

And yet not at your father's? What do you propose to do, then?

GREGERS.

Ah, if I only knew t h a t, Hialmar, I shouldn't be so badly off! But when one has the misfortune to be called Gregers—! "Gregers"—and then "Werle" after it; did you ever hear anything so hideous?

HIALMAR.

Oh, I don't think so at all.

GREGERS.

Ugh! Bah! I feel I should like to spit upon the fellow that answers to such a name. But when a man is once for all doomed to be Gregers—Werle in this world, as I am——

HIALMAR.

[*Laughs.*] Ha ha! If you weren't Gregers Werle, what would you like to be?

GREGERS.

If I could choose, I should like best to be a clever dog.

GINA.

A dog!

HEDVIG.

[*Involuntarily.*]   Oh no!

GREGERS.

Yes, an amazingly clever dog; one that goes to the bottom after wild ducks when they dive and bite themselves fast in tangle and sea-weed, down among the ooze.

HIALMAR.

Upon my word now, Gregers—I don't in the least know what you're driving at.

GREGERS.

Oh well, you might not be much the wiser if you did. It's understood, then, that I move in early to-morrow morning. [*To* GINA.] I won't give you any trouble; I do everything for myself. [*To* HIALMAR.]   We can talk about the rest to-morrow.—Good-night, Mrs. Ekdal. [*Nods to* HEDVIG.]   Good-night.

GINA.

Good-night, Mr. Werle.

HEDVIG.

Good-night.

HIALMAR.

[*Who has lighted a candle.*]   Wait a moment; I must show you a light; the stairs are sure to be dark.

[GREGERS *and* HIALMAR *go out by the passage door.*

GINA.

[*Looking straight before her, with her sewing in her lap.*] Wasn't that queer-like talk about wanting to be a dog?

HEDVIG.

Do you know, mother—I believe he meant something quite different by that.

GINA.

Why, what s h o u l d he mean?

HEDVIG.

Oh, I don't know; but it seemed to me he meant something different from what he said—all the time.

GINA.

Do you think so?   Yes, it was sort of queer.

HIALMAR.

[*Comes back.*]   The lamp was still burning.   [*Puts out the candle and sets it down.*]   Ah, now one can get a mouthful of food at last.   [*Begins to eat the bread and butter.*]   Well, you see, Gina—if only you keep your eyes open——

GINA.

How, keep your eyes open——?

HIALMAR.

Why, haven't we at last had the luck to get the room let?   And just think—to a person like Gregers—a good old friend.

GINA.

Well, I don't know what to say about it.

HEDVIG.

Oh mother, you'll see; it'll be such fun!

HIALMAR.

You're very strange.   You were so bent upon getting the room let before; and now you don't like it.

GINA.

Yes I do, Ekdal; if it had only been to some one else—— But what do you suppose Mr. Werle will say?

HIALMAR.

Old Werle?   It doesn't concern him.

GINA.

But surely you can see that there's something amiss between them again, or the young man wouldn't be leaving home. You know very well those two can't get on with each other.

HIALMAR.

Very likely not, but——

GINA.

And now Mr. Werle may fancy it's you that has egged him on——

HIALMAR.

Let him fancy so, then! Mr. Werle has done a great deal for me; far be it from me to deny it. But that doesn't make me everlastingly dependent upon him.

GINA.

But, my dear Ekdal, maybe grandfather'll suffer for it. He may lose the little bit of work he gets from Gråberg.

HIALMAR.

I could almost say: so much the better! Is it not humiliating for a man like me to see his grey-haired father treated as a pariah? But now I believe the fulness of time is at hand. [*Takes a fresh piece of bread and butter.*] As sure as I have a mission in life, I mean to fulfil it now!

HEDVIG.

Oh yes, father, do!

GINA.

Hush! Don't wake him!

HIALMAR.

[*More softly.*] I w i l l fulfil it, I say. The day shall come when—— And that is why I say it's a good thing we have let the room; for that makes me more independent. The man who has a mission in life must be independent. [*By the arm-chair, with emotion.*] Poor old white-haired father! Rely on your Hialmar. He has broad shoulders—strong shoulders, at any rate. You shall yet wake up some fine day and—— [*To* GINA.] Do you not believe it?

GINA.

[*Rising.*] Yes, of course I do; but in the meantime suppose we see about getting him to bed.

HIALMAR.

Yes, come.   [*They take hold of the old man carefully.*

ACT THIRD

HIALMAR EKDAL'S *studio. It is morning: the daylight shines through the large window in the slanting roof; the curtain is drawn back.*

HIALMAR *is sitting at the table, busy retouching a photograph; several others lie before him. Presently* GINA, *wearing her hat and cloak, enters by the passage door; she has a covered basket on her arm.*

HIALMAR.

Back already, Gina?

GINA.

Oh yes, one can't let the grass grow under one's feet. [*Sets her basket on a chair, and takes off her things.*

HIALMAR.

Did you look in at Gregers' room?

GINA.

Yes, that I did. It's a rare sight, I can tell you; he's made a pretty mess to start off with.

HIALMAR.

How so?

GINA.

He was determined to do everything for himself, he said; so he sets to work to light the stove, and what must

324

he do but screw down the damper till the whole room is full of smoke.   Ugh!   There was a smell fit to——

HIALMAR.

Well, really!

GINA.

But that's not the worst of it; for then he thinks he'll put out the fire, and goes and empties his water-jug into the stove, and so makes the whole floor one filthy puddle.

HIALMAR.

How annoying!

GINA.

I've got the porter's wife to clear up after him, pig that he is!   But the room won't be fit to live in till the afternoon.

HIALMAR.

What's he doing with himself in the meantime?

GINA.

He said he was going out for a little while.

HIALMAR.

I looked in upon him too, for a moment—after you had gone.

GINA.

So I heard.   You've asked him to lunch.

HIALMAR.

Just to a little bit of early lunch, you know.   It's his first day—we can hardly do less.   You've got something in the house, I suppose?

GINA.

I shall have to find something or other.

HIALMAR.

And don't cut it too fine, for I fancy Relling and Molvik are coming up too. I just happened to meet Relling on the stairs, you see; so I had to——

GINA.

Oh, are we to have those two as well?

HIALMAR.

Good Lord—a couple more or less can't make any difference.

OLD EKDAL.

[*Opens his door and looks in.*] I say, Hialmar—— [*Sees* GINA.] Oh!

GINA.

Do you want anything, grandfather?

EKDAL.

Oh no, it doesn't matter. H'm!   [*Retires again.*

GINA.

[*Takes up the basket.*] Be sure you see that he doesn't go out.

HIALMAR.

All right, all right. And, Gina, a little herring-salad wouldn't be a bad idea; Relling and Molvik were out on the loose again last night.

GINA.

If only they don't come before I'm ready for them——

HIALMAR.

No, of course they won't; take your own time.

GINA.

Very well; and meanwhile you can be working a bit.

HIALMAR.

Well, I a m working! I am working as hard as I can!

GINA.

Then you'll have that job off your hands, you see.
      [*She goes out to the kitchen with her basket.*

HIALMAR *sits for a time pencilling away at the photograph, in an indolent and listless manner.*

EKDAL.

[*Peeps in, looks round the studio, and says softly:*]   Are you busy?

HIALMAR.

Yes, I'm toiling at these wretched pictures——

EKDAL.

Well well, never mind,—since you're so busy—h'm!
      [*He goes out again; the door stands open.*

HIALMAR.

[*Continues for some time in silence; then he lays down his brush and goes over to the door.*] Are y o u busy, father?

EKDAL.

[*In a grumbling tone, within.*]   If you're busy, I'm busy too.   H'm!

HIALMAR.

Oh, very well, then.   [*Goes to his work again.*

EKDAL.

[*Presently, coming to the door again.*] H'm; I say, Hialmar, I'm not so v e r y busy, you know.

HIALMAR.

I thought you were writing.

EKDAL.

Oh, devil take it! can't Gråberg wait a day or two? After all, it's not a matter of life and death.

HIALMAR.

No; and you're not his slave either.

EKDAL.

And about that other business in there——

HIALMAR.

Just what I was thinking of.   Do you want to go in? Shall I open the door for you?

EKDAL.

Well, it wouldn't be a bad notion.

HIALMAR.

[*Rises.*]   Then we'd have t h a t off our hands.

EKDAL.

Yes, exactly.   It's got to be ready first thing to-morrow.
It i s to-morrow, isn't it?   H'm?

HIALMAR.

Yes, of course it's to-morrow.

   [HIALMAR *and* EKDAL *push aside each his half of
   the sliding door.   The morning sun is shining in
   through the skylights; some doves are flying about;
   others sit cooing, upon the perches; the hens are
   heard clucking now and then, further back in the
   garret.*

HIALMAR.

There; now you can get to work, father.

EKDAL.

[*Goes in.*]   Aren't you coming too?

HIALMAR.

Well really, do you know——; I almost think——
[*Sees* GINA *at the kitchen door.*]   I ?   No; I haven't time;
I must work.—But now for our new contrivance——

   [*He pulls a cord, a curtain slips down inside, the
   lower part consisting of a piece of old sailcloth, the
   upper part of a stretched fishing net.   The floor of
   the garret is thus no longer visible.*

HIALMAR.

[*Goes to the table.*] So! Now, perhaps I can sit in peace for a little while.

GINA.

Is he rampaging in there again?

HIALMAR.

Would you rather have had him slip down to Madam Eriksen's. [*Seats himself.*] Do you want anything? You know you said——

GINA.

I only wanted to ask if you think we can lay the table for lunch here?

HIALMAR.

Yes; we have no early appointment, I suppose?

GINA.

No, I expect no one to-day except those two sweethearts that are to be taken together.

HIALMAR.

Why the deuce couldn't they be taken together another day!

GINA.

Don't you know, I told them to come in the afternoon, when you are having your nap.

HIALMAR.

Oh, that's capital. Very well, let us have lunch here then.

GINA.

All right; but there's no hurry about laying the cloth; you can have the table for a good while yet.

HIALMAR.

Do you think I am not sticking at my work? I'm at it as hard as I can!

GINA.

Then you'll be free later on, you know.
[*Goes out into the kitchen again. Short pause.*

EKDAL.

[*In the garret doorway, behind the net.*] Hialmar!

HIALMAR.

Well?

EKDAL.

Afraid we shall have to move the water-trough, after all.

HIALMAR.

What else have I been saying all along?

EKDAL.

H'm—h'm—h'm. [*Goes away from the door again.*
[HIALMAR *goes on working a little; glances towards the garret and half rises.* HEDVIG *comes in from the kitchen.*

HIALMAR.

[*Sits down again hurriedly.*] What do you want?

HEDVIG.

I only wanted to come in beside you, father.

HIALMAR.

[*After a pause.*] What makes you go prying around like that? Perhaps you are told off to watch me?

HEDVIG.

No, no.

HIALMAR.

What is your mother doing out there?

HEDVIG.

Oh, mother's in the middle of making the herring-salad. [*Goes to the table.*] Isn't there any little thing I could help you with, father?

HIALMAR.

Oh no. It is right that I should bear the whole burden—so long as my strength holds out. Set your mind at rest, Hedvig; if only your father keeps his health——

HEDVIG.

Oh no, father! You mustn't talk in that horrid way. [*She wanders about a little, stops by the doorway and looks into the garret.*

HIALMAR.

Tell me, what is he doing?

HEDVIG.

I think he's making a new path to the water-trough.

HIALMAR.

He can never manage t h a t by himself! And here am I doomed to sit——!

HEDVIG.

[*Goes to him.*] Let m e take the brush, father; I c a n do it, quite well.

HIALMAR.

Oh nonsense; you will only hurt your eyes.

HEDVIG.

Not a bit.   Give me the brush.

HIALMAR.

[*Rising.*]   Well, it won't take more than a minute or two.

HEDVIG.

Pooh, what harm can it do then?   [*Takes the brush.*] There! [*Seats herself.*]   I can begin upon this one.

HIALMAR.

But mind you don't hurt your eyes! Do you hear? *I* won't be answerable; you do it on your own responsibility—understand that.

HEDVIG.

[*Retouching.*]   Yes yes, I understand.

Hialmar.

You are quite clever at it, Hedvig.   Only a minute or
two, you know.
> [*He slips through by the edge of the curtain into the
> garret.*   Hedvig *sits at her work.*   Hialmar *and*
> Ekdal *are heard disputing inside.*

Hialmar.

[*Appears behind the net.*]   I say, Hedvig—give me
those pincers that are lying on the shelf.   And the chisel.
[*Turns away inside.*]   Now you shall see, father.   Just
let me show you first what I mean!
> [Hedvig *has fetched the required tools from the shelf,
> and hands them to him through the net.*

Hialmar.

Ah, thanks.   I didn't come a moment too soon.
> [*Goes back from the curtain again; they are heard
> carpentering and talking inside.*   Hedvig *stands
> looking in at them.   A moment later there is a
> knock at the passage door; she does not notice it.*

Gregers Werle.

[*Bareheaded, in indoor dress, enters and stops near the
door.*]   H'm——!

Hedvig.

[*Turns and goes towards him.*]   Good morning.   Please
come in.

Gregers.

Thank you.   [*Looking towards the garret.*]   You seem
to have workpeople in the house.

HEDVIG.

No, it is only father and grandfather. I'll tell them you are here.

GREGERS.

No no, don't do that; I would rather wait a little
                    [*Seats himself on the sofa.*

HEDVIG.

It looks so untidy here——
                    [*Begins to clear away the photographs.*

GREGERS.

Oh, don't take them away.   Are those prints that have to be finished off ?

HEDVIG.

Yes, they are a few I was helping father with.

GREGERS.

Please don't let me disturb you.

HEDVIG.

Oh no.
    [*She gathers the things to her and sits down to work;*
    GREGERS *looks at her, meanwhile, in silence.*

GREGERS.

Did the wild duck sleep well last night ?

HEDVIG.

Yes, I think so, thanks.

GREGERS.

[*Turning towards the garret.*] It looks quite different by day from what it did last night in the moonlight.

HEDVIG.

Yes, it changes ever so much. It looks different in the morning and in the afternoon; and it's different on rainy days from what it is in fine weather.

GREGERS.

Have you noticed that?

HEDVIG.

Yes, how could I help it?

GREGERS.

Are you, too, fond of being in there with the wild duck?

HEDVIG.

Yes, when I can manage it——

GREGERS.

But I suppose you haven't much spare time; you go to school, no doubt.

HEDVIG.

No, not now; father is afraid of my hurting my eyes.

GREGERS.

Oh; then he reads with you himself?

HEDVIG.

Father has promised to read with me; but he has never had time yet.

GREGERS.

Then is there nobody else to give you a little help?

HEDVIG.

Yes, there is Mr. Molvik; but he is not always exactly —quite——

GREGERS.

Sober?

HEDVIG.

Yes, I suppose that's it!

GREGERS.

Why, then you must have any amount of time on your hands.   And in there I suppose it is a sort of world by itself?

HEDVIG.

Oh yes, quite.   And there are such lots of wonderful things.

GREGERS.

Indeed?

HEDVIG.

Yes, there are big cupboards full of books; and a great many of the books have pictures in them.

GREGERS.

Aha!

HEDVIG.

And there's an old bureau with drawers and flaps, and a big clock with figures that go out and in. But the clock isn't going now.

GREGERS.

So time has come to a standstill in there—in the wild duck's domain.

HEDVIG.

Yes. And then there's an old paint-box and things of that sort; and all the books.

GREGERS.

And you read the books, I suppose?

HEDVIG.

Oh yes, when I get the chance. Most of them are English though, and I don't understand English. But then I look at the pictures.—There is one great big book called "Harrison's History of London."[1] It must be a hundred years old; and there are such heaps of pictures in it. At the beginning there is Death with an hour-glass and a woman. I think that is horrid. But then there are all the other pictures of churches, and castles, and streets, and great ships sailing on the sea.

GREGERS.

But tell me, where did all those wonderful things come from?

[1] *A New and Universal History of the Cities of London and West-minster*, by Walter Harrison. London, 1775, folio.

HEDVIG.

Oh, an old sea captain once lived here, and he brought them home with him.　They used to call him "The Flying Dutchman."　That was curious, because he wasn't a Dutchman at all.

GREGERS.

Was he not?

HEDVIG.

No.　But at last he was drowned at sea; and so he left all those things behind him.

GREGERS.

Tell me now—when you are sitting in there looking at the pictures, don't you wish you could travel and see the real world for yourself?

HEDVIG.

Oh no!　I mean always to stay at home and help father and mother.

GREGERS.

To retouch photographs?

HEDVIG.

No, not only that.　I should love above everything to learn to engrave pictures like those in the English books.

GREGERS.

H'm.　What does your father say to that?

HEDVIG.

I don't think father likes it; father is strange about such things. Only think, he talks of my learning basket-making, and straw-plaiting! But I don't think t h a t would be much good.

GREGERS.

Oh no, I don't think so either.

HEDVIG.

But father was right in saying that if I had learnt basket-making I could have made the new basket for the wild duck.

GREGERS.

So you could; and it was you that ought to have done it, wasn't it?

HEDVIG.

Yes, for it's m y wild duck.

GREGERS.

Of course it is.

HEDVIG.

Yes, it belongs to m e. But I lend it to father and grandfather as often as they please.

GREGERS.

Indeed? What do they do with it?

HEDVIG.

Oh, they look after it, and build places for it, and so on.

GREGERS.

I see; for no doubt the wild duck is by far the most distinguished inhabitant of the garret?

HEDVIG.

Yes, indeed she is; for she is a r e a l wild fowl, you know. And then she is so much to be pitied; she has no one to care for, poor thing.

GREGERS.

She has no family, as the rabbits have——

HEDVIG.

No. The hens too, many of them, were chickens together; but she has been taken right away from all her friends. And then there is so much that is strange about the wild duck. Nobody knows her, and nobody knows where she came from either.

GREGERS.

And she has been down in the depths of the sea.

HEDVIG.

[*With a quick glance at him, represses a smile and asks:*] Why do you say "the depths of the sea"?

GREGERS.

What else should I say?

HEDVIG.

You could say "the bottom of the sea."[1]

GREGERS.

Oh, mayn't I just as well say the depths of the sea?

HEDVIG.

Yes; but it sounds so strange to me when other people speak of the depths of the sea.

GREGERS.

Why so? Tell me why?

HEDVIG.

No, I won't; it's so stupid.

GREGERS.

Oh no, I am sure it's not. Do tell me why you smiled.

HEDVIG.

Well, this is the reason: whenever I come to realise suddenly—in a flash—what is in there, it always seems to me that the whole room and everything in it should be called "the depths of the sea."—But that is so stupid.

GREGERS.

You mustn't say that.

[1] Gregers here uses the old-fashioned expression "havsens bund," while Hedvig would have him use the more commonplace "havets bund" or "havbunden."

HEDVIG.

Oh yes, for you know it is only a garret.

GREGERS.

[*Looks fixedly at her.*]   Are you so sure of that?

HEDVIG.

[*Astonished.*]   That it's a garret?

GREGERS.

Are you quite certain of it?
  [HEDVIG *is silent, and looks at him open-mouthed.*
    GINA *comes in from the kitchen with the table
    things.*

GREGERS.

[*Rising.*]   I have come in upon you too early.

GINA.

Oh, you must be somewhere; and we're nearly ready
now, any way.   Clear the table, Hedvig.
  [HEDVIG *clears away her things; she and* GINA *lay
    the cloth during what follows.*   GREGERS *seats him-
    self in the arm-chair, and turns over an album.*

GREGERS.

I hear you can retouch, Mrs. Ekdal.

GINA.

[*With a side glance.*]   Yes, I can.

GREGERS.

That was exceedingly lucky.

GINA.

How—lucky?

GREGERS.

Since Ekdal took to photography, I mean.

HEDVIG.

Mother can take photographs too.

GINA.

Oh, yes; I was bound to learn t h a t.

GREGERS.

So it is really you that carry on the business, I suppose?

GINA.

Yes, when Ekdal hasn't time himself——

GREGERS.

He is a great deal taken up with his old father, I daresay.

GINA.

Yes; and then you can't expect a man like Ekdal to do nothing but take car-de-visits of Dick, Tom and Harry.

GREGERS.

I quite agree with you; but having once gone in for the thing——

GINA.

You can surely understand, Mr. Werle, that Ekdal's not like one of your common photographers.

GREGERS.

Of course not; but still——
                    [*A shot is fired within the garret.*

GREGERS.

[*Starting up.*] What's that?

GINA.

Ugh! now they're firing again!

GREGERS.

Have they firearms in there?

HEDVIG.

They are out shooting.

GREGERS.

What! [*At the door of the garret.*] Are you shooting, Hialmar?

HIALMAR.

[*Inside the net.*] Are you there? I didn't know; I was so taken up—— [*To* HEDVIG.] Why did you not let us know?
                    [*Comes into the studio.*

GREGERS.

Do you go shooting in the garret?

HIALMAR.

[*Showing a double-barrelled pistol.*] Oh, only with this thing.

GINA.

Yes, you and grandfather will do yourselves a mischief some day with that there pigstol.

HIALMAR.

[*With irritation.*] I believe I have told you that this kind of firearm is called a p i s t o l .

GINA.

Oh, that doesn't make it much better, that I can see.

GREGERS.

So you have become a sportsman too, Hialmar.

HIALMAR.

Only a little rabbit-shooting now and then. Mostly to please father, you understand.

GINA.

Men are strange beings; they must always have something to pervert theirselves with.

HIALMAR.

[*Snappishly.*] Just so; we must always have something to d i v e r t ourselves with.

GINA.

Yes, that's just what I say.

HIALMAR.

H'm. [*To* GREGERS.] You see the garret is fortunately so situated that no one can hear us shooting. [*Lays the pistol on the top shelf of the bookcase.*] Don't touch the pistol, Hedvig! One of the barrels is loaded; remember that.

GREGERS.

[*Looking through the net.*] You have a fowling-piece too, I see.

HIALMAR.

That is father's old gun. It's of no use now; something has gone wrong with the lock. But it's fun to have it all the same; for we can take it to pieces now and then, and clean and grease it, and screw it together again.— Of course, it's mostly father that fiddle-faddles with all that sort of thing.

HEDVIG.

[*Beside* GREGERS.] Now you can see the wild duck properly.

GREGERS.

I was just looking at her. One of her wings seems to me to droop a bit.

HEDVIG.

Well, no wonder; her wing was broken, you know.

GREGERS.

And she trails one foot a little. Isn't that so?

HIALMAR.

Perhaps a very little bit.

HEDVIG.

Yes, it was by that foot the dog took hold of her.

HIALMAR.

But otherwise she hasn't the least thing the matter with her; and that is simply marvellous for a creature that has a charge of shot in her body, and has been between a dog's teeth——

GREGERS.

[*With a glance at* HEDVIG.]——and that has lain in the depths of the sea—so long.

HEDVIG.

[*Smiling.*] Yes.

GINA.

[*Laying the table.*] That blessëd wild duck! What a lot of fuss you do make over her.

HIALMAR.

H'm;—will lunch soon be reådy?

GINA.

Yes, directly. Hedvig, you must come and help me now.   [GINA *and* HEDVIG *go out into the kitchen.*

HIALMAR.

[*In a low voice.*] I think you had better not stand there looking in at father; he doesn't like it. [GREGERS *moves away from the garret door.*] Besides I may as well shut up before the others come. [*Claps his hands to drive the fowls back.*]　Shh—shh, in with you!　[*Draws up the curtain and pulls the doors together.*]　All the contrivances are my own invention.　It's really quite amusing to have things of this sort to potter with, and to put to rights when they get out of order.　And it's absolutely necessary, too; for Gina objects to having rabbits and fowls in the studio.

GREGERS.

To be sure; and I suppose the studio is your wife's special department?

HIALMAR.

As a rule, I leave the everyday details of business to her; for then I can take refuge in the parlour and give my mind to more important things.

GREGERS.

What things may t h e y be, Hialmar?

HIALMAR.

I wonder you have not asked t h a t question sooner. But perhaps you haven't heard of the invention?

GREGERS.

The invention?　No.

HIALMAR.

Really?　Have you not?　Oh no, out there in the wilds——

GREGERS.

So you have invented something, have you?

HIALMAR.

It is not quite completed yet; but I am working at it. You can easily imagine that when I resolved to devote myself to photography, it wasn't simply with the idea of taking likenesses of all sorts of commonplace people.

GREGERS.

No; your wife was saying the same thing just now.

HIALMAR.

I swore that if I consecrated my powers to this handi-craft, I would so exalt it that it should become both an art and a science. And to that end I determined to make this great invention.

GREGERS.

And what is the nature of the invention? What purpose does it serve?

HIALMAR.

Oh, my dear fellow, you mustn't ask for details yet. It takes time, you see. And you must not think that my motive is vanity. It is not for my own sake that I am working. Oh no; it is my life's mission that stands before me night and day.

GREGERS.

What is your life's mission?

HIALMAR.

Do you forget the old man with the silver hair?

GREGERS.

Your poor father? Well, but what can you do for him?

HIALMAR.

I can raise up his self-respect from the dead, by restoring the name of Ekdal to honour and dignity.

GREGERS.

Then that is your life's mission?

HIALMAR.

Yes. I will rescue the shipwrecked man. For shipwrecked he was, by the very first blast of the storm. Even while those terrible investigations were going on, he was no longer himself. That pistol there—the one we use to shoot rabbits with—has played its part in the tragedy of the house of Ekdal.

GREGERS.

The pistol? Indeed?

HIALMAR.

When the sentence of imprisonment was passed—he had the pistol in his hand——

GREGERS.

Had he——?

HIALMAR.

Yes; but he dared not use it. His courage failed him. So broken, so demoralised was he even then! Oh, can you understand it? He, a soldier; he, who had shot nine bears, and who was descended from two lieutenant-colonels—one after the other of course. Can you understand it, Gregers?

GREGERS.

Yes, I understand it well enough.

HIALMAR.

I cannot. And once more the pistol played a part in the history of our house. When he had put on the grey clothes and was under lock and key—oh, that was a terrible time for me, I can tell you. I kept the blinds drawn down over both my windows. When I peeped out, I saw the sun shining as if nothing had happened. I could not understand it. I saw people going along the street, laughing and talking about indifferent things. I could not understand it. It seemed to me that the whole of existence must be at a standstill—as if under an eclipse.

GREGERS.

I felt like that too, when my mother died.

HIALMAR.

It was in such an hour that Hialmar Ekdal pointed the pistol at his own breast.

GREGERS.

You too thought of——!

HIALMAR.

Yes.

GREGERS.

But you did not fire?

HIALMAR.

No. At the decisive moment I won the victory over myself. I remained in life. But I can assure you it takes some courage to choose life under circumstances like those.

GREGERS.

Well, that depends on how you look at it.

HIALMAR.

Yes, indeed, it takes courage. But I am glad I was firm: for now I shall soon perfect my invention; and Dr. Relling thinks, as I do myself, that father may be allowed to wear his uniform again. I will demand that as my sole reward.

GREGERS.

So t h a t is what he meant about his uniform——?

HIALMAR.

Yes, that is what he most yearns for. You can't think how my heart bleeds for him. Every time we celebrate any little family festival—Gina's and my wedding-day, or whatever it may be—in comes the old man in the lieutenant's uniform of happier days. But if he only hears a knock at the door—for he daren't show himself to strangers, you know—he hurries back to his room again as fast as his old legs can carry him. Oh, it's heart-rending for a son to see such things!

GREGERS.

How long do you think it will take you to finish your invention?

HIALMAR.

Come now, you mustn't expect me to enter into particulars like that. An invention is not a thing completely under one's own control. It depends largely on inspiration—on intuition—and it is almost impossible to predict when the inspiration may come.

GREGERS.

But it's advancing?

HIALMAR.

Yes, certainly, it is advancing. I turn it over in my mind every day; I am full of it. Every afternoon, when I have had my dinner, I shut myself up in the parlour, where I can ponder undisturbed. But I can't be goaded to it; it's not a bit of good; Relling says so too.

GREGERS.

And you don't think that all that business in the garret draws you off and distracts you too much?

HIALMAR.

No no no; quite the contrary. You mustn't say that. I cannot be everlastingly absorbed in the same laborious train of thought. I must have something alongside of it to fill up the time of waiting. The inspiration, the intuition, you see—when it comes, it comes, and there's an end of it.

GREGERS.

My dear Hialmar, I almost think you have something of the wild duck in you.

HIALMAR.

Something of the wild duck? How do you mean?

GREGERS.

You have dived down and bitten yourself fast in the undergrowth.

HIALMAR.

Are you alluding to the well-nigh fatal shot that has broken my father's wing—and mine too?

GREGERS.

Not exactly to t h a t. I don't say that your wing has been broken; but you have strayed into a poisonous marsh, Hialmar; an insidious disease has taken hold of you, and you have sunk down to die in the dark.

HIALMAR.

I? To die in the dark? Look here, Gregers, you must really leave off talking such nonsense.

GREGERS.

Don't be afraid; I shall find a way to help you up again. I too have a mission in life now; I found it yesterday.

Hialmar.

That's all very well; but you will please leave m e out of it. I can assure you that—apart from my very natural melancholy, of course—I am as contented as any one can wish to be.

Gregers.

Your contentment is an effect of the marsh poison.

Hialmar.

Now, my dear Gregers, pray do not go on about disease and poison; I am not used to that sort of talk. In m y house nobody ever speaks to me about unpleasant things.

Gregers.

Ah, t h a t I can easily believe.

Hialmar.

It's not good for me you see. And there a r e no marsh poisons here, as you express it. The poor photographer's roof is lowly, I know—and my circumstances are narrow. But I am an inventor, and I am the breadwinner of a family. That exalts me above my mean surroundings.—Ah, here comes lunch!

Gina *and* Hedvig *bring bottles of ale, a decanter of brandy, glasses, etc. At the same time,* Relling *and* Molvik *enter from the passage; they are both without hat or overcoat.* Molvik *is dressed in black.*

Gina.

[*Placing the things upon the table.*] Ah, you two have come in the nick of time.

RELLING.

Molvik got it into his head that he could smell herring-salad, and then there was no holding him.—Good morning again, Ekdal.

HIALMAR.

Gregers, let me introduce you to Mr. Molvik. Doctor—— Oh, you know Relling, don't you?

GREGERS.

Yes, slightly.

RELLING.

Oh, Mr. Werle, junior! Yes, we two have had one or two little skirmishes up at the Höidal works. You've just moved in?

GREGERS.

I moved in this morning.

RELLING.

Molvik and I live right under you; so you haven't far to go for the doctor and the clergyman, if you should need anything in that line.

GREGERS.

Thanks, it's not quite unlikely; for yesterday we were thirteen at table.

HIALMAR.

Oh, come now, don't let us get upon unpleasant subjects again!

RELLING.

You may make your mind easy, Ekdal; I'll be hanged if the finger of fate points to y o u.

HIALMAR.

I should hope not, for the sake of my family.   But let us sit down now, and eat and drink and be merry.

GREGERS.

Shall we not wait for your father?

HIALMAR.

No, his lunch will be taken in to him later.   Come along!
> [*The men seat themselves at table, and eat and drink.* GINA *and* HEDVIG *go in and out and wait upon them.*

RELLING.

Molvik was frightfully screwed yesterday, Mrs. Ekdal.

GINA.

Really?   Yesterday again?

RELLING.

Didn't you hear him when I brought him home last night.

GINA.

No, I can't say I did.

RELLING.

That was a good thing, for Molvik was disgusting last night.

GINA.

Is that true, Molvik?

MOLVIK.

Let us draw a veil over last night's proceedings. That sort of thing is totally foreign to my better self.

RELLING.

[*To* GREGERS.]   It comes over him like a sort of possession, and then I have to go out on the loose with him. Mr. Molvik is dæmonic, you see.

GREGERS.

Dæmonic?

RELLING.

Molvik is dæmonic, yes.

GREGERS.

H'm.

RELLING.

And dæmonic natures are not made to walk straight through the world; they must meander a little now and then.—Well, so you still stick up there at those horrible grimy works?

GREGERS.

I have stuck there until now.

RELLING.

And did you ever manage to collect that claim you went about presenting?

GREGERS.

Claim? [*Understands him.*] Ah, I see.

HIALMAR.

Have you been presenting claims, Gregers?

GREGERS.

Oh, nonsense.

RELLING.

Faith, but he has, though! He went round to all the cottars' cabins presenting something he called "the claim of the ideal."

GREGERS.

I was young then.

RELLING.

You're right; you were very young. And as for the claim of the ideal—you never got it honoured while *I* was up there.

GREGERS.

Nor since either.

RELLING.

Ah, then you've learnt to knock a little discount off, I expect.

GREGERS.

Never, when I have a true man to deal with.

HIALMAR.

No, I should think not, indeed.   A little butter, Gina.

RELLING.

And a slice of bacon for Molvik.

MOLVIK.

Ugh! not bacon!   [*A knock at the garret door.*

HIALMAR.

Open the door, Hedvig; father wants to come out.
  [HEDVIG *goes over and opens the door a little way;*
    EKDAL *enters with a fresh rabbit-skin; she closes
    the door after him.*

EKDAL.

Good morning, gentlemen!   Good sport to-day.   Shot
a big one.

HIALMAR.

And you've gone and skinned it without waiting for
m e——!

EKDAL.

Salted it too.   It's good tender meat, is rabbit; it's
sweet; it tastes like sugar.   Good appetite to you, gentlemen!   [*Goes into his room*

MOLVIK.

  [*Rising.*]   Excuse me——; I can't——; I must get
downstairs immediately——

RELLING.

Drink some soda water, man!

MOLVIK.

[*Hurrying away.*]   Ugh—ugh!
                    [*Goes out by the passage door.*

RELLING.

[*To* HIALMAR.]   Let us drain a glass to the old hunter.

HIALMAR.

[*Clinks glasses with him.*]   To the undaunted sportsman who has looked death in the face!

RELLING.

To the grey-haired——   [*Drinks.*]   By-the-bye, is his
hair grey or white?

HIALMAR.

Something between the two, I fancy; for that matter,
he has very few hairs left of any colour.

RELLING.

Well well, one can get through the world with a wig.
After all, you are a happy man, Ekdal; you have your
noble mission to labour for——

HIALMAR.

And I do labour, I can tell you.

RELLING.

And then you have your excellent wife, shuffling quietly in and out in her felt slippers, with that see-saw walk of hers, and making everything cosy and comfortable about you.

HIALMAR.

Yes, Gina—[*Nods to her*]—you are a good helpmate on the path of life.

GINA.

Oh, don't sit there cricketizing me.

RELLING.

And your Hedvig too, Ekdal!

HIALMAR.

[*Affected.*] The child, yes! The child before everything! Hedvig, come here to me. [*Strokes her hair.*] What day is it to-morrow, eh?

HEDVIG.

[*Shaking him.*] Oh no, you're not to say anything, father!

HIALMAR.

It cuts me to the heart when I think what a poor affair it will be; only a little festivity in the garret——

HEDVIG.

Oh, but that's just what I like!

RELLING.

Just you wait till the wonderful invention sees the light, Hedvig!

HIALMAR.

Yes indeed—then you shall see——! Hedvig, I have resolved to make your future secure. You shall live in comfort all your days. I will demand—something or other—on your behalf. T h a t shall be the poor inventor's sole reward.

HEDVIG.

[*Whispering, with her arms round his neck.*] Oh, you dear, kind father!

RELLING.

[*To* GREGERS.] Come now, don't you find it pleasant, for once in a way, to sit at a well-spread table in a happy family circle?

HIALMAR.

Ah yes, I really prize these social hours.

GREGERS.

For my part, I don't thrive in marsh vapours.

RELLING.

Marsh vapours?

HIALMAR.

Oh, don't begin with that stuff again!

Gina.

Goodness knows there's no vapours in t h i s house, Mr. Werle; I give the place a good airing every blessed day.

Gregers.

[*Leaves the table.*]   No airing y o u can give will drive out the taint I mean.

Hialmar.

Taint!

Gina.

Yes, what do you say to that, Ekdal!

Relling.

Excuse me—may it not be you yourself that have brought the taint from those mines up there?

Gregers.

It is like you to call what I bring into this house **a** taint.

Relling.

[*Goes up to him.*]   Look here, Mr. Werle, junior: I have a strong suspicion that you are still carrying about that "claim of the ideal" large as life, in your coat-tail pocket.

Gregers.

I carry it in my breast.

Relling.

Well, wherever you carry it, I advise you not to come dunning us with it here, so long as *I* am on the premises.

GREGERS.

And if I do so none the less?

RELLING.

Then you'll go head-foremost down the stairs; now I've warned you.

HIALMAR.

[*Rising.*] Oh, but Relling——!

GREGERS.

Yes, you may turn me out——

GINA.

[*Interposing between them.*] We can't have that, Relling. But I must say, Mr. Werle, it ill becomes you to talk about vapours and taints, after all the mess you made with your stove.   [*A knock at the passage door.*

HEDVIG.

Mother, there's somebody knocking.

HIALMAR.

There now, we're going to have a whole lot of people!

GINA.

I'll go—— [*Goes over and opens the door, starts, and draws back.*] Oh—oh dear!

WERLE, *in a fur coat, advances one step into the room.*

WERLE.

Excuse me; but I think my son is staying here.

GINA.

[*With a gulp.*]   Yes.

HIALMAR.

[*Approaching him.*]   Won't you do us the honour to——?

WERLE.

Thank you, I merely wish to speak to my son.

GREGERS.

What is it?   Here I am.

WERLE.

I want a few words with you, in your room.

GREGERS.

In my room?   Very well——   [*About to go.*

GINA.

No, no, your room's not in a fit state——

WERLE.

Well then, out in the passage here; I want to have a few words with you alone.

HIALMAR.

You can have them here, sir.   Come into the parlour, Relling.

> [HIALMAR *and* RELLING *go off to the right.*   GINA *takes* HEDVIG *with her into the kitchen.*

GREGERS.

[*After a short pause.*]   Well, now we are alone.

WERLE.

From something you let fall last evening, and from your coming to lodge with the Ekdals, I can't help inferring that you intend to make yourself unpleasant to me, in one way or another.

GREGERS.

I intend to open Hialmar Ekdal's eyes. He shall see his position as it really is—that is all.

WERLE.

Is t h a t the mission in life you spoke of yesterday?

GREGERS.

Yes. You have left me no other.

WERLE.

Is it I, then, that have crippled your mind, Gregers?

GREGERS.

You have crippled my whole life. I am not thinking of all that about mother—— But it's thanks to you that I am continually haunted and harassed by a guilty conscience.

WERLE.

Indeed! It is your conscience that troubles you, is it?

GREGERS.

I ought to have taken a stand against you when the
trap was set for Lieutenant Ekdal.   I ought to have cau-
tioned him; for I had a misgiving as to what was in the
wind.

WERLE.

Yes, that was the time to have spoken.

GREGERS.

I did not dare to, I was so cowed and spiritless.   I
was mortally afraid of you—not only then, but long afterwards.

WERLE.

You have got over that fear now, it appears.

GREGERS.

Yes, fortunately.   The wrong done to old Ekdal, both
by me and by—others, can never be undone; but Hialmar I can rescue from all the falsehood and deception
that are bringing him to ruin.

WERLE.

Do you think t h a t will be doing him a kindness?

GREGERS.

I have not the least doubt of it.

WERLE.

You think our worthy photographer is the sort of man
to appreciate such friendly offices?

GREGERS.

Yes, I do.

WERLE.

H'm—we shall see.

GREGERS.

Besides, if I am to go on living, I must try to find some cure for my sick conscience.

WERLE.

It will never be sound. Your conscience has been sickly from childhood. That is a legacy from your mother, Gregers—the only one she left you.

GREGERS.

[*With a scornful half-smile.*] Have you not yet forgiven her for the mistake you made in supposing she would bring you a fortune?

WERLE.

Don't let us wander from the point.—Then you hold to your purpose of setting young Ekdal upon what you imagine to be the right scent?

GREGERS.

Yes, that is my fixed resolve.

WERLE.

Well, in that case I might have spared myself this visit; for of course it is useless to ask whether you will return home with me?

GREGERS.

Quite useless.

WERLE.

And I suppose you won't enter the firm either?

GREGERS.

No.

WERLE.

Very good.   But as I am thinking of marrying again, your share in the property will fall to you at once.[1]

GREGERS.

[*Quickly.*]   No, I do not want that.

WERLE.

You don't want it?

GREGERS.

No, I dare not take it, for conscience' sake.

WERLE.

[*After a pause.*]   Are you going up to the works again?

GREGERS.

No; I consider myself released from your service.

WERLE.

But what are you going to do?

[1] By Norwegian law, before a widower can marry again, a certain proportion of his property must be settled on his children by his former marriage.

GREGERS.

Only to fulfil my mission; nothing more.

WERLE.

Well, but afterwards? What are you going to live upon?

GREGERS.

I have laid by a little out of my salary.

WERLE.

How long will t h a t last?

GREGERS.

I think it will last m y time.

WERLE.

What do you mean?

GREGERS.

I shall answer no more questions.

WERLE.

Good-bye then, Gregers.

GREGERS.

Good-bye.   [WERLE *goes*

HIALMAR.

[*Peeping in.*]   He's gone, isn't he?

GREGERS.

Yes.

HIALMAR *and* RELLING *enter; also* GINA *and* HEDVIG
from the kitchen.

RELLING.

That luncheon-party was a failure.

GREGERS.

Put on your coat, Hialmar; I want you to come for a
long walk with me.

HIALMAR.

With pleasure.   What was it your father wanted?
Had it anything to do with me?

GREGERS.

Come along.   We must have a talk.   I'll go and put
on my overcoat.   [*Goes out by the passage door.*

GINA.

You shouldn't go out with him, Ekdal.

RELLING.

No, don't you do it.   Stay where you are.

HIALMAR.

[*Gets his hat and overcoat.*]   Oh, nonsense!   When a
friend of my youth feels impelled to open his mind to me
in private——

RELLING.

But devil take it—don't you see that the fellow's mad, cracked, demented!

GINA.

There, what did I tell you! His mother before him had crazy fits like that sometimes.

HIALMAR.

The more need for a friend's watchful eye. [*To* GINA.] Be sure you have dinner ready in good time. Good-bye for the present. [*Goes out by the passage door.*

RELLING.

It's a thousand pities the fellow didn't go to hell through one of the Höidal mines.

GINA.

Good Lord! what makes you say that?

RELLING.

[*Muttering.*] Oh, I have my own reasons.

GINA.

Do you think young Werle is really mad?

RELLING.

No, worse luck; he's no madder than most other people. But one disease he has certainly got in his system.

GINA.

What is it that's the matter with him?

RELLING.

Well, I'll tell you, Mrs. Ekdal.   He is suffering from an acute attack of integrity.

GINA.

Integrity?

HEDVIG.

Is that a kind of disease?

RELLING.

Yes, it's a national disease; but it only appears sporadically.   [*Nods to* GINA.]   Thanks for your hospitality.
[*He goes out by the passage door.*

GINA.

[*Moving restlessly to and fro.*]   Ugh, that Gregers Werle—he was always a wretched creature.

HEDVIG.

[*Standing by the table, and looking searchingly at her.*] I think all this is very strange.

ACT FOURTH

HIALMAR EKDAL'S *studio. A photograph has just been taken; a camera with the cloth over it, a pedestal, two chairs, a folding table, etc., are standing out in the room. Afternoon light; the sun is going down; a little later it begins to grow dusk.*

GINA *stands in the passage doorway, with a little box and a wet glass plate in her hand, and is speaking to somebody outside.*

GINA.

Yes, certainly. When I make a promise I keep it. The first dozen shall be ready on Monday. Good afternoon.

> [*Some one is heard going downstairs.* GINA *shuts the door, slips the plate into the box, and puts it into the covered camera.*

HEDVIG.

[*Comes in from the kitchen.*] Are they gone?

GINA.

[*Tidying up.*] Yes, thank goodness, I've got rid of them at last.

HEDVIG.

But can you imagine why father hasn't come home yet?

GINA.

Are you sure he's not down in Relling's room?

376

HEDVIG.

No, he's not; I ran down the kitchen stair just now and asked.

GINA.

And his dinner standing and getting cold, too.

HEDVIG.

Yes, I can't understand it.   Father's always so careful to be home to dinner!

GINA.

Oh, he'll be here directly, you'll see.

HEDVIG.

I wish he would come; everything seems so queer today.

GINA.

[*Calls out.*]   There he is!

HIALMAR EKDAL *comes in at the passage door.*

HEDVIG.

[*Going to him.*]   Father!   Oh what a time we've been waiting for you!

GINA.

[*Glancing sidelong at him.*]   You've been out a long time, Ekdal.

HIALMAR.

[*Without looking at her.*]   Rather long, yes.
[*He takes off his overcoat;* GINA *and* HEDVIG *go to
help him; he motions them away.*

GINA.

Perhaps you've had dinner with Werle?

HIALMAR.

[*Hanging up his coat.*]   No.

GINA.

[*Going towards the kitchen door.*]   Then I'll bring some
in for you.

HIALMAR.

No; let the dinner alone.   I want nothing to eat.

HEDVIG.

[*Going nearer to him.*]   Are you not well, father?

HIALMAR.

Well?   Oh yes, well enough.   We have had a tiring
walk, Gregers and I.

GINA.

You didn't ought to have gone so far, Ekdal, you're
not used to it.

HIALMAR.

H'm; there's many a thing a man must get used to in
this world.   [*Wanders about the room.*]   Has any one been
here whilst I was out?

GINA.

Nobody but the two sweethearts.

HIALMAR.

No new orders?

GINA.

No, not to-day.

HEDVIG.

There will be some to-morrow, father, you'll see.

HIALMAR.

I hope there will; for to-morrow I am going to set to work in real earnest.

HEDVIG.

To-morrow!   Don't you remember what day it is to-morrow?

HIALMAR.

Oh yes, by-the-bye——.   Well, the day after, then. Henceforth I mean to do everything myself; I shall take all the work into my own hands.

GINA.

Why, what can be the good of that, Ekdal?   It'll only make your life a burden to you.   I can manage the photography all right; and you can go on working at your invention.

HEDVIG.

And think of the wild duck, father,—and all the hens and rabbits and——!

Hialmar.

Don't talk to me of all that trash!   From to-morrow I will never set foot in the garret again.

Hedvig.

Oh but, father, you promised that we should have a little party——

Hialmar.

H'm, true.   Well then, from the day after to-morrow. I should almost like to wring that cursëd wild duck's neck!

Hedvig.

[*Shrieks.*]   The wild duck!

Gina.

Well I never!

Hedvig.

[*Shaking him.*]   Oh no, father; you know it's m y wild duck!

Hialmar.

That is why I don't do it.   I haven't the heart to— for your sake, Hedvig.   But in my inmost soul I feel that I ought to do it.   I ought not to tolerate under my roof a creature that has been through t h o s e hands.

Gina.

Why, good gracious, even if grandfather did g e t it from that poor creature, Pettersen——

HIALMAR.

[*Wandering about.*] There are certain claims—what shall I call them?—let me say claims of the ideal—certain obligations, which a man cannot disregard without injury to his soul.

HEDVIG.

[*Going after him.*] But think of the wild duck,—the poor wild duck!

HIALMAR.

[*Stops.*] I tell you I will spare it—for your sake. Not a hair of its head shall be—I mean, it shall be spared. There are greater problems than that to be dealt with. But you should go out a little now, Hedvig, as usual; it is getting dusk enough for you now.

HEDVIG.

No, I don't care about going out now.

HIALMAR.

Yes do; it seems to me your eyes are blinking a great deal; all these vapours in here are bad for you. The air is heavy under this roof.

HEDVIG.

Very well then, I'll run down the kitchen stair and go for a little walk. My cloak and hat?—oh, they're in my own room. Father—be sure you don't do the wild duck any harm whilst I'm out.

HIALMAR.

Not a feather of its head shall be touched. [*Draws her to him.*] You and I, Hedvig—we two——! Well, go along.

[HEDVIG *nods to her parents and goes out through the kitchen.*

HIALMAR.

[*Walks about without looking up.*] Gina.

GINA.

Yes?

HIALMAR.

From to-morrow—or, say, from the day after to-morrow—I should like to keep the household account-book myself.

GINA.

Do you want to keep the accounts too, now?

HIALMAR.

Yes; or to check the receipts at any rate.

GINA.

Lord help us! t h a t ' s soon done.

HIALMAR.

One would hardly think so; at any rate you seem to make the money go a very long way. [*Stops and looks at her.*] How do you manage it?

GINA.

It's because me and Hedvig, we need so little.

HIALMAR.

Is it the case that father is very liberally paid for the copying he does for Mr. Werle?

GINA.

I don't know as he gets anything out of the way. I don't know the rates for that sort of work.

HIALMAR.

Well, what does he get, about? Let me hear!

GINA.

Oh, it varies; I daresay it'll come to about as much as he costs us, with a little pocket-money over.

HIALMAR.

As much as he costs us! And you have never told me this before!

GINA.

No, how could I tell you? It pleased you so much to think he got everything from you.

HIALMAR.

And he gets it from Mr. Werle.

GINA.

Oh well, he has plenty and to spare, he has.

HIALMAR.

Light the lamp for me, please!

GINA.

[*Lighting the lamp.*] And of course we don't know as it's Mr. Werle himself; it may be Gråberg——

HIALMAR.

Why attempt such an evasion?

GINA.

I don't know; I only thought——

HIALMAR.

H'm!

GINA.

It wasn't me that got grandfather that copying. It was Bertha, when she used to come about us.

HIALMAR.

It seems to me your voice is trembling.

GINA.

[*Putting the lamp-shade on.*] Is it?

HIALMAR.

And your hands are shaking, are they not?

GINA.

[*Firmly.*] Come right out with it, Ekdal. What has he been saying about me?

Hialmar.

Is it true—c a n it be true that—that there was an—an understanding between you and Mr. Werle, while you were in service there?

· Gina.

That's not true. Not at that time. Mr. Werle did come after me, that's a fact. And his wife thought there was something in it, and then she made such a hocus-pocus and hurly-burly, and she hustled me and bustled me about so, that I left her service.

Hialmar.

But afterwards, then?

Gina.

Well, then I went home. And mother—well, she wasn't the woman you took her for, Ekdal; she kept on worrying and worrying at me about one thing and another—for Mr. Werle was a widower by that time.

Hialmar.

Well, and then?

Gina.

I suppose you've got to know it. He gave me no peace until he'd had his way.

Hialmar.

[*Striking his hands together*.] And this is the mother of my child! How could you hide this from me?

GINA.

Yes, it was wrong of me; I ought certainly to have told you long ago.

HIALMAR.

You should have told me at the very first;—then I should have known the sort of woman you were.

GINA.

But would you have married me all the same?

HIALMAR.

How can you dream that I would?

GINA.

That's just why I didn't dare tell you anything, then. For I'd come to care for you so much, you see; and I couldn't go and make myself utterly miserable——

HIALMAR.

[*Walks about.*]   And this is my Hedvig's mother.   And to know that all I see before me—[*Kicks at a chair*]—all that I call my home—I owe to a favoured predecessor! Oh that scoundrel Werle!

GINA.

Do you repent of the fourteen—the fifteen years as we've lived together?

HIALMAR.

[*Placing himself in front of her.*]   Have y o u not every day, every hour, repented of the spider's-web of deceit

you have spun around me ? Answer me that! How could
you help writhing with penitence and remorse ?

Gina.

Oh, my dear Ekdal, I've had all I could do to look
after the house and get through the day's work——

Hialmar.

Then you never think of reviewing your past ?

Gina.

No; Heaven knows I'd almost forgotten those old
stories.

Hialmar.

Oh, this dull, callous contentment! To me there is
something revolting about it. Think of it—never so
much as a twinge of remorse!

Gina.

But tell me, Ekdal—what would have become of you
if you hadn't had a wife like me ?

Hialmar.

Like you——!

Gina.

Yes; for you know I've always been a bit more practical and wide-awake than you. Of course I'm a year
or two older.

Hialmar.

What would have become of me!

GINA.

You'd got into all sorts of bad ways when first you met me; that you can't deny.

HIALMAR.

"Bad ways" do you call them? Little do you know what a man goes through when he is in grief and despair—especially a man of my fiery temperament.

GINA.

Well, well, that may be so. And I've no reason to crow over you, neither; for you turned a moral of a husband, that you did, as soon as ever you had a house and home of your own.—And now we'd got everything so nice and cosy about us; and me and Hedvig was just thinking we'd soon be able to let ourselves go a bit, in the way of both food and clothes.

HIALMAR.

In the swamp of deceit, yes.

GINA.

I wish to goodness that detestable being had never set his foot inside our doors!

HIALMAR.

And I, too, thought my home such a pleasant one. That was a delusion. Where shall I now find the elasticity of spirit to bring my invention into the world of reality? Perhaps it will die with me; and then it will be your past, Gina, that will have killed it.

GINA.

[*Nearly crying.*] You mustn't say such things, Ekdal. Me, that has only wanted to do the best I could for you, all my days!

HIALMAR.

I ask you, what becomes of the breadwinner's dream? When I used to lie in there on the sofa and brood over my invention, I had a clear enough presentiment that it would sap my vitality to the last drop. I felt even then that the day when I held the patent in my hand—that day—would bring my—release. And then it was my dream that you should live on after me, the dead inventor's well-to-do widow.

GINA.

[*Drying her tears.*] No, you mustn't talk like that, Ekdal. May the Lord never let me see the day I am left a widow!

HIALMAR.

Oh, the whole dream has vanished. It is all over now. All over!

GREGERS WERLE *opens the passage door cautiously and looks in.*

GREGERS.

May I come in?

HIALMAR.

Yes, come in.

[*Comes forward, his face beaming with satisfaction, and holds out both his hands to them.*] Well, dear friends——! [*Looks from one to the other, and whispers to* HIALMAR.] Have you not done it yet?

HIALMAR.

[*Aloud.*] It is done.

GREGERS.

It is?

HIALMAR.

I have passed through the bitterest moments of my life.

GREGERS.

But also, I trust, the most ennobling.

HIALMAR.

Well, at any rate, we have got through it for the present.

GINA.

God forgive you, Mr. Werle.

GREGERS.

[*In great surprise.*]   But I don't understand this.

HIALMAR.

What don't you understand?

GREGERS.

After so great a crisis—a crisis that is to be the starting-point of an entirely new life—of a communion founded on truth, and free from all taint of deception——

HIALMAR.

Yes yes, I know; I know that quite well.

GREGERS.

I confidently expected, when I entered the room, to find the light of transfiguration shining upon me from both husband and wife. And now I see nothing but dulness, oppression, gloom——

GINA.

Oh, is that it?   [*Takes off the lamp-shade.*

GREGERS.

You will not understand me, Mrs. Ekdal. Ah well, y o u, I suppose, need time to——. But you, Hialmar? Surely you feel a new consecration after the great crisis.

HIALMAR.

Yes, of course I do. That is—in a sort of way.

GREGERS.

For surely nothing in the world can compare with the joy of forgiving one who has erred, and raising her up to oneself in love.

HIALMAR.

Do you think a man can so easily throw off the effects of the bitter cup I have drained?

GREGERS.

No, not a c o m m o n man, perhaps. But a man like y o u——!

HIALMAR.

Good God! I know that well enough. But you must keep me up to it, Gregers. It takes time, you know.

GREGERS.

You have m u c h of the wild duck in you, Hialmar.

RELLING *has come in at the passage door.*

RELLING.

Oho! is the wild duck to the fore again?

HIALMAR.

Yes; Mr. Werle's wing-broken victim.

RELLING.

Mr. Werle's——? So it's h i m you are talking about?

HIALMAR.

Him and—ourselves.

RELLING.

[*In an undertone to* GREGERS.] May the devil fly away with you!

HIALMAR.

What is that you are saying?

RELLING.

Only uttering a heartfelt wish that this quack-salver would take himself off. If he stays here, he is quite equal to making an utter mess of life, for both of you.

GREGERS.

These two will not make a mess of life, Mr. Relling. Of course I won't speak of Hialmar—him we know. But she, too, in her innermost heart, has certainly something loyal and sincere——

GINA.

[*Almost crying.*] You might have let me alone for what I was, then.

RELLING.

[*To* GREGERS.] Is it rude to ask what you really want in this house?

GREGERS.

To lay the foundations of a true marriage.

RELLING.

So you don't think Ekdal's marriage is good enough as it is?

GREGERS.

No doubt it is as good a marriage as most others, worse luck.   But a t r u e marriage it has yet to become.

HIALMAR.

You have never had eyes for the claims of the ideal, Relling.

RELLING.

Rubbish, my boy!—But excuse me, Mr. Werle: how many—in round numbers—how many true marriages have you seen in the course of your life?

GREGERS.

Scarcely a single one.

RELLING.

Nor I either.

GREGERS.

But I have seen innumerable marriages of the opposite kind. And it has been my fate to see at close quarters what ruin such a marriage can work in two human souls.

HIALMAR.

A man's whole moral basis may give away beneath his feet; t h a t is the terrible part of it.

RELLING.

Well, I can't say I've ever been exactly married, so I don't pretend to speak with authority. But this I know, that the c h i l d enters into the marriage problem. And you must leave the child in peace.

HIALMAR.

Oh—Hedvig! my poor Hedvig!

RELLING.

Yes, you must be good enough to keep Hedvig outside of all this. You two are grown-up people; you are free, in God's name, to make what mess and muddle you please of your life. But you must deal cautiously with Hedvig, I tell you; else you may do her a great injury.

HIALMAR.

An injury!

RELLING.

Yes, or she may do herself an injury—and perhaps others too.

GINA.

How can you know that, Relling?

HIALMAR.

Her sight is in no immediate danger, is it?

RELLING.

I am not talking about her sight. Hedvig is at a critical age. She may be getting all sorts of mischief into her head.

GINA.

That's true—I've noticed it already! She's taken to carrying on with the fire, out in the kitchen. She calls it playing at house-on-fire. I'm often scared for fear she really sets fire to the house.

RELLING.

You see; I thought as much.

GREGERS.

[*To* RELLING.] But how do you account for that?

RELLING.

[*Sullenly.*] Her constitution's changing, sir.

HIALMAR.

So long as the child has m e——! So long as *I* am
above ground——!   [*A knock at the door.*

GINA.

Hush, Ekdal; there's some one in the passage. [*Calls
out.*]   Come in!

                  [MRS. SÖRBY, *in walking dress, comes in.*

MRS. SÖRBY.

Good evening

GINA.

[*Going towards her.*]   Is it really you, Bertha?

MRS. SÖRBY.

Yes, of course it is.   But I'm disturbing you, I'm
afraid?

HIALMAR.

No, not at all; an emissary from t h a t house——

MRS. SÖRBY.

[*To* GINA.]   To tell the truth, I hoped your men-folk
would be out at this time.   I just ran up to have a little
chat with you, and to say good-bye.

GINA.

Good-bye?   Are you going away, then?

MRS. SÖRBY.

Yes, to-morrow morning,—up to Höidal.   Mr. Werle
started this afternoon.   [*Lightly to* GREGERS.]   He asked
me to say good-bye for him.

GINA.

Only fancy——!

HIALMAR.

So Mr. Werle has gone? And now you are going
after him?

MRS. SÖRBY.

Yes, what do you say to t h a t, Ekdal?

HIALMAR.

I say: beware!

GREGERS.

I must explain the situation. My father and Mrs.
Sörby are going to be married.

HIALMAR.

Going to be married!

GINA.

Oh Bertha! So it's come to that at last!

RELLING.

[*His voice quivering a little.*] This is surely not true?

MRS. SÖRBY.

Yes, my dear Relling, it's true enough.

RELLING.

You are going to marry again?

Mrs. Sörby.

Yes, it looks like it.   Werle has got a special licence, and we are going to be married quite quietly, up at the works.

Gregers.

Then I must wish you all happiness, like a dutiful stepson.

Mrs. Sörby.

Thank you very much—if you mean what you say.   I certainly hope it will lead to happiness, both for Werle and for me.

Relling.

You have every reason to hope that.   Mr. Werle never gets drunk—so far as I know; and I don't suppose he's in the habit of thrashing his wives, like the late lamented horse-doctor.

Mrs. Sörby.

Come now, let Sörby rest in peace.   He had his good points too.

Relling.

Mr. Werle has better ones, I have no doubt.

Mrs. Sörby.

He hasn't frittered away all that was good in him, at any rate.   The man who does that must take the consequences.

Relling.

I shall go out with Molvik this evening.

Mrs. Sörby.

You mustn't do that, Relling. Don't do it—for my sake.

Relling.

There's nothing else for it. [*To* Hialmar.] If you're going with us, come along.

Gina.

No, thank you. Ekdal doesn't go in for t h a t sort of dissertation.

Hialmar.

[*Half aloud, in vexation.*] Oh, do hold your tongue!

Relling.

Good-bye, Mrs.—Werle.

　　　　　[*Goes out through the passage door.*

Gregers.

[*To* Mrs. Sörby.] You seem to know Dr. Relling pretty intimately.

Mrs. Sörby.

Yes, we have known each other for many years. At one time it seemed as if things might have gone further between us.

Gregers.

It was surely lucky for you that they did not.

Mrs. Sörby.

You may well say that. But I have always been wary of acting on impulse. A woman can't afford absolutely to throw herself away.

GREGERS.

Are you not in the least afraid that I may let my father know about this old friendship?

MRS. SÖRBY.

Why, of course I have told him all about it myself

GREGERS.

Indeed?

MRS. SÖRBY.

Your father knows every single thing that can, with any truth, be said about me. I have told him all; it was the first thing I did when I saw what was in his mind.

GREGERS.

Then you have been franker than most people, I think.

MRS. SÖRBY.

I have always been frank. We women find that the best policy.

HIALMAR.

What do you say to that, Gina?

GINA.

Oh, we're not all alike, us women aren't. Some are made one way, some another.

MRS. SÖRBY.

Well, for my part, Gina, I believe it's wisest to do as I've done. And Werle has no secrets either, on his side.

That's really the great bond between us, you see.   Now
he can talk to me as openly as a child.   He has never
had the chance to do that before.   Fancy a man like
him, full of health and vigour, passing his whole youth
and the best years of his life in listening to nothing but
penitential sermons!   And very often the sermons had
for their text the most imaginary offences—at least so I
understand.

GINA.

That's true enough.

GREGERS.

If you ladies are going to follow up this topic, I had
better withdraw.

MRS. SÖRBY.

You can stay so far as that's concerned.   I shan't say
a word more.   But I wanted you to know that I had done
nothing secretly or in an underhand way.   I may seem
to have come in for a great piece of luck; and so I have,
in a sense.   But after all, I don't think I am getting any
more than I am giving.   I shall stand by him always,
and I can tend and care for him as no one else can, now
that he is getting helpless.

HIALMAR.

Getting helpless?

GREGERS.

[To MRS. SÖRBY.]   Hush, don't speak of that here.

MRS. SÖRBY.

There is no disguising it any longer, however much he
would like to.   He is going blind.

HIALMAR.

[*Starts.*]   Going blind ?   That's strange.   He too going blind!

GINA.

Lots of people do.

MRS. SÖRBY.

And you can imagine what t h a t means to a business man.   Well, I shall try as well as I can to make my eyes take the place of his.   But I mustn't stay any longer; I have such heaps of things to do.—Oh, by-the-bye, Ekdal, I was to tell you that if there is anything Werle can do for you, you must just apply to Gråberg.

GREGERS.

That offer I am sure Hialmar Ekdal will decline with thanks.

MRS. SÖRBY.

Indeed ?   I don't think he used to be so——

GINA.

No, Bertha, Ekdal doesn't need anything from Mr. Werle now.

HIALMAR.

[*Slowly, and with emphasis.*]   Will you present my compliments to your future husband, and say that I intend very shortly to call upon Mr. Gråberg——

GREGERS.

What!   You don't really mean that ?

HIALMAR.

To call upon Mr. Gråberg, I say, and obtain an account of the sum I owe his principal. I will pay that debt of honour—ha ha ha! a debt of honour, let us call it! In any case, I will pay the whole, with five per cent. interest.

GINA.

But, my dear Ekdal, God knows we haven't got the money to do it.

HIALMAR.

Be good enough to tell your future husband that I am working assiduously at my invention. Please tell him that what sustains me in this laborious task is the wish to free myself from a torturing burden of debt. That is my reason for proceeding with the invention. The entire profits shall be devoted to releasing me from my pecuniary obligations to your future husband.

MRS. SÖRBY.

Something has happened here.

HIALMAR.
Yes, you are right.

MRS. SÖRBY.

Well, good-bye. I had something else to speak to you about, Gina; but it must keep till another time. Good-bye.

[HIALMAR *and* GREGERS *bow silently.* GINA *follows* MRS. SÖRBY *to the door.*

HIALMAR.

Not beyond the threshold, Gina!
[MRS. SÖRBY *goes*; GINA *shuts the door after her.*

HIALMAR.

There now, Gregers; I have got that burden of debt off my mind.

GREGERS.

You soon will, at all events.

HIALMAR.

I think my attitude may be called correct.

GREGERS.

You are the man I have always taken you for.

HIALMAR.

In certain cases, it is impossible to disregard the claim of the ideal.   Yet, as the breadwinner of a family, I cannot but writhe and groan under it.   I can tell you it is no joke for a man without capital to attempt the repayment of a long-standing obligation, over which, so to speak, the dust of oblivion had gathered.   But it cannot be helped: the Man in me demands his rights.

GREGERS.

[*Laying his hand on* HIALMAR'S *shoulder.*]   My dear Hialmar—was it not a good thing I came?

HIALMAR.

Yes.

GREGERS.

Are you not glad to have had your true position made clear to you?

HIALMAR.

[*Somewhat impatiently.*] Yes, of course I am. But there is one thing that is revolting to my sense of justice.

GREGERS.

And what is that?

HIALMAR.

It is that—but I don't know whether I ought to express myself so unreservedly about your father.

GREGERS.

Say what you please, so far as I am concerned.

HIALMAR.

Well then, is it not exasperating to think that it is not I, but he, who will realise the true marriage?

GREGERS.

How can you say such a thing?

HIALMAR.

Because it is clearly the case. Isn't the marriage between your father and Mrs. Sörby founded upon complete confidence, upon entire and unreserved candour on both sides? They hide nothing from each other, they keep no secrets in the background; their relation is based, if I may put it so, on mutual confession and absolution.

GREGERS.

Well, what then?

HIALMAR.

Well, is not that the whole thing? Did you not yourself say that this was precisely the difficulty that had to be overcome in order to found a true marriage?

GREGERS.

But this is a totally different matter, Hialmar. You surely don't compare either yourself or your wife with those two——? Oh, you understand me well enough.

HIALMAR.

Say what you like, there is something in all this that hurts and offends my sense of justice. It really looks as if there were no just providence to rule the world.

GINA.

Oh no, Ekdal; for God's sake don't say such things.

GREGERS.

H'm; don't let us get upon those questions.

HIALMAR.

And yet, after all, I cannot but recognise the guiding finger of fate. He is going blind.

GINA.

Oh, you can't be sure of that.

HIALMAR.

There is no doubt about it.　At all events there ought not to be; for in that very fact lies the righteous retribution.　He has hoodwinked a confiding fellow creature in days gone by— —

GREGERS.

I fear he has hoodwinked many.

HIALMAR.

And now comes inexorable, mysterious Fate, and demands Werle's own eyes.

GINA.

Oh, how dare you say such dreadful things!　You make me quite scared.

HIALMAR.

It is profitable, now and then, to plunge deep into the night side of existence.

HEDVIG, *in her hat and cloak, comes in by the passage door. She is pleasurably excited, and out of breath.*

GINA.

Are you back already?

HEDVIG.

Yes, I didn't care to go any farther.　It was a good thing, too; for I've just met some one at the door.

HIALMAR.

It must have been that Mrs. Sörby.

HEDVIG.

Yes.

HIALMAR.

[*Walks up and down.*] I hope you have seen her for the last time.

[*Silence.* HEDVIG, *discouraged, looks first at one and then at the other, trying to divine their frame of mind.*

HEDVIG.

[*Approaching, coaxingly.*] Father.

HIALMAR.

Well—what is it, Hedvig?

HEDVIG.

Mrs. Sörby had something with her for me.

HIALMAR.

[*Stops.*] For you?

HEDVIG.

Yes. Something for to-morrow.

GINA.

Bertha has always given you some little thing on your birthday.

HIALMAR.

What is it?

HEDVIG.

Oh, you mustn't see it now. Mother is to give it to me to-morrow morning before I'm up.

HIALMAR.

What is all this hocus-pocus that I am to be kept in the dark about!

HEDVIG.

[*Quickly.*]   Oh no, you may see it if you like.   It's a big letter.   [*Takes the letter out of her cloak pocket.*

HIALMAR.

A letter too?

HEDVIG.

Yes, it is only a letter.   The rest will come afterwards, I suppose.   But fancy—a letter!   I've never had a letter before.   And there's "Miss" written upon it. [*Reads.*] "Miss Hedvig Ekdal."   Only fancy—that's me!

HIALMAR.

Let me see that letter.

HEDVIG.

[*Hands it to him.*]   There it is.

HIALMAR.

That is Mr. Werle's hand.

GINA.

Are you sure of that, Ekdal?

HIALMAR.

Look for yourself.

GINA.

Oh, what do *I* know about such-like things?

HIALMAR.

Hedvig, may I open the letter—and read it?

HEDVIG.

Yes, of course you may, if you want to.

GINA.

No, not to-night, Ekdal; it's to be kept till to-morrow.

HEDVIG.

[*Softly.*]   Oh, can't you let him read it!   It's sure to
be something good; and then father will be glad, and
everything will be nice again.

HIALMAR.

I may open it then?

HEDVIG.

Yes do, father.   I'm so anxious to know what it is.

HIALMAR.

Well and good.   [*Opens the letter, takes out a paper,
reads it through, and appears bewildered.*]   What is
this——!

GINA.

What does it say?

HEDVIG.

Oh yes, father—tell us!

HIALMAR.

Be quiet.   [*Reads it through again; he has turned pale,
but says with self-control:*]   It is a deed of gift, Hedvig.

HEDVIG.

Is it? What sort of gift am I to have?

HIALMAR.

Read for yourself.
[HEDVIG *goes over and reads for a time by the lamp.*

HIALMAR.

[*Half-aloud, clenching his hands.*] The eyes! The eyes—and then that letter!

HEDVIG.

[*Leaves off reading.*] Yes, but it seems to me that it's grandfather that's to have it.

HIALMAR.

[*Takes the letter from her.*] Gina—can you understand this?

GINA.

I know nothing whatever about it; tell me what's the matter.

HIALMAR.

Mr. Werle writes to Hedvig that her old grandfather need not trouble himself any longer with the copying, but that he can henceforth draw on the office for a hundred crowns a month——

GREGERS.

Aha!

HEDVIG.

A hundred crowns, mother! I read that.

GINA.

What a good thing for grandfather!

HIALMAR.

——a hundred crowns a month so long as he needs it —that means, of course, so long as he lives.

GINA.

Well, so he's provided for, poor dear.

HIALMAR.

But there is more to come. You didn't read that, Hedvig. Afterwards this gift is to pass on to you.

HEDVIG.

To me! The whole of it?

HIALMAR.

He says that the same amount is assured to you for the whole of your life. Do you hear that, Gina?

GINA.

Yes, I hear.

HEDVIG.

Fancy—all that money for me! [*Shakes him.*] Father, father, aren't you glad——?

HIALMAR.

[*Eluding her.*] Glad! [*Walks about.*] Oh what vistas—what perspectives open up before me! It is Hedvig, Hedvig that he showers these benefactions upon!

GINA.

Yes, because it's Hedvig's birthday——

HEDVIG.

And you'll get it all the same, father! You know quite well I shall give all the money to you and mother.

HIALMAR.

To mother, yes! There we have it.

GREGERS.

Hialmar, this is a trap he is setting for you.

HIALMAR.

Do you think it's another trap?

GREGERS.

When he was here this morning he said: Hialmar Ekdal is not the man you imagine him to be.

HIALMAR.

Not the man——!

GREGERS.

That you shall see, he said.

HIALMAR.

He meant you should see that I would let myself be bought off——!

HEDVIG.

Oh, mother what does all this mean?

GINA.

Go and take off your things.
[HEDVIG *goes out by the kitchen door, half-crying.*

GREGERS.

Yes, Hialmar—now is the time to show who was right, he or I.

HIALMAR.

[*Slowly tears the paper across, lays both pieces on the table, and says:*]   Here is my answer.

GREGERS.

Just what I expected.

HIALMAR.

[*Goes over to* GINA, *who stands by the stove, and says in a low voice:*]   Now please make a clean breast of it. If the connection between you and him was quite over when you—came to care for me, as you call it—why did he place us in a position to marry?

GINA.

I suppose he thought as he could come and go in our house.

HIALMAR.

Only t h a t ? Was not he afraid of a possible contingency?

GINA.

I don't know what you mean.

HIALMAR.

I want to know whether—your child has the right to live under my roof.

GINA.

[*Draws herself up; her eyes flash.*] Y o u ask that!

HIALMAR.

You shall answer me this one question: Does Hedvig belong to me—or——? Well!

GINA.

[*Looking at him with cold defiance.*] I don't know.

HIALMAR.

[*Quivering a little.*] You don't know!

GINA.

How should *I* know? A creature like m e——

HIALMAR.

[*Quietly turning away from her.*] Then I have nothing more to do in this house.

GREGERS.

Take care, Hialmar! Think what you are doing!

HIALMAR.

[*Puts on his overcoat.*] In this case, there is nothing for a man like me to think twice about.

GREGERS.

Yes indeed, there are endless things to be considered. You three must be together if you are to attain the true frame of mind for self-sacrifice and forgiveness.

HIALMAR.

I don't want to attain it. Never, never! My hat! [*Takes his hat.*] My home has fallen in ruins about me. [*Bursts into tears.*] Gregers, I have no child!

HEDVIG.

[*Who has opened the kitchen door.*] What is that you're saying? [*Coming to him.*] Father, father!

GINA.

There, you see!

HIALMAR.

Don't come near me, Hedvig! Keep far away. I cannot bear to see you. Oh! those eyes——! Good-bye.
[*Makes for the door.*

HEDVIG.

[*Clinging close to him and screaming loudly.*] No! no! Don't leave me!

GINA.

[*Cries out.*] Look at the child, Ekdal! Look at the child !

HIALMAR.

I will not! I cannot! I must get out—away from all this!
　　[*He tears himself away from* HEDVIG, *and goes out by the passage door.*

HEDVIG.

[*With despairing eyes.*] He is going away from us, mother! He is going away from us! He will never come back again!

GINA.

Don't cry, Hedvig.   Father's sure to come back again.

HEDVIG.

[*Throws herself sobbing on the sofa.*] No, no, he'll never come home to us any more.

GREGERS.

Do you believe I meant all for the best, Mrs. Ekdal?

GINA.

Yes, I daresay you did; but God forgive you, all the same.

HEDVIG.

[*Lying on the sofa.*] Oh, this will kill me! What have I done to him ?   Mother, you must fetch him home again!

GINA.

Yes yes yes; only be quiet, and I'll go out and look for him. [*Puts on her outdoor things.*] Perhaps he's gone in to Relling's. But you mustn't lie there and cry. Promise me!

HEDVIG.

[*Weeping convulsively.*] Yes, I'll stop, I'll stop; if only father comes back!

GREGERS.

[*To* GINA, *who is going.*] After all, had you not better leave him to fight out his bitter fight to the end?

GINA.

Oh, he can do that afterwards. First of all, we must get the child quieted. [*Goes out by the passage door.*

HEDVIG.

[*Sits up and dries her tears.*] Now you must tell me what all this means. Why doesn't father want me **any** more?

GREGERS.

You mustn't ask that till you are a big girl—quite grown-up.

HEDVIG.

[*Sobs.*] But I can't go on being as miserable as this till I'm grown-up.—I think I know what it is.—Perhaps I'm not really father's child.

GREGERS.

[*Uneasily.*] How could t h a t be?

HEDVIG.

Mother might have found me.   And perhaps father has just got to know it; I've read of such things.

GREGERS.

Well, but if it were so——

HEDVIG.

I think he might be just as fond of me for all that. Yes, fonder almost.   We got the wild duck in a present, you know, and I love it so dearly all the same.

GREGERS.

[*Turning the conversation.*]   Ah, the wild duck, by-the-bye!   Let us talk about the wild duck a little, Hedvig.

HEDVIG.

The poor wild duck!   He doesn't want to see it any more either.   Only think, he wanted to wring its neck!

GREGERS.

Oh, he won't do that.

HEDVIG.

No; but he said he would like to.   And I think it was horrid of father to say it; for I pray for the wild duck every night, and ask that it may be preserved from death and all that is evil.

GREGERS.

[*Looking at her.*]   Do you say your prayers every night?

HEDVIG.

Yes.

GREGERS.

Who taught you to do that?

HEDVIG.

I myself; one time when father was very ill, and had leeches on his neck, and said that death was staring him in the face.

GREGERS.

Well?

HEDVIG.

Then I prayed for him as I lay in bed; and since then I have always kept it up.

GREGERS.

And now you pray for the wild duck too?

HEDVIG.

I thought it was best to bring in the wild duck; for she was so weakly at first.

GREGERS.

Do you pray in the morning, too?

HEDVIG.

No, of course not.

GREGERS.

Why not in the morning as well?

HEDVIG.

In the morning it's light, you know, and there's nothing in particular to be afraid of.

GREGERS.

And your father was going to wring the neck of the wild duck that you love so dearly?

HEDVIG.

No; he said he ought to wring its neck, but he would spare it for my sake; and that was kind of father.

GREGERS.

[*Coming a little nearer.*] But suppose y o u were to sacrifice the wild duck of your own free will for h i s sake.

HEDVIG.

[*Rising.*] The wild duck!

GREGERS.

Suppose you were to make a free-will offering, for his sake, of the dearest treasure you have in the world!

HEDVIG.

Do you think t h a t would do any good?

GREGERS.

Try it, Hedvig.

HEDVIG.

[*Softly, with flashing eyes.*] Yes, I will try it.

GREGERS.

Have you really the courage for it, do you think?

HEDVIG.

I'll ask grandfather to shoot the wild duck for me.

GREGERS.

Yes, do.   But not a word to your mother about it.

HEDVIG.

Why not?

GREGERS.

She doesn't understand us.

HEDVIG.

The wild duck!   I'll try it to-morrow morning.
[GINA *comes in by the passage door.*

HEDVIG.

[*Going towards her.*]   Did you find him, mother?

GINA.

No, but I heard as he had called and taken Relling with him.

GREGERS.

Are you sure of that?

GINA.

Yes, the porter's wife said so.   Molvik went with them too, she said.

GREGERS.

This evening, when his mind so sorely needs to wrestle in solitude——!

GINA.

[*Takes off her things.*]   Yes, men are strange creatures, so they are.   The Lord only knows where Relling has dragged him to!   I ran over to Madam Eriksen's, but they weren't t h e r e.

HEDVIG.

[*Struggling to keep back her tears.*]   Oh, if he should never come home any more!

GREGERS.

He w i l l come home again.   I shall have news to give him to-morrow; and then you shall see h o w he comes home.   You may rely upon that, Hedvig, and sleep in peace.   Good-night.

[*He goes out by the passage door.*

HEDVIG.

[*Throws herself sobbing on* GINA's *neck.*]   Mother, mother!

GINA.

[*Pats her shoulder and sighs.*]   Ah yes; Relling was right, he was.   That's what comes of it when crazy creatures go about presenting the claims of the—what-you-may-call-it.

ACT FIFTH

HIALMAR EKDAL'S *studio. Cold, grey, morning light. Wet snow lies upon the large panes of the sloping roof-window.*

GINA *comes from the kitchen with an apron and bib on, and carrying a dusting-brush and a duster; she goes towards the sitting-room door. At the same moment* HEDVIG *comes hurriedly in from the passage.*

GINA.

[*Stops.*] Well?

HEDVIG.

Oh, mother, I almost think he's down at Relling's——

GINA.

There, you see!

HEDVIG.

——because the porter's wife says she could hear that Relling had two people with him when he came home last night.

GINA.

That's just what I thought.

HEDVIG.

But it's no use his being there, if he won't come up to us.

424

GINA.

I'll go down and speak to him at all events.

OLD EKDAL, *in dressing-gown and slippers, and with a lighted pipe, appears at the door of his room.*

EKDAL.

Hialmar—— Isn't Hialmar at home?

GINA.

No, he's gone out.

EKDAL.

So early? And in such a tearing snowstorm? Well well; just as he pleases; I can take my morning walk alone.
   [*He slides the garret door aside;* HEDVIG *helps him; he goes in; she closes it after him.*

HEDVIG.

[*In an undertone.*] Only think, mother, when poor grandfather hears that father is going to leave us.

GINA.

Oh, nonsense; grandfather mustn't hear anything about it. It was a heaven's mercy he wasn't at home yesterday in all that hurly-burly.

HEDVIG.

Yes, but—— [GREGERS *comes in by the passage door.*

GREGERS.

Well, have you any news of him?

GINA.

They say he's down at Relling's.

GREGERS.

At Relling's!   Has he really been out with those creatures?

GINA.

Yes, like enough.

GREGERS.

When he ought to have been yearning for solitude, to collect and clear his thoughts——

GINA.

Yes, you may well say so.

RELLING *enters from the passage.*

HEDVIG.

[*Going to him.*]   Is father in your room?

GINA.

[*At the same time.*]   Is he there?

RELLING.

Yes, to be sure he is.

HEDVIG.

And you never let us know!

RELLING.

Yes; I'm a brute.   But in the first place I had to look after the other brute; I mean our dæmonic friend, of course; and then I fell so dead asleep that——

GINA.

What does Ekdal say to-day?

RELLING.

He says nothing whatever.

HEDVIG.

Doesn't he speak?

RELLING.

Not a blessed word.

GREGERS.

No no; I can understand that very well.

GINA.

But what's he doing then?

RELLING.

He's lying on the sofa, snoring.

GINA.

Oh is he?   Yes, Ekdal's a rare one to snore.

HEDVIG.

Asleep?   Can he sleep?

RELLING.

Well, it certainly looks like it.

GREGERS.

No wonder, after the spiritual conflict that has rent him——

GINA.

And then he's never been used to gadding about out of doors at night.

HEDVIG.

Perhaps it's a good thing that he's getting some sleep, mother.

GINA.

Of course it is; and we must take care we don't wake him up too early. Thank you, Relling. I must get the house cleaned up a bit now, and then—— Come and help me, Hedvig.

[GINA *and* HEDVIG *go into the sitting-room.*

GREGERS.

[*Turning to* RELLING.] What is your explanation of the spiritual tumult that is now going on in Hialmar Ekdal?

RELLING.

Devil a bit of a spiritual tumult have *I* noticed in him.

GREGERS.

What! Not at such a crisis, when his whole life has been placed on a new foundation——? How can you think that such an individuality as Hialmar's——?

RELLING.

Oh, individuality—he! If he ever had any tendency to the abnormal developments you call individuality, I can assure you it was rooted out of him while he was still in his teens.

GREGERS.

That would be strange indeed,—considering the loving care with which he was brought up.

RELLING.

By those two high-flown, hysterical maiden aunts, you mean?

GREGERS.

Let me tell you that they were women who never forgot the claim of the ideal—but of course you will only jeer at me again.

RELLING.

No, I'm in no humour for that. I know all about those ladies; for he has ladled out no end of rhetoric on the subject of his "two soul-mothers." But I don't think he has much to thank them for. Ekdal's misfortune is that in his own circle he has always been looked upon as a shining light——

GREGERS.

Not without reason, surely. Look at the depth of his mind!

RELLING.

I have never discovered it. That his father believed in it I don't so much wonder; the old lieutenant has been an ass all his days.

GREGERS.

He has had a child-like mind all his days; that is what you cannot understand.

Relling.

Well, so be it.   But then, when our dear, sweet Hialmar went to college, he at once passed for the great light of the future amongst his comrades too!   He was handsome, the rascal—red and white—a shop-girl's dream of manly beauty; and with his superficially emotional temperament, and his sympathetic voice, and his talent for declaiming other people's verses and other people's thoughts——

Gregers.

[*Indignantly.*]   Is it Hialmar Ekdal you are talking about in this strain?

Relling.

Yes, with your permission; I am simply giving you an inside view of the idol you are grovelling before.

Gregers.

I should hardly have thought I was quite stone blind.

Relling.

Yes you are—or not far from it.   You are a sick man, too, you see.

Gregers.

You are right there.

Relling.

Yes.   Yours is a complicated case.   First of all there is that plaguy integrity-fever; and then—what's worse—you are always in a delirium of hero-worship; you must always have something to adore, outside yourself.

GREGERS.

Yes, I must certainly seek it outside myself.

RELLING.

But you make such shocking mistakes about every new phœnix you think you have discovered. Here again you have come to a cotter's cabin with your claim of the ideal; and the people of the house are insolvent.

GREGERS.

If you don't think better than that of Hialmar Ekdal, what pleasure can you find in being everlastingly with him?

RELLING.

Well, you see, I'm supposed to be a sort of a doctor— save the mark! I can't but give a hand to the poor sick folk who live under the same roof with me.

GREGERS.

Oh, indeed! Hialmar Ekdal is sick too, is he!

RELLING.

Most people are, worse luck.

GREGERS.

And what remedy are you applying in Hialmar's case?

RELLING.

My usual one. I am cultivating the life-illusion[1] in him.

---

[1] "Livslögnen," literally "the life-lie."

GREGERS.

Life—illusion? I didn't catch what you said.

RELLING.

Yes, I said illusion. For illusion, you know, is the stimulating principle.

GREGERS.

May I ask with what illusion Hialmar is inoculated?

RELLING.

No, thank you; I don't betray professional secrets to quacksalvers. You would probably go and muddle his case still more than you have already. But my method is infallible. I have applied it to Molvik as well. I have made him "dæmonic." That's the blister I have to put on h i s neck.

GREGERS.

Is he not really dæmonic then?

RELLING.

What the devil do you mean by dæmonic! It's only a piece of gibberish I've invented to keep up a spark of life in him. But for that, the poor harmless creature would have succumbed to self-contempt and despair many a long year ago. And then the old lieutenant! But he has hit upon his own cure, you see.

GREGERS.

Lieutenant Ekdal? What of him?

Relling.

Just think of the old bear-hunter shutting himself up in that dark garret to shoot rabbits! I tell you there is not a happier sportsman in the world than that old man pottering about in there among all that rubbish. The four or five withered Christmas-trees he has saved up are the same to him as the whole great fresh Höidal forest; the cock and the hens are big game-birds in the fir-tops; and the rabbits that flop about the garret-floor are the bears he has to battle with—the mighty hunter of the mountains!

Gregers.

Poor unfortunate old man! Yes; he has indeed had to narrow the ideals of his youth.

Relling.

While I think of it, Mr. Werle, junior—don't use that foreign word: ideals. We have the excellent native word: lies.

Gregers.

Do you think the two things are related?

Relling.

Yes, just about as closely as typhus and putrid fever.

Gregers.

Dr. Relling, I shall not give up the struggle until I have rescued Hialmar from your clutches!

Relling.

So much the worse for him. Rob the average man of his life-illusion, and you rob him of his happiness at the same stroke. [*To* HEDVIG, *who comes in from the sitting-room.*] Well, little wild-duck-mother, I'm just going down to see whether papa is still lying meditating upon that wonderful invention of his.

[*Goes out by the passage door.*

GREGERS.

[*Approaches* HEDVIG.] I can see by your face that you have not yet done it.

HEDVIG.

What? Oh, that about the wild duck! No.

GREGERS.

I suppose your courage failed when the time came.

HEDVIG.

No, that wasn't it. But when I awoke this morning and remembered what we had been talking about, it seemed so strange.

GREGERS.

Strange?

HEDVIG.

Yes, I don't know——. Yesterday evening, at the moment, I thought there was something so delightful about it; but since I have slept and thought of it again, it somehow doesn't seem worth while.

GREGERS.

Ah, I thought you could not have grown up quite unharmed in this house.

HEDVIG.

I don't care about that, if only father would come up——

GREGERS.

Oh, if only your eyes had been opened to that which gives life its value—if you possessed the true, joyous, fearless spirit of sacrifice, you would soon see h o w he would come up to you.—But I believe in you still, Hedvig.

[*He goes out by the passage door.*

[HEDVIG *wanders about the room for a time; she is on the point of going into the kitchen when a knock is heard at the garret door.* HEDVIG *goes over and opens it a little; old* EKDAL *comes out; she pushes the door to again.*

EKDAL.

H'm, it's not much fun to take one's morning walk alone.

HEDVIG.

Wouldn't you like to go shooting, grandfather?

EKDAL.

It's not the weather for it to-day. It's so dark there, you can scarcely see where you're going.

HEDVIG.

Do you never want to shoot anything besides the rabbits?

EKDAL.

Do you think the rabbits aren't good enough?

HEDVIG.

Yes, but what about the wild duck?

EKDAL.

Ho-ho! are you afraid I shall shoot your wild duck?
Never in the world.   Never.

HEDVIG.

No, I suppose you couldn't; they say it's very difficult
to shoot wild ducks.

EKDAL.

Couldn't!   Should rather think I could.

HEDVIG.

How would you set about it, grandfather?—I don't
mean with m y wild duck, but with others?

EKDAL.

I should take care to shoot them in the breast, you
know; that's the surest place.   And then you must
shoot against the feathers, you see—not the way of the
feathers.

HEDVIG.

Do they die then, grandfather?

EKDAL.

Yes, they die right enough—when you shoot properly.
Well, I must go and brush up a bit.   H'm—understand
—h'm.   [Goes into his room.

*HEDVIG waits a little, glances towards the sitting-
room door, goes over to the bookcase, stands on tip-
toe, takes the double-barrelled pistol down from the
shelf, and looks at it.   GINA, with brush and duster,
comes from the sitting-room.   HEDVIG hastily lays
down the pistol, unobserved.*

GINA.

Don't stand raking amongst father's things, Hedvig.

HEDVIG.

[*Goes away from the bookcase.*]   I was only going to
tidy up a little.

GINA.

You'd better go into the kitchen, and see if the coffee's
keeping hot; I'll take his breakfast on a tray, when I go
down to him.

    [*HEDVIG goes out.   GINA begins to sweep and clean
up the studio.   Presently the passage door is opened
with hesitation, and HIALMAR EKDAL looks in.   He
has on his overcoat, but not his hat; he is unwashed,
and his hair is dishevelled and unkempt.   His eyes
are dull and heavy.*

GINA.

[*Standing with the brush in her hand, and looking at
him.*]   Oh, there now, Ekdal—so you've come after all?

HIALMAR.

[*Comes in and answers in a toneless voice.*]   I come—
only to depart again immediately.

GINA.

Yes, yes, I suppose so.   But, Lord help us! what a sight you are!

HIALMAR.

A sight?

GINA.

And your nice winter coat too!   Well, that's done for.

HEDVIG.

[*At the kitchen door.*]   Mother, hadn't I better——?
[*Sees* HIALMAR, *gives a loud scream of joy, and runs to him.*]   Oh, father, father!

HIALMAR.

[*Turns away and makes a gesture of repulsion.*]   Away, away, away!   [*To* GINA.]   Keep her away from me, I say!

GINA.

[*In a low tone.*]   Go into the sitting-room, Hedvig.
[HEDVIG *does so without a word.*

HIALMAR.

[*Fussily pulls out the table-drawer.*]   I must have my books with me.   Where are my books?

GINA.

Which books?

HIALMAR.

My scientific books, of course; the technical magazines I require for my invention.

GINA.

[*Searches in the bookcase.*]   Is it these here paper-covered ones?

HIALMAR.

Yes, of course

GINA.

[*Lays a heap of magazines on the table.*]   Shan't I get Hedvig to cut them for you?

HIALMAR.

I don't require to have them cut for me.   [*Short silence.*

GINA.

Then you're still set on leaving us, Ekdal?

HIALMAR.

[*Rummaging amongst the books.*]   Yes, that is a matter of course, I should think.

GINA.

Well, well.

HIALMAR.

[*Vehemently.*]   How can I live here, to be stabbed to the heart every hour of the day?

GINA.

God forgive you for thinking such vile things of me.

HIALMAR.

Prove——!

GINA.

I think it's y o u as has got to prove.

HIALMAR.

After a past like yours?   There are certain claims—I may almost call them claims of the ideal——

GINA.

But what about grandfather?   What's to become of h i m, poor dear?

HIALMAR.

I know my duty; my helpless father will come with me. I am going out into the town to make arrangements——. H'm—[*hesitatingly*] has any one found my hat on the stairs?

GINA.

No.   Have you lost your hat?

HIALMAR.

Of course I had it on when I came in last night; there's no doubt about that; but I couldn't find it this morning.

GINA.

Lord help us! where h a v e you been to with those two ne'er-do-weels?

HIALMAR.

Oh, don't bother me about trifles.   Do you suppose I am in the mood to remember details?

GINA.

If only you haven't caught cold, Ekdal.

[*Goes out into the kitchen.*

HIALMAR.

[*Talks to himself in a low tone of irritation, whilst he empties the table-drawer.*] You're a scoundrel, Relling!— You're a low fellow!—Ah, you shameless tempter!—I wish I could get some one to stick a knife into you!

[*He lays some old letters on one side, finds the torn document of yesterday, takes it up and looks at the pieces; puts it down hurriedly as* GINA *enters.*

GINA.

[*Sets a tray with coffee, etc., on the table.*] Here's a drop of something hot, if you'd fancy it. And there's some bread and butter and a snack of salt meat.

HIALMAR.

[*Glancing at the tray.*] Salt meat? Never under this roof! It's true I have not had a mouthful of solid food for nearly twenty-four hours; but no matter.—My memoranda! The commencement of my autobiography! What has become of my diary, and all my important papers? [*Opens the sitting-room door but draws back.*] She is there too!

GINA.

Good Lord! the child must be s o m e w h e r e!

HIALMAR.

Come out.

[*He makes room,* HEDVIG *comes, scared, into the studio.*

Hialmar.

[*With his hand upon the door-handle, says to* Gina:] In these, the last moments I spend in my former home, I wish to be spared from interlopers——

[*Goes into the room.*

Hedvig.

[*With a bound towards her mother, asks softly, trembling.*] Does that mean me?

Gina.

Stay out in the kitchen, Hedvig; or, no—you'd best go into your own room. [*Speaks to* Hialmar *as she goes in to him.*] Wait a bit, Ekdal; don't rummage so in the drawers; *I* know where everything is.

Hedvig.

[*Stands a moment immovable, in terror and perplexity, biting her lips to keep back the tears; then she clenches her hands convulsively, and says softly:*] The wild duck.

[*She steals over and takes the pistol from the shelf, opens the garret door a little way, creeps in, and draws the door to after her.*

[Hialmar *and* Gina *can be heard disputing in the sitting-room.*

Hialmar.

[*Comes in with some manuscript books and old loose papers, which he lays upon the table.*] That portmanteau is of no use! There are a thousand and one things I must drag with me.

GINA.

[*Following with the portmanteau.*]   Why not leave all
the rest for the present, and only take a shirt and a pair
of woollen drawers with you?

HIALMAR.

Whew!—all these exhausting preparations——!
   [*Pulls off his overcoat and throws it upon the sofa.*

GINA.

And there's the coffee getting cold.

HIALMAR.

H'm.
   [*Drinks a mouthful without thinking of it, and then
      another.*

GINA.

[*Dusting the backs of the chairs.*]   A nice job you'll
have to find such another big garret for the rabbits.

HIALMAR.

What!   Am I to drag all those rabbits with me too?

GINA.

You don't suppose grandfather can get on without his
rabbits.

HIALMAR.

He must just get used to doing without them.   Have
not *I* to sacrifice very much greater things than rabbits!

GINA.

[*Dusting the bookcase.*]   Shall I put the flute in the portmanteau for you?

HIALMAR.

No.   No flute for me.   But give me the pistol!

GINA.

Do you want to take the pigstol with you?

HIALMAR.

Yes.   My loaded pistol.

GINA.

[*Searching for it.*]   It's gone.   He must have taken it in with him.

HIALMAR.

Is he in the garret?

GINA.

Yes, of course he's in the garret.

HIALMAR.

H'm—poor lonely old man.
  [*He takes a piece of bread and butter, eats it, and finishes his cup of coffee.*

GINA.

If we hadn't have let that room, you could have moved in there.

HIALMAR.

And continued to live under the same roof with——!
Never,—never!

GINA.

But couldn't you put up with the sitting-room for a
day or two? You could have it all to yourself.

HIALMAR.

Never within these walls!

GINA.

Well then, down with Relling and Molvik.

HIALMAR.

Don't mention those wretches' names to me! The
very thought of them almost takes away my appetite.—
Oh no, I must go out into the storm and the snow-drift,
—go from house to house and seek shelter for my father
and myself.

GINA.

But you've got no hat, Ekdal! You've been and lost
your hat, you know.

HIALMAR.

Oh those two brutes, those slaves of all the vices! A
hat must be procured. [*Takes another piece of bread and
butter.*] Some arrangement must be made. For I have
no mind to throw away my life, either.

[*Looks for something on the tray.*

GINA.

What are you looking for?

HIALMAR.

Butter.

GINA.

I'll get some at once.   [*Goes out into the kitchen.*

HIALMAR.

[*Calls after her.*]   Oh it doesn't matter; dry bread is good enough for m e.

GINA.

[*Brings a dish of butter.*]   Look here; this is fresh churned.
> [*She pours out another cup of coffee for him; he seats himself on the sofa, spreads more butter on the already buttered bread, and eats and drinks awhile in silence.*

HIALMAR.

Could I, without being subject to intrusion—intrusion of a n y sort—could I live in the sitting-room there for a day or two?

GINA.

Yes, to be sure you could, if you only would.

HIALMAR.

For I see no possibility of getting all father's things out in such a hurry.

GINA.

And besides, you've surely got to tell him first as you don't mean to live with us others no more.

HIALMAR.

[*Pushes away his coffee cup.*]　Yes, there is that too; I shall have to lay bare the whole tangled story to him——. I must turn matters over; I must have breathing-time; I cannot take all these burdens on my shoulders in a single day.

GINA.

No, especially in such horrible weather as it is outside.

HIALMAR.

[*Touching* WERLE'S *letter.*]　I see that paper is still lying about here.

GINA.

Yes, *I* haven't touched it.

HIALMAR.

So far as I am concerned it is mere waste paper——

GINA.

Well, *I* have certainly no notion of making any use of it.

HIALMAR.

——but we had better not let it get lost all the same;— in all the upset when I move, it might easily——

GINA.

I'll take good care of it, Ekdal.

HIALMAR.

The donation is in the first instance made to father, and it rests with him to accept or decline it.

GINA.

[*Sighs.*] Yes, poor old father——.

HIALMAR.

To make quite safe—— Where shall I find some gum?

GINA.

[*Goes to the bookcase.*] Here's the gum-pot.

HIALMAR.

And a brush?

GINA.

The brush is here too.   [*Brings him the things.*

HIALMAR.

[*Takes a pair of scissors.*] Just a strip of paper at the back——[*Clips and gums.*] Far be it from me to lay hands upon what is not my own—and least of all upon what belongs to a destitute old man—and to—the other as well.—There now. Let it lie there for a time; and when it is dry, take it away. I wish never to see that document again. Never!

GREGERS WERLE *enters from the passage.*

GREGERS.

[*Somewhat surprised.*]   What,—are you sitting here, Hialmar?

HIALMAR.

[*Rises hurriedly.*]   I had sunk down from fatigue.

GREGERS.

You have been having breakfast, I see.

HIALMAR.

The body sometimes makes its claims felt too.

GREGERS.

What have you decided to do?

HIALMAR.

For a man like me, there is only one course possible. I am just putting my most important things together. But it takes time, you know.

GINA.

[*With a touch of impatience.*]   Am I to get the room ready for you, or am I to pack your portmanteau?

HIALMAR.

[*After a glance of annoyance at* GREGERS.]   Pack—and get the room ready!

GINA.

[*Takes the portmanteau.*] Very well; then I'll put in the shirt and the other things.

    [*Goes into the sitting-room and draws the door to after her.*

GREGERS.

[*After a short silence.*] I never dreamed that this would be the end of it. Do you really feel it a necessity to leave house and home?

HIALMAR.

[*Wanders about restlessly.*] What would you have me do?—I am not fitted to bear unhappiness, Gregers. I must feel secure and at peace in my surroundings.

GREGERS.

But can you not feel that here? Just try it. I should have thought you had firm ground to build upon now—if only you start afresh. And remember, you have your invention to live for.

HIALMAR.

Oh don't talk about my invention. It's perhaps still in the dim distance.

GREGERS.

Indeed!

HIALMAR.

Why, great heavens, what would you have me invent? Other people have invented almost everything already. It becomes more and more difficult every day——

GREGERS.

And you have devoted so much labour to it.

HIALMAR.

It was that blackguard Relling that urged me to it.

GREGERS.

Relling?

HIALMAR.

Yes, it was he that first made me realise my aptitude for making some notable discovery in photography.

GREGERS.

Aha—it was Relling!

HIALMAR.

Oh, I have been so truly happy over it!   Not so much for the sake of the invention itself, as because Hedvig believed in it—believed in it with a child's whole eagerness of faith.—At least, I have been fool enough to go and imagine that she believed in it.

GREGERS.

Can you really think that Hedvig has been false towards you?

HIALMAR.

I can think anything now.   It is Hedvig that stands in my way.   She will blot out the sunlight from my whole life.

GREGERS.

Hedvig! Is it Hedvig you are talking of? How should s h e blot out your sunlight?

HIALMAR.

[*Without answering.*] How unutterably I have loved that child! How unutterably happy I have felt every time I came home to my humble room, and she flew to meet me, with her sweet little blinking eyes. Oh, confiding fool that I have been! I loved her unutterably;— and I yielded myself up to the dream, the delusion, that she loved me unutterably in return.

GREGERS.

Do you call t h a t a delusion?

HIALMAR.

How should I know? I can get nothing out of Gina; and besides, she is totally blind to the ideal side of these complications. But to you I feel impelled to open my mind, Gregers. I cannot shake off this frightful doubt —perhaps Hedvig has never really and honestly loved me.

GREGERS.

What would you say if she were to give you a proof of her love? [*Listens.*] What's that? I thought I heard the wild duck——?

HIALMAR.

It's the wild duck quacking. Father's in the garret.

GREGERS.

Is he? [*His face lights up with joy.*] I say you may yet have proof that your poor misunderstood Hedvig loves you!

HIALMAR.

Oh, what proof can she give me? I dare not believe in any assurances from that quarter.

GREGERS.

Hedvig does not know what deceit means.

HIALMAR.

Oh Gregers, that is just what I cannot be sure of. Who knows what Gina and that Mrs. Sörby may many a time have sat here whispering and tattling about? And Hedvig usually has her ears open, I can tell you. Perhaps the deed of gift was not such a surprise to her, after all. In fact, I'm not sure but that I noticed something of the sort.

GREGERS.

What spirit is this that has taken possession of you?

HIALMAR.

I have had my eyes opened. Just you notice;—you'll see, the deed of gift is only a beginning. Mrs. Sörby has always been a good deal taken up with Hedvig; and now she has the power to do whatever she likes for the child. They can take her from me whenever they please.

GREGERS.

Hedvig will never, never leave you.

HIALMAR.

Don't be so sure of that.   If only they beckon to her
and throw out a golden bait——!   And oh! I have loved
her so unspeakably!   I would have counted it my highest
happiness to take her tenderly by the hand and lead her,
as one leads a timid child through a great dark empty
room!—I am cruelly certain now that the poor photographer in his humble attic has never really and truly
been anything to her.   She has only cunningly contrived
to keep on a good footing with him until the time came.

GREGERS.

You don't believe that yourself, Hialmar.

HIALMAR.

That is just the terrible part of it—I don't know what
to believe,—I never can know it.   But can you really
doubt that it must be as I say ?   Ho-ho, you have far too
much faith in the claim of the ideal, my good Gregers!
If those others came, with the glamour of wealth about
them, and called to the child:—"Leave him: come to us:
here life awaits you——! "

GREGERS.

[*Quickly.*]   Well, what then ?

HIALMAR.

If I then asked her: Hedvig, are you willing to re-
nounce that life for me ?   [*Laughs scornfully.*]   No thank
you!   You would soon hear what answer I should get.
            [*A pistol shot is heard from within the garret.*

GREGERS.

[*Loudly and joyfully.*]　Hialmar!

HIALMAR.

There now; he must needs go shooting too.

GINA.

[*Comes in.*]　Oh Ekdal, I can hear grandfather blazing away in the garret by hisself.

HIALMAR.

I'll look in——

GREGERS.

[*Eagerly, with emotion.*]　Wait a moment!　Do you know what that was?

HIALMAR.

Yes, of course I know.

GREGERS.

No you don't know.　But *I* do.　That was the proof!

HIALMAR.

What proof?

GREGERS.

It was a child's free-will offering.　She has got your father to shoot the wild duck.

HIALMAR.

To shoot the wild duck!

GINA.

Oh, think of that——!

HIALMAR.

What was t h a t for?

GREGERS.

She wanted to sacrifice to you her most cherished possession; for then she thought you would surely come to love her again.

HIALMAR.

[*Tenderly, with emotion.*]   Oh, poor child!

GINA.

What things she does think of!

GREGERS.

She only wanted your love again, Hialmar.   She could not live without it.

GINA.

[*Struggling with her tears.*]   There, you can see for yourself, Ekdal.

HIALMAR.

Gina, where is she?

GINA.

[*Sniffs.*]   Poor dear, she's sitting out in the kitchen, I dare say.

HIALMAR.

[*Goes over, tears open the kitchen door, and says:*]　Hedvig, come, come in to me!　[*Looks round.*]　No, she's not here.

GINA.

Then she must be in her own little room.

HIALMAR.

[*Without.*]　No, she's not here either.　[*Comes in.*] She must have gone out.

GINA.

Yes, you wouldn't have her anywheres in the house.

HIALMAR.

Oh, if she would only come home quickly, so that I can tell her—— Everything will come right now, Gregers; now I believe we can begin life afresh.

GREGERS.

[*Quietly.*]　I knew it; I knew the child would make amends.

OLD EKDAL *appears at the door of his room; he is in full uniform, and is busy buckling on his sword.*

HIALMAR.

[*Astonished.*]　Father!　Are you there?

GINA.

Have you been firing in your room?

EKDAL.

[*Resentfully, approaching.*] So you go shooting alone, do you, Hialmar?

HIALMAR.

[*Excited and confused.*] Then it wasn't you that fired that shot in the garret?

EKDAL.

M e that fired? H'm.

GREGERS.

[*Calls out to* HIALMAR.] She has shot the wild duck herself!

HIALMAR.

What can it mean? [*Hastens to the garret door, tears it aside, looks in and calls loudly:*] Hedvig!

GINA.

[*Runs to the door.*] Good God, what's that!

HIALMAR.

[*Goes in.*] She's lying on the floor!

GREGERS.

Hedvig! lying on the floor! [*Goes in to* HIALMAR.

GINA.

[*At the same time.*] Hedvig! [*Inside the garret.*] No, no, no!

E DAL.

Ho-ho! does s h e go shooting too, now?

[HIALMAR, GINA, *and* GREGERS *carry* HEDVIG *into the studio; in her dangling right hand she holds the pistol fast clasped in her fingers.*

HIALMAR.

[*Distracted.*] The pistol has gone off. She has wounded herself. Call for help! Help!

GINA.

[*Runs into the passage and calls down.*] Relling! Relling! Doctor Relling; come up as quick as you can!

[HIALMAR *and* GREGERS *lay* HEDVIG *down on the sofa.*

EKDAL.

[*Quietly.*] The woods avenge themselves.

HIALMAR.

[*On his knees beside* HEDVIG.] She'll soon come to now. She's coming to——; yes, yes, yes.

GINA.

[*Who has come in again.*] Where has she hurt herself? I can't see anything——

[RELLING *comes hurriedly, and immediately after him* MOLVIK; *the latter without his waistcoat and necktie, and with his coat open.*

RELLING.

What's the matter here?

GINA.

They say Hedvig has shot herself.

HIALMAR.

Come and help us!

RELLING.

Shot herself!
   [*He pushes the table aside and begins to examine her.*

HIALMAR.

[*Kneeling and looking anxiously up at him.*]   It can't
be dangerous?   Speak, Relling!   She is scarcely bleed-
ing at all.   It can't be dangerous?

RELLING.

How did it happen?

HIALMAR.

Oh, we don't know——!

GINA.

She wanted to shoot the wild duck.

RELLING.

The wild duck?

HIALMAR.

The pistol must have gone off.

RELLING.

H'm.   Indeed.

EKDAL.

The woods avenge themselves. But I'm not afraid, all the same.

[*Goes into the garret and closes the door after him.*

HIALMAR.

Well, Relling,—why don't you say something?

RELLING.

The ball has entered the breast.

HIALMAR.

Yes, but she's coming to!

RELLING.

Surely you can see that Hedvig is dead.

GINA.

[*Bursts into tears.*] Oh my child, my child!

GREGERS.

[*Huskily.*] In the depths of the sea——

HIALMAR.

[*Jumps up.*] No, no, she m u s t live! Oh, for God's sake, Relling—only a moment—only just till I can tell her how unspeakably I loved her all the time!

RELLING.

The bullet has gone through her heart. Internal hemorrhage. Death must have been instantaneous.

HIALMAR.

And I! I hunted her from me like an animal! And she crept terrified into the garret and died for love of me! [*Sobbing.*] I can never atone to her! I can never tell her——! [*Clenches his hands and cries, upwards.*] O thou above——! If thou be indeed! Why hast thou done this thing to me?

GINA.

Hush, hush, you mustn't go on that awful way. We had no right to keep her, I suppose.

MOLVIK.

The child is not dead, but sleepeth.

RELLING.

Bosh!

HIALMAR.

[*Becomes calm, goes over to the sofa, folds his arms, and looks at* HEDVIG.] There she lies so stiff and still.

RELLING.

[*Tries to loosen the pistol.*] She's holding it so tight, so tight.

GINA.

No, no, Relling, don't break her fingers; let the pigstol be.

HIALMAR.

She shall take it with her.

GINA.

Yes, let her.   But the child mustn't lie here for a show. She shall go to her own room, so she shall.   Help me, Ekdal.

[HIALMAR *and* GINA *take* HEDVIG *between them.*

HIALMAR.

[*As they are carrying her.*]   Oh Gina, Gina, can you survive this!

GINA.

We must help each other to bear it.   For n o w at least she belongs to both of us.

MOLVIK.

[*Stretches out his arms and mumbles.*]   Blessed be the Lord; to earth thou shalt return; to earth thou shalt return——

RELLING.

[*Whispers.*]   Hold your tongue, you fool; you're drunk. [HIALMAR *and* GINA *carry the body out through the kitchen door.* RELLING *shuts it after them.* MOL- VIK *slinks out into the passage.*

RELLING.

[*Goes over to* GREGERS *and says:*]   No one shall ever convince me that the pistol went off by accident.

GREGERS.

[*Who has stood terrified, with convulsive twitchings.*] Who can say how the dreadful thing happened?

RELLING.

The powder has burnt the body of her dress. She must have pressed the pistol right against her breast and fired.

GREGERS.

Hedvig has not died in vain. Did you not see how sorrow set free what is noble in him?

RELLING.

Most people are ennobled by the actual presence of death. But how long do you suppose this nobility will last in h i m?

GREGERS.

Why should it not endure and increase throughout his life?

RELLING.

Before a year is over, little Hedvig will be nothing to him but a pretty theme for declamation.

GREGERS.

How dare you say that of Hialmar Ekdal?

RELLING.

We will talk of this again, when the grass has first withered on her grave. Then you'll hear him spouting about "the child too early torn from her father's heart;" then you'll see him steep himself in a syrup of sentiment and self-admiration and self-pity. Just you wait!

GREGERS.

If you are right and I am wrong, then life is not worth living.

RELLING.

Oh, life would be quite tolerable, after all, if only we could be rid of the confounded duns that keep on pestering us, in our poverty, with the claim of the ideal.

GREGERS.

[*Looking straight before him.*]   In that case, I am glad that my destiny is what it is.

RELLING.

May I inquire,—what is your destiny?

GREGERS.

[*Going.*]   To be the thirteenth at table.

RELLING.

The devil it is.

THE END.